# CONTENTS

# INTRODUCTION

When Thackeray visited Limerick on Ireland's western coast, prior to the Great Famine, he observed that the poverty of the inhabitants was not paralleled even in St. Giles which had lately achieved notoriety as one of the worst of London's rookeries, those conglomerations of mean tenements and sanitary disasters which so troubled the Victorian social conscience. This was not his first experience of Irish poverty; on the approach to Dublin from Dun Laoghaire he had passed (in his own words), 'more shabbiness than a Londoner will see in the course of his home peregrinations for a year'. But Thackeray could only see the outside of the houses; it was his imagination which carried him into the interiors, to the broken table and chairs, the teapot without spout, the ragged and sloppy table-cloth, where the lady was in dubious curl papers and the gentleman in a flaring dressing-gown all ragged at the elbows.[1] Detailed comments such as these may be most informative even when made by a man who is only passing through the district. However, if we want to know about life in such communities, to discover whether they were one undifferentiated mass of poverty or whether there were important gradations between one occupational group and another, perhaps between one street and another, it is obvious that we must approach a source of a very different character and the one which most readily springs to mind, as in theory it included everyone within its grasp, is the census.[2] Unfortunately the takers of the official British censuses, content to get some idea of where population was rising or falling, consistently omitted to put the questions on rent, earnings and number of rooms occupied by each family which would throw most light on the structure of Victorian society. The gap left by their neglect was filled only by various unofficial census takers, amongst whom doctors and clergymen were particularly prominent.

Such interest in the lives of their less fortunate neighbours was not new to the nineteenth century. On the Continent priest and pastor from Spain to Scandinavia were accustomed to enquiring into the morals of their parishioners and even in England a surprisingly large number of Anglican clergymen drew up lists in which each resident was named and placed in his respective household.[3] Yet it is only in the nineteenth century that the practice began of questioning an individual not merely about his age and occupation, but about his membership of Friendly Societies, and the amount of money he spent on the education of his children, while at the same time taking a careful note of the condition and quality of his clothing and furniture. It would be easy to interpret this interest as over-reaction by the establishment when faced with large sections of the urban populace listening to radical agitators rather than the local minister, and that only when the differences between rich and poor were wide or widening were the latter likely to be thought worthy of study.

Clearly, however, many other factors were involved – particularly the growth in numbers of a middle class who found that their employment as administrators or doctors brought them increasingly in contact with the poor or at least with the problems created by their existence. One might even go further and query whether the great social and economic changes of the period did indeed result in an intensification of class differences, but this would be beyond the scope of the present enquiry. Certainly no claim is made here that the four censuses which we have decided to reproduce, out of the many which survive for the period, take us very far in this direction. Our brief will simply be to discover what prompted the respective investigators to indulge in such arduous employment as census taking[4] and assess the result of their labours. Although the general applicability of their findings may be questioned, there can be little doubt that their observations have a lot to teach us about what life was like for the mass of the inhabitants of Dublin in 1798 and three segments of the working class London of the 1840s – a London rookery, Church Lane, St. Giles, and, east of the City, two adjoining areas forming part of the parish of St. George in the East. Not surprisingly the documents vary widely in scope and style and there is more to be learned from the four years' analysis of St. George in the East by the Royal Statistical Society than from the single table which is all that survives – perhaps all that ever existed – of Queckett's.

It is logical, however, to begin with the earliest and the only one of our documents to cover a whole city – the Dublin census of 1798 which we owe to the labours of an Anglican clergyman, the Vicar of the far from prosperous parish of St. Catherine's. It is also the one which has least to tell us about society at the time, consisting in its printed form, if we except for the moment the introductory essay, merely of totals of males, females and houses (distinguishing the uninhabited from the inhabited) in each street, lane and court in the city. Whitelaw had available some other tables, which were deemed too detailed for publication, which showed for each house its state of repair and number of stories, as well as the class of inhabitants ('upper and middle', servants and 'lower class'). Even here we have this rather peculiar three-class division yet there is nothing on family structure. The occupation of the proprietor (not inevitably a resident himself) is recorded but not that of the other inmates. In any case it is now only possible to speculate on all that might have been gained from discovering which houses were back to back and which were let out in poor tenements, since the detailed sheets, lodged in Dublin Castle for safety, were later transferred to the Dublin Record Office and blown up in the 1920s.[5] All that survives are the two specimen streets, one respectable (York Street) and one poor (The Poddle).[6] Much more can be expected should it be possible to trace Whitelaw's list of the Protestant population of St. Catherine's (the list was never apparently lodged in the Castle) which specified age, sex and occupation of every individual, adding for the children some detail on their schooling.

Of the accuracy of the figures he does give there can be little doubt. In order to ascertain the true population, no room even in the most wretched habitation was left unvisited and although Whitelaw employed assistants, none were permitted to survey streets on their own until the accuracy of their work had been measured by starting them on streets which a colleague, or Whitelaw himself, had already covered. The most difficult areas he reserved for himself. The same meticulous care for detail characterised all his other undertakings from his *System of Geography* which involved him in learning the art of engraving when the engravings which he had commissioned failed to come up to his high standards, to his map of the canals of Ireland for which he navigated the entire system from the Liffey to the Shannon recording the position of every lock and bridge.[7] With the census Whitelaw claimed he was greatly helped by the willingness of the population to co-operate, first through fear of appearing to oppose an undertaking which was known to have the government's blessing, and then from an expectation that the government was considering some action to relieve their wants. In addition he had available the lists of the residents of each house which the inmates were required under a civic regulation to affix to their doors, but these lists Whitelaw found generally unreliable in lower class areas, frequently illegible and short of the total number of persons by one third or even one half. None of this detracts in any way from what was a considerable achievement in completing a census of any sort in Dublin at the time and later attempts were to be less rather than more accurate.[8]

As a gazetteer it could hardly be bettered but as such it reflects only one aspect of his life's work – his interest in geography – and not his parochial concerns, the reorganisation of existing and the establishment of new schools for the poor, including one for apprentices, and the relief and loans to the weavers when economic depression forced thousands out of business. Some inkling of these interests is to be gleaned, however, from his introductory essay in which he comments on the unwholesome habitations of the mass of the labouring poor. He saw clearly in 1798, as the Royal Statistical Society was to do later, that the heart of the problem lay in the high rents which the poor were just not able to pay without sharing their dwellings, and sometimes even their rooms, with other families. His recommendations were essentially practical – the worst houses were to be pulled down and the manufactories whose evil effects were so clearly established, slaughter houses, glass houses, lime kilns, distilleries, removed from the midst of a crowded population (pages 53, 62).

Whitelaw also came out very strongly against town dairies, which is particularly interesting in view of a claim recently put forward that the fall in infant mortality in English cities in the late 18th century is to be ascribed partly to such dairies having increased the opportunity of purchasing fresh milk.[9] As far as Dublin is concerned, there can be little doubt that Whitelaw was right in thinking that butter and milk originating from cows confined in narrow yards and filthy stalls and 'fed on grains, still-wash and decayed vegetables, the refuse of the root-market', were not likely to be of much benefit to the people who consumed them. All this was in addition to the hazard to public health caused by the failure to remove the dung, yet the picture was not entirely black. Overcrowding even amongst the poor was probably less of a problem than it had been previously, while his careful inspection of the narrowest courts and lanes shown on old maps of Dublin revealed that the majority in his day consisted of workshops rather than dwelling houses and that many other courts had completely disappeared.

From Dublin in 1798 we turn to the London parish of St. Giles, but to a street in which in 1847 two out of every three inhabitants were of Irish origin or descent.[10] Church Lane was undoubtedly selected by the Royal Statistical Society because of its exceptional poverty although there is plenty of evidence that this was only one of a number of such streets in the area.[11] Disraeli had seen the rich and the poor as constituting two separate nations mutually ignorant of each other's habits, and the astonishment of the Society that the poor could possess so little and exist in such confined dwellings, is clearly visible even in this factual room-by-room survey of beds, furniture and fitments. As to the accuracy of the information there can be little doubt, as each room in the 12 houses was visited in person by at least one member of the Committee and by the paid agent, who had, for the most part, only to record what they saw – for example, whether the furniture was in a good or bad state of repair – rather than what they were told, as would have been the case with an enquiry which concerned itself with ages or other personal details of the inhabitants. Included on the Committee were some of the most prominent members of the Society (the list alone of their contributions to the Society's Journal is most impressive), yet it is the much neglected agent who survives in name only (A. Balfour) who was of paramount importance. It was, after all, a very slightly amended version of his notebook which made up the bulk of the Report and in addition a considerable amount of the preparation and organisation of the research might have devolved upon him, given that many of the senior members were, according to their own description, 'men of business' and therefore unable to engage full-time in statistical pursuits.[12] Such enquiries were later discontinued by the Society but this was because of their cost and not because the agents' work had been found unreliable. Indeed the only possible reason for doubting the Report's accuracy would appear to stem from the speed with which the enquiry got under way. Appointed in December 1847, the Committee had concluded its deliberations in time for the Report to appear in the Journal of the following year. On the other hand the amount of information which it was decided to gather was quite modest and in one respect the Committee had a certain advantage, even over an enquiry by the local Medical Officer of Health, in that the inhabitants may have been less inclined to conceal instances of rooms illegally occupied.[13]

The interest of the members in the plight of the poor has not always been sufficiently stressed, yet in fact it went so far that one might justifiably talk of their commitment to the principle of sanitary reform; and it was to lead the Society some distance from the impartial recording of facts which it might be thought should have been its sole concern. In this case it seems not unlikely that the Committee hoped that the speedy publication of its Report which showed an average of over 38 persons to each house, more than 7 persons in each room, and 5 persons to a bed[15] would bring about some improvement. If so, it was to be disappointed, for the Medical Officer for St. Giles was to refer to Church Lane in much the same terms as the Statistical Society for at least a further decade.[16] And the Committee's far from novel proposal to substitute clean but cheap homes for the insanitary ones, when half-heartedly acted upon in later years, was to bring but little succour to those classes for whom it was primarily intended, who ended up herded into what remained of the sub-standard accommodation.[17] It was no coincidence that Church Lane immediately adjoined one of the major 'improvements' of the mid-Victorian era, New Oxford Street.

It was also possible, however, to blame overcrowding on other factors, particularly the large Irish exodus as a result of famine. The nature of the Statistical Society enquiry naturally prevented any search for an explanation although some passing references to the length of time some of the Irish had been in London, and more especially the comment on the numbers of empty rooms, could be taken as implying that the Committee members saw the nature of the problem as lying elsewhere, perhaps with the sheer inability of the inhabitants to meet the room rent without sharing with other families.

Somewhat more thought for this subject was given by Horace Mann whose Report on the mortality in Church Lane was appended to the Society's study. Mann clearly had access both to the enumerator's books of the 1841 census and to the medical records of the workhouse, which is presumably why it was thought that his contribution was worthy of publication. He concluded that as the Irish were relatively more numerous in 1847 than in 1841, it was their arrival which was responsible for the increased overcrowding and higher mortality of the later years. In fact it is possible to use his figures to show that the English had also increased in numbers – perhaps by as much as 30 per cent.[18] This issue could in any case only be resolved if we knew how long the Irish had been resident in London, information which Mann failed to elicit. Nor is this the only place where his argument breaks down for want of sufficient data. His study of mortality, for instance, proceeded without the records of those who had died in either the hospitals or the workhouse. Some of the other gaps he attempted to fill with a series of improbable assumptions: that the overall population fluctuated little between 1838 and 1844 and that the increase in population, when it occurred, was the same in the twelve houses covered by the Statistical Society's survey as in the street as a whole. Yet the one factor which stands out above all others when one compares the two censuses is the immense variation in the numbers of inhabitants in particular houses at the two dates. For a house to double or even triple the numbers of its inmates within the six years was not uncommon yet there were others which were no more crowded in 1847 than they had been earlier and some actually saw a decline. So great is the variation indeed that one is almost ready to question the accuracy of the earlier census, particularly when several – although by no means all – of the houses in which the greatest increase occurred possessed rooms reached from narrow back yards which it is conceivable that an enumerator with a large district to cover may have omitted altogether or recorded separately. Despite its weaknesses, however, the study contains some interesting material. It shows that fever cases were very unevenly distributed between the houses despite the universal overcrowding, poverty and dirt, those who struggled to keep their rooms clean and furniture whole being mown down with the rest. It is a pity that there is insufficient detail on the background, particularly on the ages, of the members of the various families for the issue to be pursued further.

No such problem occurs with the second survey by the Royal Statistical Society which was an altogether more ambitious undertaking. It took as its base an area immediately to the west of Cannon Street Road, easily discernible on a contemporary Carey's Map and even on a modern plan despite the fact that many of the courts and lanes have disappeared. It looks an impossibly small area to have contained the seven thousand odd inhabitants which the survey encompassed yet it was selected not on the grounds of poverty but because it was deemed representative of working-class London, an assumption (it amounted to little more than this) whose veracity we investigate below. The Society's examination was wide-ranging, concerning itself not only with the standard of accommodation – persons per room, persons per bed – but with earnings (both of the household head and of other family members) and rent; with the standard of living of the inhabitants – whether their rooms and furniture were clean, how many times in a week they ate 'animal food' – and even with their taste in books and pictures: the data presented for the most part according to the occupation of the household head.

As with their previous survey, we know very little of the actual mechanics of the taking of the census and although it seems that agents were used,[19] the greater amount of analysis attempted probably meant more work for the Committee members. This they shared out between them so that those investigating issues such as place of birth, period of residence, membership of friendly societies, were unaware of the plans of their colleagues concentrating on fertility and mortality. This seems the only logical inference to draw from the fact that some of the tables appear twice in an article of only moderate length. With rather more certainty it can be said that the Committee took as its model the earlier survey of the Westminster poor[20] since the range of questions was much the same, the principal difference being the absence of the occupational breakdown which of course is what renders the St. George in the East survey so interesting.

Unfortunately we can do no more here than draw attention to its findings. The Committee thought some were of general application, as in the case of more children being born – yet fewer lost – to couples who married before the age of 25 compared with those who married later in life, but the other results are no less interesting. It emerged, for instance, that one quarter of the population had animal food just once or twice a week. The same proportion were without books of any description, a third possessed no pictures, two thirds had been in their present house less than three years. On the positive side, the clothing of the inhabitants was described as generally clean if sometimes insufficient and attendance at school, if only for a comparatively few years, was universal. Infant mortality was less than half that of Liverpool, lower than the figure for England and Wales as a whole, lower even than in Surrey, although all these calculations included both rich and poor. By the tenth year, however, the position had changed dramatically, with life expectancy now lower than for the majority of the other populations with which it could be compared. The Committee made no comment on this but it is difficult to believe that the infant mortality figure can be genuine even allowing for the bias arising through the method of data collection (for example, only unbroken marriages were examined). One possibility could be that in the early years of marriage, couples had lived elsewhere and the Committee was even inclined to exonerate the environment of Whitechapel of blame for the mortality of all but the children of the most recently married couples. Yet these families, being generally smaller, might well have been the most mobile and in the absence of any evidence on how long inhabitants had been in the district (as opposed to a particular house) further speculation seems pointless.[21]

Elsewhere the Committee's reaction can be equally unexpected – a population which gives every impression of being highly mobile, it thought stable, given the frequency with which men had to move with their trade into the many different parts of London. A degree of crowding which gave figures of 2·0 persons to a room and 2·4 to a bed it thought, perhaps with Church Lane in mind, only moderate. A considerable amount of time was devoted to speculating how frequently the 'serious' books, which included the Bible, were actually read but this is one thing which even it did not attempt to measure statistically.

One serious fault in the Committee's work, however, was that it based its calculations on what were in some cases very small numbers and that it ignored all those cases where for one reason or another the relevant information had not been gathered. When the latter numbers are large – as with the 630 families whose readership of newspapers was not ascertained – it is impossible to decide whether the proportions which are of most interest (in this case 2 per cent who stated positively that they did not read a newspaper) have any validity. It is also somewhat surprising that the Committee did not make more use of the materials which it collected.[22] For example although it insisted (p. 199) that 'occupation was the circumstance which brings in its train the most numerous and most potent of the influences which affect the relative condition of all' in the end it made no use of its own classification except to observe that those who lived in most comfort in proportion to their earnings were the German sugar bakers and the mates of vessels. Others, such as the gunsmiths, were criticised for failing to make full use of their higher earnings.

Complaints such as these are voiced frequently but for once we have a chance to check, to see who translated his earnings into a higher standard of living by purchasing most animal food, who kept his rooms the cleanest and filled with the best furniture, in whose houses books and pictures were to be found most frequently. Alternatively we can discover when rent absorbed a high proportion of a group's resources because the nature of employment or considerations of social status forced families into a certain type of accommodation. In each case what has to be measured is not so much which occupation possessed, for instance, the best accommodation and had the lowest child mortality but on what occasions the recorded level was most at variance with its position in society.[23] Theoretically it would be possible for the distribution to be absolutely even, for the clerk, for example, to have the highest earnings and spend most on rent while still having sufficient in hand to buy more books, and eat more meat than any of his neighbours. The lowly labourers would always come at the bottom of the pile, renting the cheapest accommodation, possessing least clothing and furniture. This sort of distribution will be highly improbable when the gradations between the groups are small but it is never really a strong possibility given the great variety of individual preferences.

In this connection it would be as well to repeat what was said above about the small numbers in some of the categories; to remember that at times we are measuring 7 gun-stock makers against 8 wheelwrights and that even when the numbers are larger, as with the labourers and shoemakers, they are not representative of labourers everywhere, merely of those residing in this particular section of East London. All this has to be kept in mind when we say that *in relation to their social position* sailors, shoemakers and bakers suffered least from overcrowding, that painters and porters lived in the best furnished rooms, and that policemen had a particular fondness for books. On the negative side printers seemed to have been least likely to have had meat on their table, tin workers and cigar makers to have neglected their clothing, and clerks and umbrella makers to have economised on beds. Some of the results can only be described as perplexing, even when reasonable at first sight, as for instance child mortality being lowest in families where the head was either a tailor or a butcher. This could be 'explained' by their opportunities for acquiring warm clothing and good quality meat respectively, except that neither occupation was highly rated on either account.

Further surprises are in store when we come to look at the strength of association between the several variables[24] for the most strongly linked pair are the amount earned by the head and that much smaller sum (on average about 14 per cent of the total family income)[25] contributed by other members of his family. It has sometimes been argued that the labour of the wife and children provided some compensation where the wages of the head were exceptionally poor[26], in which case the relationship would be an inverse one. Intensive competition for work of this sort, however, kept the remuneration low, some failing to find even part-time employment,[27] and the result in St. George in the East seems to have been to increase the earning power of those who were already in better circumstances than their neighbours.

Other associations in evidence were that between the possession of adequate clothing and the frequency with which rooms were cleansed, and, less obviously, between the amount spent on children's education and rent. The exact nature of the latter relationship is unclear. It is possible to think of families with considerable numbers of children needing larger accommodation and therefore spending more on rent as well as on school fees; possible also to see both as a sort of standard charge on a family's income which each met according to his ability. It should be emphasised, however, that what is being measured is how much was spent on education and not the number of children actually attending school, although the number of free places in itself seems too small to have much bearing on the calculations.

Here, unfortunately, we have to leave this material, its potential still largely unexploited, and turn to the second of the documents concerned with this survey[28] where information on place of birth, period of residence, the proportion of the population under 16, and the number of families receiving medical aid or connected with the Friendly Societies is displayed in 52 'blocks'. Not one of these characteristics featured in the Society's occupational classification and it is interesting to find as much variation in this set as in the previous. Take for instance the length of time families were said to have resided in the same house. It emerged that on average just under 40 per cent of these had only moved in within the previous year, yet it is possible to find 'blocks' where the percentage was as low as 3 per cent and others where it was as high as 75 per cent. Similarly it is possible to find 'blocks' where the proportion of those born in London was over 70 per cent, or under 30 per cent; there were 'blocks' in which no Irish were recorded and others in which they accounted for a third of all the families; even the proportion of the population under the age of 16 ranged between a low of 26 per cent and a high of 53 per cent. Random fluctuations are to be expected when numbers are small (on average there were approximately 23 houses and 34 families to each 'block') yet the fact that some 'blocks' differed in such a marked fashion from others, even those adjacent on the list, is too important to ignore. The difficulty is of course that it is impossible to translate these 'blocks' into living units. Most probably they have a geographical origin even though the total falls some way short of the number of separate streets, lanes and courts. Though it is only fair to point out that such reasoning rests on two unproven assumptions, first that the numbers in the extreme left-hand column do indeed refer to pages in the agents' notebooks[29] and second that the notebooks do mirror the agents' progress from house to house and court to court. It seems likely, and the evidence will not allow us to put it any more strongly, that within what an outsider might assume was a homogeneous district there existed a whole series of what might almost be termed neighbourhood 'cultures' – streets or sections of streets where sufficient residents possessed certain characteristics in common, be it nationality, age[30] or the frequency with which they shared their dwellings with another family, which set them somewhat apart from the generality.

A logical extension of this is to test for possible association between the variables. It might be thought, for example, that when the proportion of migrants in the population was high (measured either by place of birth or by the length of time that the family had resided in a particular dwelling) there would be more instances of two or more families to a house, particularly as many would be forced to take lodgings[31] before they were able to find accommodation more suited to their needs. Between the two districts[32] there are certainly substantial differences, the second emerging as the one with the rapid turnover in population and the large number of tenement dwellings. But other differences, not usually associated with areas of high migration, are equally important, especially the high proportion of children in the population, nor indeed is there much sign of one of the most frequent types of migrant – the unmarried lodger. A further problem is that the association between migration and a high family-to-house ratio breaks down altogether when we come to look at the first district in isolation. Preliminary work suggests that there was no relationship, either positive or negative, between any of the variables so far considered (with the sole exception that here families with children seem less likely to have had to share a house with another family) and that we are in fact looking at two different types of migration to two distinct, although adjoining districts.

Rather similar work can be carried out on the last of the documents in the present collection – the Reverend W. A. Queckett's census of the area lying immediately east of Cannon Street Road. Queckett is by no means an obscure figure. Besides his autobiography,[33] described in his *Dictionary of National Biography* entry as 'gossiping', his concern for the poor brought him to the attention of Charles Dickens who featured him in two articles in *Household Words*.[34] When Dickens wrote of eastern St. George's with its 'scores of houses, of six rooms, holding six families, scores of houses, of five rooms holding five families; hundreds of houses of four rooms, holding four families'[35] he might have had this very document in front of him for this is just what it contains, a street by street record of families, rooms and rents. Surprisingly, for a survey which gives considerable detail on the height, length and breadth of rooms, there is no statement of such essentials as the number of persons per room or even per family or house. So much information is in fact presented only as an average per house and then multiplied to give a further figure for a street, that there must be some doubt about the amount of actual enumeration that was undertaken. If, as seems likely, it was inspired by the somewhat earlier Royal Statistical Society activities, it was a very poor copy.[36]

Queckett, like Whitelaw, was badly in need of funds from wealthier parishes if the social work in which he was interested was to be continued; too much should not therefore be made of the fact that he often reported that both the water supply and drainage were poor, whereas west of the Cannon Street Road both had met with the approval of the Statistical Society. He is supported, however, by Dickens who had been much struck by the general poverty 'not always squalid, for many show the struggle for decency for appearances by a polished brass plate or door handle, with here and there bright symptoms of green paint portal and a whitened door-stone – for ever displaying the presence of a population of the humblest means'. In this case the census does provide a valuable corrective for it emphasises the great variety in living conditions, distinguishing the streets, often ill drained, where one family per room was commonplace and ceilings as well as rents were low,[37] from others, better drained, where rents per room were high (2s. 3d. and over) yet families occupied two, three or even four rooms. Even in the poorest streets, though, the poverty is unlikely to have approached that of Church Lane.

It has been pointed out often enough that there is no typical working class pattern of consumption just as there is no typical working class wage.[38] Similarly we should not be surprised at the existence of considerable differences within, as well as between, the areas we have been considering. Given this variety it is difficult to obtain any accurate picture of how different life might have been for the 'average' inhabitants in, say, St. George's, Church Lane St. Giles or Dublin. 'Into the back yard of each house . . . is flung, from the windows of each appartment, the ordure and other filth of its numerous inhabitants; from whence it is so seldom removed, that I have seen it nearly on a level with the windows of the first floor; and the moisture that . . . ouzes from this heap, having frequently no sewer to carry it off, runs into the street, by the entry leading to the staircase', wrote Whitelaw of the poorer parts of Dublin. 'The back yards are five or six feet square, . . . most of them have accumulations of filth and night-soil, and the drainage from them (which is superficial) runs through the passage of the houses into the street'; thus the Royal Statistical Society on Church Lane. The accounts are similar – the latter probably reproducing in miniature problems which existed in Dublin on a much larger scale although whether we should believe Whitelaw (p. 64) that, in some sections of this city, poverty was so widespread that prostitutes had to frequent other areas in search of custom, is another matter. One fact *is* certainly clear: the population of St. George in the East enjoyed a very much higher standard of living while in full employment. There is certainly no shortage of 'houses of ill-fame', carefully omitted in the Committee's survey. But there are other differences and it seems a trifle hard to regard the inhabitants just as representative of the grades immediately above the very poor which is all that the Committee claimed for them (p. 193). The Westminster working class, for instance, investigated by another Committee of the Society a few years earlier,[39] were probably poorer. Three quarters of all these families occupied only one room compared with only a third in

St. George's, and they owned fewer books, compensating for this with somewhat more pictures.[40] Against this it could be argued, firstly, that their rooms were better furnished (but this is a definition that is especially difficult to keep constant) and, secondly, that the rooms were considerably larger than in Queckett's section of St. George's.[41] In any case possession of two small rooms was a considerable advantage over one when, for a few extra feet, all activities of the household had to take place within the same four walls.

Nevertheless, it would be wrong to see St. George in the East as a sort of working class heaven on earth – rents were high in relation to income[42] and anything over its average of 2·0 persons per room was to be taken by the London County Council at the end of the century as constituting 'overcrowding' – just 22 per cent of all tenements being so classified in 1898.[43] On the other hand it is fairly easy to find areas of late nineteenth-century London where the overcrowding could be said to be worse than in St. George's in the 1840s.[44] Many of its inhabitants were also destined for an early grave yet here it is only right to insist on the important differences that do exist between the areas. Despite the chance of freak results due to small numbers, for only three of the twenty-eight occupational groups did child mortality rise to the 50 per cent level which is what Griffin found in the city that Thackeray had thought so poor – Limerick.[45]

In the poorer areas, the inhabitants were forever at the mercy of economic recession, epidemics, or the landlord, pub owner or shopkeeper on whom they might depend even for such a basic amenity as water. In such an inhospitable environment it is hardly surprising that the residents should often have been described as apathetic, resigned to their low places in society, the filth and stench regarded as an inconvenience if noticed at all. In Church Lane differences in life style between Irish and English carried a hint of racial tension – one harassed mother declared she accompanied her children to the privy to prevent them from being attacked. Some families had known better circumstances, others often without this advantage struggled to keep their furniture whole and rooms clean in the face of considerable odds. Such examples of 'self-help' were likely to appeal to the Committee but even in Church Lane not all found it so hard to get a living. In house 14 some 'dealers' had acquired a remarkable quantity of china while beneath them lived the lady with the valuable engravings who 'called herself a widow' and was 'supposed to obtain her living by letting the other parts of the house furnished'. It is all too easy to underestimate the human capacity to adjust to even the most straightened circumstances. Thackeray wrote[46] of Limerick 'there are long-haired girls of fourteen at every one of the windows, and dirty children everywhere. In the cellars, look at them in dingy white nightcaps over a bowl of stirabout; in the shop, paddling up and down the ruined steps, or issuing from beneath the black counter . . . sprawling at every door and court, paddling in every puddle. . . . The buzz and hum and chattering of this crowd is quite inconceivable'. This is a population which was at ease in its surroundings, if not in easy circumstances, for whom the room with the

broken chair and bed of shavings was home and the street with its piles of
refuse the world.                                                Richard Wall

Cambridge Group for the History of Population and Social Structure.
October 1973.

**Notes**

[1] Based on the opening section of William Makepeace Thackeray's *The Irish Sketch Book*, Smith, Elder and Co. pocket edition (1891).

[2] England decennially from 1801; Ireland, 1813, and decennially from 1821.

[3] Fiscal and census-type documents (e.g. Constables' Returns) predominate in the collection of pre-1801 listings held by the Cambridge Group but it was the incumbent who was responsible for the majority of the enumerations which did not owe their origin to some central directive.

[4] The census of Dublin is supposed to have occupied the Reverend James Whitelaw ten hours a day for five months. Nor was this the full extent of his labours for it was claimed that his 'careful supervision' was needed for two years and it was seven years before the work was finally published. See J. Warburton, J. Whitelaw and R. Walsh, *History of the City of Dublin* (1818) I p. viii.

[5] This emerged from a protracted correspondence with various record offices in Dublin including the Castle and the Public Record Office of Ireland between 1971 and 1973.

[6] The detailed table on York Street is to be found between pages 10 and 11, that relating to the Poddle is hidden away at the end of the parochial tables and before the alphabetical list of streets.

[7] This account has been based on the sketch of Whitelaw's life included in volume I of Warburton et al (1818).

[8] See for example Warburton et al (1818) I: appendix XI.

[9] See the article by M. W. Beaver, 'Population, infant mortality and milk' in *Population Studies* (July 1973) pp. 246–50.

[10] The Committee's own estimates (page 16) were approximately 50 per cent Irish born and 12 per cent of Irish descent. According to the summary Table 56 per cent of the rooms were occupied by Irish and only 20 per cent by English families but there was no information on nationality in a further 20 per cent of the cases. Only 4 per cent of the rooms were in 'mixed' occupancy.

[11] H. Jephson, *The Sanitary Evolution of London* (1907) *passim*. The Committee said merely that its attention had been drawn to Church Lane by one of its own members (p. 1).

[12] J. Bonar and H. W. Macrosty, *Annals of the Royal Statistical Society 1834–1934* (1934) p. 39. Such enquiries were described as both tedious and time-consuming.

[13] There were, for instance, various regulations governing the use of cellars for living accommodation and in 1859 one local Inspector complained that they were reoccupied as fast as they could be cleared (Jephson p. 110). The

Royal Statistical Society on the other hand not only found several rooms which were used during the day-time but even one in which some inmates had been sleeping.

[14] This was indeed the line taken by some members of the Society at the time. See Bonar and Macrosty, *Annals of the Royal Statistical Society* (1934).

[15] If we count as beds those piles of shavings and rags which the Committee saw in corners of some of the rooms then the number falls somewhat to just over 4 persons to a ' bed '.

[16] See for example the report quoted by Jephson, p. 109.

[17] The failure of re-housing schemes to make more than a marginal contribution to solving the housing problems of 19th century London is detailed in A. S. Wohl ' The housing of the working classes in London 1815–1914 ' in S. D. Chapman, *The history of working-class housing* (1971).

[18] Based on the relative proportions of English and Irish at the two dates. In the unlikely event of there having been no one of Irish descent in 1841 (in 1847 one eighth of the entire population was so described) then the percentage increase would be no more than about 4 per cent. It is true that Mann does say (p. 20) that he had no wish to decide between the merits of street improvements and Irish immigration as a cause of the increase in population, but by pp. 23–4 he certainly seems to have decided to pin most blame on the Irish. There were certainly more deaths in the years following the famine when Irish might be expected to have reached the street, but his only firm evidence lay in the Committee's statement that in 1847 the Irish formed 50 per cent of the total population, whereas he knew from his own work on 1841 that the Irish had then constituted no more than 40 per cent.

[19] The names of A. Balfour and J. Wardlow appear on the left-hand margin of the Table, connected with the present survey, which is reproduced below. Now located in the library of the Royal Statistical Society it is according to the present Secretary the only document to have survived from what must have been very considerable workings. The Committee, in its Report, detailed four ' stages ' of data preparation (p. 194) but the surviving Table would seem to belong to none of these. It may have been one more product of some uncoordinated research.

[20] ' Report of the Committee of the Statistical Society of London on the state of the working classes in the parishes of St. Margaret and St. John Westminster ', *Journal of the Royal Statistical Society* III. There were certain other minor differences, for instance the Westminster survey included questions on dimensions of rooms, on whether the children had been vaccinated, and on the number of families forced to share privies. On the other hand some important items are missing from the earlier survey – particularly data on earnings and on fertility and mortality.

[21] The Committee's own qualifications to its mortality analysis are set out on p. 225. See also D. Griffin, 'An enquiry into the mortality among the poor of the city of Limerick', *Journal of the Royal Statistical Society* III (1841) p. 318.

[22] One possible reason for this may have been the lack of funds which had already caused the Society to abandon the collection of raw data and restrict very carefully those eager authors who wished to insert elaborate Tables in their articles in the Journal. See Bonar and Macrosty, *Annals of the Royal Statistical Society* (1934) p. 66.

[23] Measured according to their rank when all the variables were taken together. It is hoped to spell out the procedures in more detail in a future publication.

[24] Full details of the way in which this was measured cannot be given here but in essence it consisted of counting the occasions on which the variables were distant by the same amount in the same direction from the average for each occupation.

[25] This was in fact somewhat more than the 10 per cent which was all that was added to the income of the better paid workers of Booth's late nineteenth-century London but was of course far short of what members of the family could contribute in textile districts. See J. Burnett, *A history of the cost of living* (1969) pp. 252–3.

[26] e.g. by Burnett p. 253.

[27] Points in fact made by the Committee, see pp. 203, 210.

[28] In 1973 still inadequately described by the Royal Statistical Society Library as 'A record of some form of enumeration of households' although the totals of the various columns agree exactly with those in the article in the Society's Journal. Although the table is mostly self-explanatory, the attempt to show distribution of adults not forming part of any of the co-resident nuclear families, makes for complexity, but the difficulties can be resolved by a close scrutiny of the appropriate Tables in the article. One minor discrepancy should also be noted, the proportion of children in the population is here said to include all those aged 15 and under whereas the article has it that the children are those 'under 15'. A little further light is also shown on some of the other tabulations, for instance it emerges that none of the women heading families were asked whether they read a newspaper.

[29] Suggested by the evenness of the numbers and the fact that they recommence at the place where the list has been divided into two and the name of the 'agent' inserted. The division gives us two distinct districts which we will have occasion to refer to later.

[30] The age of the household head as well as age structure in general implied by the variation in the proportion of children in the population.

[31] Unfortunately lodgers were not recorded as such in the census. Unmarried adults were classed separately (although not all in this class were necessarily lodgers – some may have been relatives) and if the entire family was in lodgings it would simply be counted as one of the families sharing that particular house.

[32] For an explanation see above note 29.

[33] W. A. Queckett, *My sayings and doings* (1887).

[34] *Household words*, 16 November 1850 and 24 January 1852.

[35] This, however, was an exaggeration for in about one third of the streets the average was at least two rooms per family.

[36] Queckett's survey is dated 1847. The population of the district was given as 17,124 and the number of houses as 2,618 which yields a ratio of 6·54 persons to a house, figures remarkably close to those for the St. Paul district of St. George in the East in the Census of 1841 (17,724, 2,641 and 6·52 respectively) but they cannot be squared with his figure for the number of families since dividing the one by the other gives an average family size of only 2·69.

[37] Rents were not noticeably as low when rooms were merely small (less than 9 feet long and 8 feet six inches wide) possibly because although ostensibly calculated *per room* they referred in some cases to two or more rooms if let as a single unit.

[38] e.g. by Burnett, *A history of the cost of living* (1969) p. 258. See also his *Plenty and want* (1968) p. 67. A weekly wage of 15 shillings gave an 'existence', 30 shillings yielded 'comfort' while 40 shillings and above took the owner into the ranks of labour aristocracy. All three were represented in the Royal Statistical Society's survey of St. George's.

[39] *Journal of the Royal Statistical Society*, III (1841).

[40] However, this plausible inverse relationship – that those who were unable to read might be inclined to acquire more pictures – is not detectable in the St. George's data.

[41] 42 per cent of the rooms were described as well-furnished compared with 31 per cent in the Statistical Society's survey of St. George in the East. 70 per cent of the rooms measured at least 12 feet by 14 feet; not one of Queckett's streets averaged rooms of this size.

[42] 15 per cent of income was devoted to rent, more than was allowed for in the 'ideal' budgets quoted by Burnett, *Plenty and want* p. 64, although for rent to absorb at least this amount of a family's income in urban areas was not unusual.

[43] Wohl, 'The housing of the working classes in London' in S. D. Chapman, *The history of working-class housing* (1971) p. 25.

[44] For example St. Giles in 1884. See Jephson, *The sanitary evolution of London* (1907), p. 314. It is important to remember that the three London censuses reproduced in this volume cover only a section of the working class community and should not therefore be used to suggest that in general overcrowding was either less or more prevalent at this period than later in the century.

[45] Griffin, 'An enquiry into the mortality among the poor of the city of Limerick', *Journal of the Royal Statistical Society*, III (1841), although the figures are subject to a certain bias because only those families who had taken sick children to the Dispensary would be included (see p. 320).

[46] Thackeray, *The Irish Sketch Book* (1891 edition) pp. 144–5.

AN

# ESSAY

ON THE

## POPULATION OF DUBLIN.

BEING THE

### RESULT OF AN ACTUAL SURVEY

TAKEN IN 1798, WITH GREAT CARE AND PRECISION,

AND ARRANGED IN A MANNER ENTIRELY NEW.

BY THE

### REV. JAMES WHITELAW, M.R.I.A.

VICAR OF ST. CATHARINE'S.

TO WHICH IS ADDED,

*The General Return of the District Committee in* 1804,

WITH

A COMPARATIVE STATEMENT OF THE TWO SURVEYS,

ALSO,

### SEVERAL OBSERVATIONS

ON THE

### PRESENT STATE

OF THE

*Poorer Parts of the City of Dublin.*

DUBLIN:

PRINTED FOR THE AUTHOR,

BY GRAISBERRY AND CAMPBELL, NO. 10, BACK-LANE.

1805.

Republished in 1974 by Gregg International Publishers Limited
Westmead, Farnborough, Hants., England

---

*May it please your Excellency,*

WHILE I feel highly gratified by your Excellency's permission, to place the Statistical Survey of the City of Dublin under your protection, I am cheered by the pleasing hope, that, in such hands, it may be the humble instrument of beneficial effects. And should the following statements, founded on absolute facts, excite your Excellency's attention to the scenes of misery which I have witnessed; should they be the means of rescuing one son of wretchedness from filth and poverty; I shall not consider that I have toiled in vain. To your Excellency's administration, every eye looks forward with hope; an administration, uniformly distinguished by attention to the *poor:*

the

the salutary influence of whose example, has already produced such a general disposition to alleviate the evils of
suffering humanity; and afforded, in the
person of your Excellency, and your
amiable Consort, a splendid proof,
that high birth, and elevated station,
are not incompatible with condescen-
sion and mercy. The benefits resulting
to this country, from measures at once
mild, conciliating, and wise, will long
be written in the hearts of Irishmen;
and, that you may long continue to
enjoy the pleasing sensations resulting
from virtuous conduct, is the sincere
prayer of,

YOUR EXCELLENCY'S OBLIGED,

AND DEVOTED,

HUMBLE SERVANT,

JAMES WHITELAW.

# ADVERTISEMENT.

The following Essay, though originally written with a view to publication, had been nearly consigned to oblivion, when his Excellency the Lord Lieutenant condescended to peruse the manuscript. It was honoured with his approbation; and, ever anxious to promote whatever might supply even a single hint towards ameliorating the state of a city, in which he is looked up to with general affection, he was pleased to express a wish to see it in print. Thus recommended, it will, I trust, interest the Public. The work, to which it refers, has, at least, the merit of originality; nothing of the kind having ever yet appeared. As its bulk, however, amounting to nearly five hundred tables in folio, rendered its publication inexpedient, the author thought that the following epitomè, giving the general result of the survey, stating the precautions taken to render it accurate, and comprising some of its most interesting tables, would be acceptable to the Public. Few capitals abound more with nuisances, unfavourable to health and comfort, than the poorer parts of Dublin. These the author investigated, during the course of the survey, with painful attention; and he has stated a few of the most prominent, with a minuteness, perhaps disgusting, and for which the purity of his intention can be the only apology. As to literary reputation, the very nature of the work precludes every idea of the kind. All the merit he claims, and to this, he presumes, he is fully entitled, is, the humble merit of unwearied toil, and patient investigation, in the search for truth; to which he may add, an anxious wish that his labours may be useful.

Dublin, June, 1805.

# ACCOUNT

## OF AN ENUMERATION OF THE

## INHABITANTS

OF

## *THE CITY OF DUBLIN.*

———

THAT national wealth and security are the result of a numerous, industrious, well-governed population, and not of widely extended dominion, is a position, I believe, universally admitted. To create, therefore, this blessing where it does not exist, and to improve it to the utmost where it does, will, naturally, be a favourite object with every prince, who is anxious for the prosperity of the people intrusted to his care. Towards the attainment of this wise and beneficent end, the first and most essential requisite is an accurate knowledge of the actual state of the population of his dominions; a knowledge which can be acquired

B                                        only

only by a faithful and intelligent survey, specifying with minute precision the different degrees of density in different districts, and pointing out the causes of this variation, whether local, accidental, or artificial. With this preliminary information, a wise government may do much; without it, the best intended efforts will be ill-directed and ineffectual. And yet, in the acquisition of a knowledge so really useful, how little has been done by the enlightened nations of Europe! Several ingenious men indeed have, in their studies, entered into curious calculations on the subject, but founded on such insufficient facts, on such bold assumptions, and uncertain conjectures, that the result of their labours, inapplicable to any practical purpose, can scarcely gratify a rational curiosity. How widely different from each other are the different calculations of the population of England;* varying from five to nine millions? That of her immense capital is a matter of equal uncertainty; and of our own metropolis, the population has been

* This was written before the late census.

been variously stated, from 128,570, at which number it was estimated by Dr. Rutty in 1753, to 300 000, which seems at present the popular idea.

Struck with this strange diversity of opinion, anxious to ascertain the truth, and influenced, perhaps, by a laudable ambition of being the first to offer to the public, what it has often wished for in vain, an accurate well arranged census of a considerable capital, I availed myself of the favourable opportunity offered by the unhappy situation of this city at the commencement of the late rebellion; and, with the sanction of Government, but at my own private expence and toil, began a census of the inhabitants of the city of Dublin, early in the month of Ma , 1798.

When I first entered on the business, I conceived that I should have little more to do than to transcribe carefully the list of inhabitants affixed to the door of each house by order of the Lord Mayor. As the families of the middle and upper classes always contained some individual who was competent to the task, and as few had
any

any motive to conceal or misrepresent, I
found their lists, in general, extremely correct: but among the lower class, which
forms the great mass of the population of
this city, the case was very different. The
lists on the doors of their wretched habitations, presented generally to view a con-
fused chaos of names, frequently illegible,
and generally short of the actual number,
by a third, or even one-half. This I at
first imputed to design, but was afterwards
convinced that it proceeded from ignorance
and incapacity. In order effectually to obvi-
ate this difficulty, my assistants and I, un-
deterred by the dread of infectious diseases,
undismayed by degrees of filth, stench, and
darkness inconceivable, by those who have
not experienced them, explored, in the burn-
ing months of the summer of 1798, every
room of these wretched habitations, from
the cellar to the garret, and on the spot
ascertained their population. In this business I expected opposition, but experienced
none. So universal, at this period, was the
dread of being suspected of disaffection,
and so powerful was the secretary's seal
and

and signature, that every person seemed anxious to assist; and, when this terror gradually subsided, a rumour circulated that I was employed by Government to take an account of the poor inhabitants, prepara- tory to the adoption of some system for the relief of their necessities; which produced a similar effect, from a far more pleasing mo- tive. In the course of the survey, one only of our number received a serious insult. In attempting to remonstrate with a butcher of Ormond-market, on the incorrectness of his list, the human brute flung at him a quantity of blood and offals.

I was at first much embarrassed by the in- experience of my assistants. I employed them, therefore, in taking surveys of streets which I had already surveyed myself, until I disco- vered that they had attained a sufficient de- gree of accuracy. I never, however, relied on their returns with implicit confidence, but made them frequently act as checks on each other. Two or more of them frequently sur- veyed the same street in succession, without any communication with each other, and, if any material variation occurred, I investigated

tignted it myself on the spot. I was, besides, constantly engaged, during the continuance of the survey, in taking the population of the poorest and most thickly inhabited houses of the poorest streets, as these were most likely to produce confusion and error, in order to serve as checks on their returns. Hence it happens that, in the poorer parts of the city, there are few streets that have not been twice, and some even three times surveyed,

In a country, where difference of religious opinions has been the source of so much misery, to ascertain the number belonging to each religious sect would be gratifying to many, and particularly at a period when animosities, that were supposed to be nearly extinguished, have been unfortunately revived. The calculations, or, to speak more properly, the conjectures on this subject, are so various and discordant, that I was anxious to determine the point, as far as it concerned the capital. On a nearer view, however, I found it a subject of extreme delicacy: the temper of the times seemed to discourage enquiry, and I was obliged, though with reluctance, to relinquish the idea. On this subject, however, I

shall

shall take the liberty to intimate, that truth may be sufficiently approximated by a little exertion on the part of the Protestant clergy. In their domiciliary visits, they may easily ascertain the number of their respective flocks, with sufficient accuracy, while engaged in the performance of an essential and pleasing part of their duty, and without giving alarm to any by the parade of a census. There may, at first view, seem to be some difficulty in discovering the habitations of poor Protestant room-keepers; but the parish registers of births and marriages, which, in consequence of the repeated injunctions of the late and present Archbishops of Dublin, are now, I believe, kept with accuracy,. will generally serve as guides where to find them; and, as each poor room-keeper has generally some knowledge of those of his own communion in his neighbourhood, the clergyman, who is willing to exert himself, will seldom want the necessary information. I should not have suggested this mode with so much confidence, had not experience convinced me that it is practicable. I have myself, by the means proposed, obtained a complete list of the Protes-

tant

tant inhabitants of the parish of St. Catharine, at once the largest, and nearly the poorest in this city; which specifies the age, sex, and occupation of every individual; together with their state of education, if children; and such other circumstances as may be singularly useful to a parish minister, in the execution of an indispensable, but too much neglected duty. The number of Protestants, deducted from the gross population of each parish, as ascertained by the present survey, will shew the number of those of the Church of Rome, without any material error, except, perhaps, in St. Catharine's parish, where allowance must be made for a considerable number of Quakers.

The materials, thus collected, with the incessant toil of at least ten hours each day, during five successive months, were next to be arranged. The plan I have adopted, I trust, is such, that the work may be considered as a correct and faithful picture of the actual state of Dublin in the year 1798, and may, at any future period, be compared as such with its then existing state, in order to discover, at a single glance, the changes, whether for better or worse, which have taken place in the lapse of
time.

time. For this purpose, not only the position of every house is given, with the population, and the proprietor's name and occupation; but its elevation or number of stories; whether it is modern built or old; and whether, with respect to its state of repair, it is good, midling, bad, or ruinous, are all expressed by appropriate marks. The width of the streets at either end is also given, with its commencement and termination, and the intersections of other streets, lanes, &c. with their breadth where they enter it. If the contiguity of the houses be interrupted by a dead wall, waste ground, or any other object, its position and extent in yards are carefully marked. Public buildings are placed in their proper situations. The position of the different sides of each street, with respect to the points of the compass, with the parish in which it is situate, are expressed; and if the boundary line between two parishes cross it, the houses between which it passes are accurately noted. This seeming multiplicity of objects, with a variety of others unnecessary to detail, are, I think, minutely delineated, without the slightest confusion. For the truth

c of

of this statement I must refer to the work itself, where it may be observed, that each page
is divided into six columns by strong lines.
The first of these columns is subdivided into
four by finer lines; of which the first contains
the number of houses in regular order; the
second the number actually on the door; the
third its state of repair, in which the letters
n, g, m, b, r, express *new*, *good*, *midling*,
*bad*, *ruinous;* and the fourth column gives
the elevation expressed in stories above the
ground floor.    The second column, titled *Upper and middle Classes*, subdivided into three,
gives the males, females, and total of that
description in each house;  while the third
column gives the servants of ditto, similarly
divided,   The fourth column, titled *Lower
Class*, exhibits the great mass of the labouring
poor,  working manufacturers, &c. who are
not in the service of others, similarly divided.
The fifth column gives the grand total, divided
into males and females; and the last column
contains the name and occupation of the proprietor, if resident; if not, the letters **P. T.**
intimate that he has it set in poor tenements.
On the left-hand margin of the page, the extent

tent of each side of the street is marked, with
its direction with respect to the cardinal points;
and, on the right-hand margin, the parish or
parishes, in which the whole or different parts
of it are situate.

The examination of a few pages of the work
will, I hope, shew that its claim to perspicuity
is not unfounded. But, as it is accessible to
few, and its bulk (two folio volumes) renders
its publication inexpedient, I have, for the satisfaction of the reader, annexed the table,
containing York-street, as a sample of the
method I have adopted. Immediately after
the name, its breadth at either end is given,
in feet and inches. In the first horizontal
space, Aungier-street is written, intimating
that it commences at, and is numbered from
thence; then follow the houses, in regular succession, from No. 1 to No. 13, where their
contiguity is interrupted by the intersection of
French-street, which is here twenty-nine feet
wide. The series of houses is again resumed,
until again interrupted by Proud's-lane, only
eighteen feet wide, which is succeeded by a
dead wall of forty-three yards to Lord Roden's
house, where the south side of York-street,

as

as appears by the left-hand margin, terminates in Stephen's-green. From the Green we
return along the north side, in which we first
meet a dead wall of eighty yards bounding
the Quakers burial ground, and from thence
a continuity of houses to Aungier-street, interrupted only by the intersection of Mercer-
street, thirty-one feet wide; and, by directing
the eye to the right-hand margin, we find
that the entire street is in St. Peter's parish.

Giving the breadth of the streets, and
noting their waste or unbuilt on spaces,
may, perhaps, seem to some superfluous:
but such persons will please to recollect,
that these are points which plans seldom
ascertain. In some of our latest productions,
the narrowest alleys are widened into respectable streets; while streets that have but
a few straggling houses, or that exist only
in idea, are represented as completely occupied by buildings. I am anxious, besides,
to give posterity a work, which may enable
them to compare the same street with itself
at very distant periods, in order to discover its
improvement or decline; and, in such a point
of view, these are most essential features.

The

The corner or angle houses are, it is obvious, situate in two streets; and hence it is necessary to specify in which of them they are numbered.

The limits of several of the parishes are so very irregular, that streets of a very moderate extent frequently pay ministers money to three different incumbents. This is the case with the Poddle, (see the table). The north side of this street commences we find from Francis-street, in which the corner house is numbered; and by the left-hand margin we see, that the ten first houses between Francis-street and Patrick-street belong to the parish of St. Nicholas Without: the 11th and 12th, between Patrick-street and Upper Kevin's-street, belong to the Deanery of St. Patrick; the 13th, 14th, and 15th, on the south side, to St. Nicholas Without; and the remainder of the south side to St, Luke's. This is so clearly expressed, that any person of common understanding, with the table in his hand, might instantly find the limits on the spot, not only by the numbers of the houses, but where these may happen to be erased or altered, which frequently happens, by their relative situation with respect to the intersecting streets.

From

From the survey of the squares, streets, lanes, alleys, courts, &c. of the city of Dublin, thus arranged with persevering patience, the tables of the population of its parishes were formed. In these, the first column expresses the streets or parts of streets that compose it; the second, third, fourth, and fifth, give their population properly arranged; the sixth exhibits the number of houses in each street, distinguished into inhabited and waste; the seventh shews the average population to an inhabited house, both for the entire parish, and its principal streets; and, finally, the left-hand margin serves an an index to the page, where the particular survey of each street, &c. may be found.

I have annexed these parochial tables, but in an abridged form; the population being divided into males and females only, and not ranged according to their classes, as in the original work.

From the addition of the totals of these parochial tables, I formed the following general table of the population of Dublin, in which I have retained the classification of the inhabitants, and hope it will be satisfactory to the reader.

To

To the total of this table, viz. . . . . . . 172,091

We must add for the Garrison, about . 7,000

Royal Hospital . . . . . . . . . . . . . 400

Foundling Hospital, in July 1798 . . . 558

St. Patrick's Hospital, do. . . . . . . . 155

House of Industry, do. . . . . . . . . . 1,637

Trinity College, at present 597, in 1798 529

Castle . . . . . . . . . . . . . . . . . . 000

Total population of Dublin, in 1798, } 182,370*
may be estimated at . . . . . . }

As a salutary precaution against the revival of that disaffection, which in 1798 pervaded the poorer parts of Dublin, Government, in 1803, ordered that the city and its immediate vicinity should be divided into 53 wards or districts, which, from motives of œconomy, were afterwards réduced to the present number of 21. These were entrusted to the inspection of Conservators, who were directed to make accurate lists of the population of their respective districts. As I have reason to believe that this work was generally

* This is on the supposition, that the population of Ormond-market and Spring-garden was nearly the same in 1798 and 1804; and I am ignorant of any cause that could have produced a material change.

rally executed with care, and in some instances with minute precision, I am happy that the polite attention of my worthy and ingenious friend, M. Handcock, Esq. Deputy Muster-Master-General, has enabled me to lay its general result before the public. It is arranged, in the following table, in such a manner, as to shew the population, both of the former, and at present existing districts. As no return was made by the Conservators for the districts of Grange-Gorman, Broadstone, and Grand Canal, distinguished in the table by an asterism*, I have supplied the deficiency from my survey. To the district of St. Kevin's, No. 37, I have added 13 houses, and 95 souls, the population of Old Portobello, omitted by the Conservators of that district; and I shall add a comparative view of the general result of the two surveys in 1798 and 1804.

## Population of Dublin in 1804 as returned by the District Committee.

| | PRESENT DISTRICTS. | | | | FORMER DISTRICTS. | | |
|---|---|---|---|---|---|---|---|
| Nos. | NAMES. | Houses. | Population. | Nos. | NAMES. | Houses. | Population. |
| 1 | Barrack, | 638 | 5673 | 1 | Barrack, | 228 | 3157 |
| | | | | 2 | Mountpelier, | 410 | 2516 |
| | | | | 3 | Aughrim, | | |
| 2 | House of Industry, | 458 | 3104 | 4 | Grange-Gorman,* | 154 | 883 |
| | | | | 7 | House of Industry, | 146 | 1482 |
| | | | | 8 | Broadstone,* | 158 | 739 |
| 3 | Smithfield, | 706 | 9432 | 5 | Smithfield, | 310 | 3143 |
| | | | | 6 | St. Michan's, | 396 | 6289 |
| 4 | King's-Inns, | 966 | 9964 | 12 | New Gaol, | 357 | 4025 |
| | | | | 13 | King's-Inns, | 609 | 5939 |
| 5 | Linen-hall, | 495 | 4025 | 9 | Royal Circus, | 186 | 1263 |
| | | | | 10 | Dorset-street, | 126 | 931 |
| | | | | 11 | Linen-hall, | 183 | 1831 |
| 6 | St. Mary's, | 876 | 9785 | 14 | St. Mary's, | 401 | 4417 |
| | | | | 21 | Henry-street, | 475 | 5368 |

D

## Population of Dublin in 1804, as returned by the District Committee, continued.

### PRESENT DISTRICTS.

| Nos. | NAMES. | Houses. | Population. |
|---|---|---|---|
| 7 | Rutland-square, | 1033 | 9663 |
| 8 | St. Thomas's, | 439 | 4780 |
| 9 | Custom-house, | 869 | 4623 |
| | Total north of the Liffey, | 6480 | 61049 |

### FORMER DISTRICTS.

| Nos. | NAMES. | Houses. | Population. |
|---|---|---|---|
| 15 | Simpson's Hospital, | 161 | 1793 |
| 16 | Rutland-square, | 159 | 1805 |
| 17 | St. George's, | 449 | 4095 |
| 18 | Mountjoy-square, | 264 | 1970 |
| 20 | St. Thomas's, | 314 | 2861 |
| 22 | Marlborough-green, | 125 | 1919 |
| 19 | Gloster-place, | 272 | 2002 |
| 23 | Custom-house, | 66 | 494 |
| 24 | North Lotts, | 186 | 841 |
| 51 | Spring-garden, | 345 | 1286 |
| | This population gives an average of 9.42 to a house, | 6480 | 61049 |

*Population of Dublin in 1804, as returned by the District Committee, continued.*

## PRESENT DISTRICTS.

| No. | NAMES. | Houses. | Population. |
|---|---|---|---|
| 10 | College, . . . . . . . | 701 | 9335 |
| 11 | Merion-square, . . . . | 725 | 6626 |
| 12 | St. Stephen's-green, . . . | 738 | 6510 |
| 13 | King William's . . . . | 1243 | 14212 |
| 14 | Castle, . . . . . | 1122 | 11683 |
| 15 | St. Kevin's, . . . . | 797 | 8338 |

## FORMER DISTRICTS.

| Nos. | NAMES. | Houses. | Population. |
|---|---|---|---|
| 25 | Grand Canal* . . . | 1 | 7 |
| 26 | St. Mark's, . . . | 294 | 3773 |
| 33 | Trinity College, . . | 406 | 5555 |
| 27 | Merion-square, . . . | 290 | 2264 |
| 32 | St. Anne's, . . . | 435 | 4362 |
| 28 | Fitzwilliam-square, . | 174 | 1686 |
| 29 | St. Stephen's-green, . | 77 | 679 |
| 30 | Harcourt-street, . . | 487 | 4145 |
| 31 | Powerscourt, . . . | 694 | 7700 |
| 34 | King William's, . . | 549 | 6512 |
| 35 | Castle, . . . . | 746 | 7406 |
| 36 | St. Peter's, . . . | 376 | 4277 |
| 37 | St. Kevin's, . . . | 316 | 3968 |
| 38 | New-street, . . . | 291 | 3170 |
| 53 | Harold's-cross, . . | 190 | 1200 |

## Population of Dublin in 1804, as returned by the District Committee, continued.

### PRESENT DISTRICTS.

| Nos. | NAMES. | Houses. | Population. |
|---|---|---|---|
| 16 | St. Patrick's, . . . . . | 1354 | 18695 |
| 17 | Usher's-island, . . . . | 785 | 7486 |
| 18 | St. Catharine's, . . . . | 1240 | 15235 |
| 19 | Weaver's-square, . . . | 470 | 6102 |
| 20 | Royal Hospital, . . . . | 493 | 5457 |
| 21 | Sandymount and Black-rock, . | 399 | 2943 |
|  | Total South of the Liffey, | 9754 | 110993 |
|  | Total Population of Dublin, &c. . . . . . | 16234 | 172042 |

### FORMER DISTRICTS.

| Nos. | NAMES. | Houses. | Population. |
|---|---|---|---|
| 42 | St. Patrick's, . . . | 822 | 11146 |
| 43 | Christ-church, . . . | 532 | 7549 |
| 44 | Usher's-island, . . . | 551 | 3281 |
| 45 | James's gate, . . . | 234 | 4205 |
| 40 | St. Luke's, . . . | 594 | 7390 |
| 41 | St. Catharine's, . . | 646 | 7845 |
| 39 | Weaver's-square, . . | 229 | 2506 |
| 46 | Marybonne-lane, . . | 241 | 3596 |
| 47 | City Bason, . . . | 187 | 1826 |
| 48 | St. James's, . . . | 127 | 1582 |
| 49 | Royal Hospital, . . | 179 | 2049 |
| 50 | Kilmainham, . . . |  |  |
| 52 | Sandymount and Black-rock, . | 399 | 2943 |
|  | This population gives an average of 11.38 to a house, . . . | 9754 | 110593 |
|  | Average, 10.51 to a house, . . . | 16234 | 172042 |

The district of Harold's-cross, with that
of Sandy-mount and Black-rock, cannot with
any propriety be considered as parts of Dublin. If, therefore, we deduct their population, the comparative statement of the surveys, in 1798 and 1804, will stand thus:

|  | Houses. | Inhabitants. |
|---|---|---|
| Population according to my survey in 1798, | 16,023 | 170,361 |
| Ormond Market not returned by me, taken from the Conservators survey, | 33 | 444 |
| Spring-garden not returned by me, as lying beyond the circular road; but properly a part of Dublin, taken from do. | 345 | 1,286 |
| Total population in 1798 - - - - | 16,401 | 172,091 |
| Population, according to the Conservators, in 1804, supplying deficiencies as above, | 16,234 | 172,042 |
| Population of the district of Harold's-cross, with that of Sandy-mount and Black-rock deducted, as not being parts of Dublin, | 589 | 4,143 |
| Total population in 1804 - - - | 15,645 | 167,899 |
| The return of 1798, therefore, exceeds that of 1804, by | 756 | 4,192 |

Of

Of the 16,023 houses, returned by me in 1798, 14,821 were inhabited, and 1,202 waste; the exact position of every one of which is distinctly marked in the survey.

If to the 16,401 houses, which I state as existing in 1798, we add 401 houses, which appear, from the returns in 1804, to have been built, in the intermediate period, in the parishes of St. Thomas and St. George only, the Conservators must have omitted 1157 houses at least, which were probably waste. In consequence of this increase of new houses, it was reasonable, that the return of the Conservators, for the districts on the north side of the Liffey, should exceed mine by 1455 souls. A greater encrease of population might indeed have been expected; but many of these 401 houses were probably untenanted in 1804, as they appear to have added only 2474 souls to the parishes of St. Thomas and St. George, which gives an average of only 6.1 to an house.

Of the above excess, of 4182 inhabitants in 1798, I found 3960 in that portion of the city westward of Fishamble street, Werburgh-street, and Bride-street; and, of these, the

the far greater part in the districts which
were the center of rebellion. But whether
this excess is only apparent, and owing to
inaccuracy in the returns of the Conservators
of these districts, or was occasioned by an
influx of rebels from the country at that
period, I do not presume to determine: nor,
indeed, am I possessed of *data* sufficient to
enable me to form any decided opinion on
the subject. It may be necessary to observe,
that a considerable number of Protestants
of condition, took shelter in Dublin just
at this period: their names, however, appeared in the lists under the head of *visitors;*
and, as they properly formed no part of its
population, they were not included in the
survey.

Ascertaining the population of Dublin is
but a part of the object I wished to attain.
The accounts of the most enlightened travel-
lers, and, indeed, the calculations of the most
intelligent natives themselves, with respect
to the population of the principal cities, not
only of the remoter parts of the world, but
of civilized Europe itself, are strangely extravagant, contradictory, and uncertain.—
This,

This, in many instances, originates in national vanity, which seems perversely to take delight in one of the most serious of national evils, an overgrown capital. It oftener, I apprehend, arises from our having no certain principle on which to found any calculation whatever; in which situation, the mind, unwilling to acknowledge ignorance, and naturally inclined to exaggeration, adopts the most extravagant guesses for sober calculation. Struck with this strange contradiction in writers of reputed veracity, I, early in the survey, formed an idea of managing it in such a manner, as would enable me to deduce from it some *data*, some fixed principles to direct us, in forming calculations of the population of cities, from such materials of acknowledged merit as do exist.

We have geometric plans, and some good ones, of most of the principal cities of Europe; and yet, from the want of the *data* to which I allude, it has not occurred to any writer, that I know of, to make any use of them in computing their population. The method I have adopted, to render them

subservient

subservient to this end, is, I believe, new. I do not offer it, however, as capable of precision, for that must be the result of actual survey alone; but I consider it as a better method of approximating truth, than most of those usually resorted to; and, in all cases, a sufficient check on that extravagance in calculation, to which I have alluded.

The density of population varies exceedingly in different quarters of the same city. Our ancestors, in times of turbulence and confusion, more anxious for security, than studious of convenience and elegance, crouded their habitations together, so as not to occupy a space too large for the purposes of defence. As domestic tranquillity became better secured, they gradually extended their quarters: persons of wealth and condition abandoned their former residence to the poorer class of citizens, built more airy houses in more spacious streets, and gradually refined into that stile of elegance that now prevails. Hence it happens that, in the ancient part of most cities, the population is dense, in proportion both to the number of houses, and the space they occupy; while, in the more modern parts, the

train

train of servants, ever attendant on opulence and luxury, gives a population, great indeed in proportion to the number of houses, but inconsiderable, if we regard the area they occupy in extensive back-grounds and spacious streets.

I therefore concluded, if I could accurately ascertain the number of souls on an area of given dimensions, such as a square English acre, actually occupied by buildings, both in the ancient and modern parts of our capital; that from hence would result rules, whereby to form a probable conjecture of the population of other cities, of which we have good geometric plans. With these *data*, all that seems necessary is, simply to measure on its plan the area of any city actually occupied by buildings; carefully distinguishing what portion of it may be considered as ancient, and what modern, and allowing to each that number of souls per acre, which was actually found to exist on an acre of the ancient or modern parts of Dublin in 1798.

The mensuration, made on the plan for this purpose, will require, it is obvious, some

some care and attention. It is usual to give us the extent of cities by their length, breadth, and circumference; but, if we aim at correctness, this method is perfectly nugatory. By circumference, I believe, we mean usually a line touching its several advanced points, and including an area, varying greatly in extent as it approximates to, or recedes from a circle. This line almost universally includes a considerable space occupied by fields and gardens. The length and breadth taken, as usual, between its most distant points, multiplied into each other, will also give an area far beyond the truth, unless the city is a square or rectangle, which scarce ever happens. I adopted, therefore, a method much more correct; and, as I propose it to the imitation of others, I shall take the liberty of explaining it somewhat at large.

I took Roque's plan of Dublin, on a scale of twenty perches Irish to an inch, for my ground-work, as I found it, on examination, a few errors in the limits of the parishes excepted, sufficiently accurate. Having corrected these errors, and added, from actual survey, the streets that have been built

built since the period of its publication, I traced round its contour a number of right lines, which separated the surrounding waste ground from the space actually occupied by buildings, and thus reduced the entire city into one great irregular polygon. This polygon I subdivided into several smaller ones, by tracing with care the boundary lines of the parishes, and also lines inclosing the area occupied by the Liffey, our great squares, the College Park, the Castle and its dependencies, and other considerable spaces not built on; and, if any parish comprehended a portion both of the ancient and modern streets, I carefully mark the line of separation. The plan thus prepared, I measured the area both of the entire polygon and its parts, and, applying to each its appropriate population, formed the following table.

On some future occasion, I shall apply this table in computing the population of the principal cities of Europe, of which we have good plans, and conclude this essay with some cursory remarks, that occurred during the course of the survey.

*Density*

## Density of Population in Dublin, A. D. 1798.

| NAMES OF PARISHES, &c. | Number of Inhabitants. | Area in English Acres. A. | R. | P. | Number of Inhabitants on an Acre. | HOUSES. Inhabited. | Waste. | Average to an Inhabited HOUSE. | |
|---|---|---|---|---|---|---|---|---|---|
| St. Paul's, . . . . . | 9904 | 88 | 0 | 37 | 112.2 | 1050 | 116 | 9.43 | |
| St. Michan's, (including Ormond-market,) . . . | 18092 | 99 | 0 | 13 | 182.6 | 1520 | 141 | 12.56 | |
| St. Mary's, . . . . . | 16654 | 115 | 0 | 33 | 144.5 | 1590 | 43 | 10.47 | |
| St. Thomas s, . . . . | 8562 | 98 | 0 | 37 | 87 1 | 892 | 82 | 9.6 | |
| St. George's, . . . . | 5096 | 53 | 3 | 21 | 96.4 | 587 | 89 | 8.68 | |
| Total occupied by buildings, North of the river Liffey, . . . | 58308 | 457 | 2 | 21 | 128.5 | 5639 | 471 | 10.35 | |
| WASTE GROUND. | | | | | | | | | |
| Oxmantown-green, in St. Paul's parish, . | | 12 | 0 | 20 | | | | The Blue-coat-hospital is on this ground. | |
| Rutland-square, in St. Mary's parish, . . | | 9 | 0 | 00 | | | | The Lying-in-hofpital is on this ground. | |
| Mountjoy's-square, in St. George's parish, . | | 3 | 0 | 11 | | | | The area of Mountjoy and Rutland-squares are taken within the railing. | |
| Total waste ground, North of the river Liffey, . | | 24 | 0 | 31 | | | | The suburb of Spring-garden is not included, as I am ignorant of its area. | |
| Total area of Dublin, North of the river Liffey, . | | 478 | 3 | 12 | | | | | |

F

## Density of Population in Dublin, A. D. 1798.

| NAMES OF PARISHES, &c. | Numbers of Inhabitants. | Area in English Acres. A. | R. | P. | Number of Inhabitants on an Acre. | HOUSES. Inhabited. | Waste. | Average to an Inhabited HOUSE. |
|---|---|---|---|---|---|---|---|---|
| St. James's, | 6104 | 59 | 1 | 36 | 102.5 | 538 | 32 | 11.34 |
| St. Catharine's, | 20176 | 112 | 1 | 28 | 179.4 | 1481 | 140 | 13.62 |
| St. Luke's, | 7241 | 31 | 0 | 21 | 232.6 | 454 | 41 | 15.95 |
| St. Nicholas, without the walls, | 12306 | 47 | 0 | 25 | 261.0 | 950 | 55 | 12.95 |
| St. Nicholas, within the walls, | 1121 | 5 | 0 | 32 | 215.0 | 107 | 10 | 10.48 |
| St. Audeon's, | 5191 | 24 | 2 | 29 | 210.0 | 415 | 53 | 12.5 |
| St. Michael's, | 2599 | 5 | 3 | 27 | 439.0 | 163 | 20 | 15.94 |
| St. John's, | 4142 | 11 | 2 | 32 | 355.0 | 295 | 31 | 14.08 |
| St. Werburgh's, | 3629 | 10 | 3 | 35 | 331.0 | 305 | 33 | 11.9 |
| St. Bridget's, or St. Bride's, | 8009 | 36 | 3 | 8 | 217.6 | 744 | 27 | 10.76 |
| St. Peter's, | 16063 | 141 | 0 | 21 | 114.0 | 1512 | 116 | 10.61 |
| St. Anne's, | 7228 | 63 | 0 | 27 | 114.0 | 711 | 36 | 10.17 |
| St. Andrew's, | 7682 | 42 | 2 | 30 | 179.8 | 709 | 63 | 10.83 |
| St. Mark's, | 8692 | 59 | 0 | 31 | 146.6 | 646 | 61 | 13.45 |
| Deanery of Christ-church, | 233 | 1 | 1 | 2 | 184.4 | 23 | 2 | 10.1 |
| Deanery of St. Patrick, | 2081 | 9 | 3 | 35 | 208.7 | 162 | 11 | 12.84 |
| Total occupied by buildings, South of the River Liffey, | 112497 | 662 | 3 | 19 | 169.7 | 9215 | 731 | 12.2 |

## Waste Ground, South of the River Liffey.

| | Area in Eng. acres. | | |
|---|---|---|---|
| | A. | R. | P. |
| Waste ground in Saint Audeon's parish, | 3 | 0 | 19 |
| *In Saint Catharine's parish.* | | | |
| Canal-harbour, stores, &c. | 23 | 2 | 4 |
| Tenter fields, | 12 | 2 | 39 |
| *In Saint Werburgh's parish.* | | | |
| Castle-garden, Castle and its dependencies, | 9 | 0 | 4 |
| *In Saint Peter's parish.* | | | |
| Saint Stephen's-green, within the wall, 17 0 2 Irish acres, including gravel walk, | 27 | 0 | 24 |
| Do. within the ditch, pasturable, 13 1 20. | | | |
| Merion-square, within the railing, | 12 | 2 | 21 |
| *In Saint Mark's parish.* | | | |
| College-park, bowling-green, &c. | 25 | 1 | 33 |
| *In Saint Anne's parish.* | | | |
| Leinster-house, offices and lawn, | 7 | 3 | 36 |
| *In Saint John's parish.* | | | |
| Old Custom-house and quay, | 0 | 3 | 25 |
| Total waste ground, South of the river Liffey, | 122 | 2 | 5 |
| Total area of Dublin, South of the river Liffey, | 785 | 1 | 24 |
| Total area of Dublin, occupied by buildings, | 1120 | 2 | 0 |
| Total waste ground in Dublin, | 146 | 2 | 36 |
| Area of the Liffey, included in Dublin, | 36 | 0 | 26 |
| Total area of Dublin, including its waste grounds and the Liffey, | 1264 | 0 | 36 |

Among the few advantages, which France
has derived from her new system, is a judicious departimental division of her territory,
founded on the united considerations of extent and population. While such a civil arrangement is favourable to the easy administration of justice, collection of revenue,
&c.; an ecclesiastical division, on similar
principles, equally facilitates the means of a
competent subsistence to the pastor, and of
spiritual comfort to his flock. Such considerations, however, seem not to have occurred in forming the ecclesiastical division
of this kingdom; in which we have country
parishes, varying in extent, from one to
thirty miles; and even in our metropolis,
as appears from a preceding table, parishes
of all dimensions; from that of St. Nicholas
Within, containing about five acres, and 1100
souls, to that of St. Catharine, comprehending
above 112 acres, and 20,000 inhabitants;
and St. Peter's, whose population, of 16,063
souls, spreads over an area, including its
squares, of 141 acres. From this very unequal extent of parishes, inconveniences obviously

viously arise. The incomes of some pastors must be incompetent to decent maintenance, while those of others will exceed it. Administering consolation to the sick and infirm, and domiciliary visits, to awaken the indolent, and rouse the profligate, who seldom enter a church, will, in the larger parishes, become extremely harassing; and hence these indispensable duties will, in consequence of the number and distance of their objects, be frequently neglected, or imperfectly performed. These inconveniences might be obviated, by a judicious partition of the city. Dublin, exclusive of its two cathedrals, has twenty churches in nineteen parishes; St. Peter's having two. It covers an area, including its squares and other waste grounds, of about 1264 acres; the twentieth part of which, viz. 63 acres, will, of course, give the average extent of a parish. And hence it may be easily computed, that, if such a division was made with tolerable judgment, a pastor, resident in a central situation, would not have a walk of more than three hundred yards to visit

visit his most distant parishioner: whereas, at present, some curates are frequently called on to attend at distances truly distressing; St. Catharine's parish being nearly an English mile, and St. Peter's considerably more than a mile and a quarter in extent. It may be said, that the income of an incumbent being generally commensurate with the extent of his parish, he possesses the means of proportioning the salary of his assistants to the extent of his exertions; but, unfortunately, that salary is fixed, and, even in the most opulent parishes, at so moderate a sum, that I may safely affirm, that no member of the community receives a compensation more inadequate to his toils and merits, than the conscientious curate of a large Dublin parish.

The parishes of this city do not vary more in extent, than in their degrees of opulence; and, as the parishes where the poor are numerous, are precisely those which possess the most scanty means of relief, while others can scarce find objects to employ their beneficence, it is obvious, that the

G                    system,

system, at present universally adopted, of
each parish providing for its own poor only,
is founded in absurdity itself. In no instance are the fatal effects of this unchristian
principle more severely felt, than in our
parochial establishments, for educating the
children of poor Protestants. We have in
this city (with regret I mention it) parishes
the most opulent, which, from their total
neglect, or languid efforts, seem unconscious
that poverty and ignorance have an existence. One parish, conscious of its utter inability to form, unaided, any establishment,
seems to have relinquished the idea in de-
spair; while, in three others, their utmost
exertions are scarcely more than sufficient
to supply a scanty salary to the master of
a day-school, with cloathing for a very
limited number of children. These, unpro-
vided with food or lodging, must, of course,
after school hours, mingle with the idle, the
profligate, and the profane; among whom,
unfortunately, we may often number their
own parents. The utter inability, of these
neglected portions of our capital, is visible
in

in the wretched state of their school-houses.
These are situate in the midst of an extremely compressed population, in narrow
streets or filthy lanes, without any back-
yards, and the ground floor, of course, occupied by the dirt-hole and necessary. In
seven of our parochial schools, that essen
tial article, the complete separation of sexes,
is neglected, and not less than eight of
them have no play-ground, except a church-
yard, generally not exceeding a few yards
in extent, and environed with lofty buildings, that interrupt a free circulation of the
air, which alone could render such a situation tolerable. Is this appropriation of the
mansions of the dead becoming in a civilized state? Is the ground, where the remains of our forefathers should repose in
holy silence, the dust over which their
children should tread with sacred awe, well
consigned to such uses in a land of christians?

The following table, which is the result
of actual observation, and minute enquiry,
will not, I hope, be uninteresting to the
public.

public. Such a simple statement of facts, will place in the strongest point of view the necessity of removing evils of such serious magnitude; and, at the same time, supply much of that preliminary knowledge, essential in forming any plan of amelioration.

From

The expence of these establishments I state thus:

BOYS SCHOOL.

| | | | |
|---|---|---|---|
| Master and mistress's salary . | £50 | 0 | 0 |
| Assistant . . . . . . . . | 25 | 0 | 0 |
| Two servant maids . . . . | 20 | 0 | 0 |
| Coals, 35 tons, at 33s. per . | 57 | 5 | 0 |
| | £152 | 5 | 0 |

GIRLS SCHOOL.

| | | | |
|---|---|---|---|
| Master and mistress . . . . . | £50 | 0 | 0 |
| Female assistant . . . . . | 25 | 0 | 0 |
| Servant maid . . . . . . | 10 | 0 | 0 |
| Coals, 35 tons, at 33s. per . . | 57 | 5 | 0 |
| | £142 | 5 | 0 |

| | | | |
|---|---|---|---|
| Thus the expence, as above, of the four establishments, will be | 599 | 0 | 0 |
| Expence, as above, of the present 17 parochial schools | 1057 | 7 | 8 |
| Difference in favour of the former | 458 | 7 | 8 |

It may be thought by some, that one assistant, in each school, is not sufficient for 120 children; but I can assure the reader, that the master of the free Protestant school, lately founded on the Coombe, by the governors of Erasmus Smith's schools, at present manages, with great ease, 150 boys, with the assistance of monitors only.

One

One of these, who are selected from the best instructed and most orderly boys, is allowed for every ten or twelve children, and receives the small gratuity of 40s. from the foundation, which, however, in a parochial school, will be unnecessary. I can assert, with great satisfaction, that this new method, which may be considered as forming a kind of seminary for future school-masters, produces in these boys, without materially retarding their own advancement, an emulation and decency of manners truly pleasing. I have, however, in the above estimate, included an assistant, as the master himself must be frequently absent as providore to the school.

It is a circumstance lamented by many, that no system of industry has been introduced at any of our parochial schools; and that children are, of course, apprenticed from them, not only ignorant of any species of useful exertion, but averse to it from habit. The sedentary occupations of knitting, spinning, and plain-work, are practised at most schools; but these, however useful, are very inadequate as the means of future subsistence.

subsistence. A better system is scarcely compatible with the contracted scale and resources of a parochial school, but might easily become an essential part of the larger establishments I recommend.

The principal superintendence of these establishments would, of course, devolve on the parochial clergy, and other governors in rotation, who would thus find the business easy, and the returns of duty distant: at the same time the attention would be unremitting, an essential point in the superintendence of a school; emulation would be excited among the governors; and individual zeal and energy, in some degree, pervade and invigorate the whole institution. Whereas, in the present system, should the incumbent be deficient in energy, his visits will be careless and unfrequent; too much will be entrusted to the master or mistress, and his school must infallibly suffer.

As to the first expence, the great objection to such a plan, I can only say, that a liberal government may do much; that, at least, two of the existing schools might, at a moderate sum, be so enlarged, as to

H answer

answer the purpose; and that the rents, at which the fifteen other schools would let, would greatly lighten the remaining expence.

In the ancient parts of this city, the streets are, with a few exceptions, generally narrow, the houses crowded together, and the reres, or back-yards, of very small extent. Of these streets, a few are the residence of the upper class of shop-keepers, and others engaged in trade; but a far greater proportion of them, with their numerous lanes and alleys, are occupied by working manufacturers, by petty shop-keepers, the labouring poor, and beggars, crowded together, to a degree distressing to humanity. A single apartment, in one of these truly wretched habitations, rates from one to two shillings per week; and, to lighten this rent, two, three, and even four families, become joint tenants. As I was usually out at very early hours on the survey, I have frequently surprized from ten to sixteen persons, of all ages and sexes, in a room, not fifteen feet square, stretched on a wad of filthy straw, swarming with vermin, and without any covering, save the
wretched

wretched rags that constituted their wear-
ing apparel. Under such circumstances, it
is not extraordinary, that I should have
frequently found from thirty to fifty individuals in a house. An intelligent clergyman, of the church of Rome, assured me,
that No. 6, Braithwaite-street, some years
since, contained one hundred and eight
souls. These, however, in 1797, were reduced to 97; and, at the period of this
survey, to 56. From a careful survey,
twice taken of Plunket-street, it appeared,
that thirty-two contiguous houses contained
917 souls, which gives an average of 28.7
to a house; and the entire Liberty averages
from about twelve to sixteen persons to
each house. This is certainly a dense
population: the best informed inhabitants,
however, assert, that it was much greater a
few years since, and to this opinion I
willingly accede. I do not, however, affirm,
that the houses, at present in existence, contained more inhabitants at any former period, though such probably was the fact;
but I am confident, that a great number
of houses, that once teemed with population,

tion, are no longer to be found. These were situate in narrow back courts and lanes, off the principal streets, and their ichnography is distinctly expressed in Roque's four-sheet map of Dublin, which I generally found minutely exact. With this map in my hand, I searched for these courts: some had totally disappeared, and their entrances had been built up; the greater part, however, I found, but their houses were mostly in ruins, or converted into warehouses or work-shops, now perfectly useless; and the few that remained were in a state of rapid decline.

This crowded population, wherever it obtains, is almost universally accompanied by a very serious evil; a degree of filth and stench inconceivable, except by such as have visited those scenes of wretchedness. Into the back-yard of each house, frequently not ten feet deep, is flung, from the windows of each apartment, the ordure and other filth of its numerous inhabitants; from whence it is so seldom removed, that I have seen it nearly on a level with the windows of the first floor; and the moisture that,

that, after heavy rains, ouzes from this heap, having frequently no sewer to carry it off, runs into the street, by the entry leading to the staircase. One instance, out of a thousand that might be given, will be sufficient. When I attempted, in the summer of 1798, to take the population of a ruinous house in Joseph's-lane, near Castle-market, I was interrupted in my progress, by an inundation of putrid blood, alive with maggots, which had, from an adjacent slaughter-yard, burst the back-door, and filled the hall to the depth of several inches. By the help of a plank, and some stepping-stones, which I procured for that purpose (for the inhabitants, without any concern, waded through it), I reached the staircase. It had rained violently, and, from the shattered state of the roof, a torrent of water made its way through every floor, from the garret to the ground. The sallow looks, and filth of the wretches, who crowded round me, indicated their situation, though they seemed insensible to the stench, which I could scarce sustain for a few minutes. In the garret, I found the entire family

of

of a poor working shoemaker, seven in number, lying in a fever, without a human being to administer to their wants. On observing that his apartment had not a door, he informed me, that his landlord, finding him not able to pay the week's rent, in consequence of his sickness, had, the preceding Saturday, taken it away, in order to force him to abandon the apartment. I counted in this stye thirty-seven persons; and computed, that its humane proprietor received out of an absolute ruin, which should be taken down by the magistrate as a public nuisance, a profit rent of above 30*l.* per annum, which he exacted, every Saturday night, with unfeeling severity. I will not disgust the reader with any further detail, and only observe, that I generally found poor room-keepers of this description, notwithstanding so many apparent causes of wretchedness, apparently at ease, and perfectly assimilated to their habitations. Filth and stench seemed congenial to their nature; they never made the smallest effort to remove them; and, if they could answer the calls of hunger, they felt, or seemed to feel, nothing else as an inconvenience.

How

How far it is the duty of the magistrate to interfere in the removal and prevention of such dreadful nuisances, or how far he is enabled to do so by the existing laws, I shall not presume to determine. I am certain, that every friend to decency and cleanliness, every person who is anxious to promote the comforts of the poor, will join me in opinion, that a police, that attends to our streets and lanes only, and that but partially, while it never bestows a thought on the back-yards of the poor, performs only half its duty. The more essential part perhaps is neglected. The stench of filth, in an open street, may be dissipated by an unobstructed current of air; but that arising from human excrement, in narrow yards, enclosed by lofty buildings, must operate with unchecked malignity.

In the course of the survey, I frequently remonstrated with the inhabitants, and particularly when I found them unemployed and idle, on their not attempting to remove their dirt; but their universal answer was, " It is not my business; if I remove it, who will pay me?" The landlord, who. in reason, should

should attend to this matter, seldom interfered. If he had an apartment in the house,
the evil was, perhaps, somewhat less, though
frequently he was the greatest brute in the
stye. I found, however, that he was generally some money-grasping wretch, who lived
in affluence, in, perhaps, a distant part of
the city, and who made a trade of renting
out such houses to the poor, with whose
concerns he never interfered, except to col-
lect his rents, generally weekly; in which,
indeed, he betrayed no remissness whatever.
Now, might not an act of the Legislature
empower the magistrate, if he have not
that power already, to make the landlord,
who has generally an exorbitant profit rent
from these miserable habitations, answerable,
under a sufficient penalty, not only for
their filth, but for their bad state of repair? This last circumstance is necessary to
be attended to, as they very frequently admit every shower of rain, and sometimes,
from their ruinous state, threaten destruction to the passenger. In July 1798, the
entire side of a house, four stories high, in
School-house-lane, fell from its foundation

into

into an adjoining yard, where it destroyed
an entire dairy of cows. I ascended the
remaining ruin, through the usual approach
of shattered stairs, stench and filth. The
floors had all sunk on the side now un-
supported, forming so many inclined planes;
and I observed, with astonishment, that the
inhabitants, above thirty in number, who
had escaped destruction by the circumstance
of the wall falling outwards, had not de-
serted their apartments. I was informed,
that it had remained some months in this
situation, and that the humane landlord
claimed, and actually received for it, the
usual rent.

To persons, unacquainted with the scenes
I have been describing, this picture will seem
overcharged; but I pledge myself, that, if
they take the trouble of enquiry, they will
find it faithfully and minutely true. I
found, I acknowledge, many exceptions.
There are landlords, who, though they pay
considerable rents for these tottering mansions themselves, shew humanity to their
lodgers, and take some little pains to render them, I cannot say more cleanly, but

I                    somewhat

somewhat less filthy. The number of these, however, are, I fear, comparatively few; and not one of them, that I know of, has reached that degree of cleanliness essential to health and comfort. I found, also, among the poor lodgers, many, who, having seen better days, were compelled by necessity to hide from the world, in these receptacles of wretchedness. These had not assimilated with the scene; their apartments bespoke a recollection of former decency, which even poverty could not obliterate; and, from the bitterness of their complaints, they seemed unhappily alive to a sense of their situation.

The most dense population, as might naturally be expected, is found within the walls of the ancient city, comprehending the parishes of St. Werburgh, St. John, St. Michael, St. Nicholas Within, the eastern part of St. Audeon, and the Deanery of Christ-Church. This space, containing an area of nearly forty-five acres English, had, in 1798, 15,683 inhabitants, in 1179 houses; which give an average of 349 souls nearly to an acre, and 13.3 to a house. There were, at that period, 137 houses waste.—

The

The density of population, however, varies within this space; for St. Nicholas Within has only 215.5 to an acre, or 10.5 to an house; while in St. Michael's it amounts to 439 to an acre, and almost 16 to a house. Such a crowded population is obviously a nuisance.

Sir William Petty, states the number of houses (I suppose inhabited houses) within the walls, in 1682, at 1145; only thirty-four less than I found them in 1798. This space having been formerly the center of commerce and wealth, the valuation of the houses was formed on a scale proportioned to their importance at that period; but though that importance is, with a few exceptions, greatly declined, the old valuation remains: and hence the minister's money, which regulates the proportion of most other taxes, is in St. John's 13s. 3d., and in St. Michael's 14s. 11½d., to a house, on an average; while, in the comparatively opulent parish of St. Peter's, it does not exceed 10s.

The existence of dairies, in the interior of the city, I have considered as a serious evil. When cows, instead of ranging through green

green pastures, and breathing a free salu-
brious air, are perpetually confined in narrow yards and filthy stalls, and fed on
grains, still-wash, and decayed vegetables,
the refuse of the root-market, their milk
and butter must necessarily be of a very inferior, and, probably, unwholesome quality.
Vast quantities of dung, thus suffered to
accumulate by neglect, continue to infect
the air; and, unless they burst their inclo-
sures, and flow, into the street, which sometimes happens, there is, I understand, no
existing law, that enables the magistrate to
interfere, however great the nuisance.

In the course of this survey, I have öften
reflected on the great disproportion between
the burial-grounds of this capital, and its
dense population; and cannot help thinking,
that a wise legislature might interfere, with
effect, in their removal, from the interior of the
city, to the neighbouring country. The idea,
that we are kneeling over the dust of what
was once most dear to us, is a fine lesson
to human vanity, and naturally produces
that humility, and solemnity of soul, with
which we ought to address the Deity.—
Hence

Hence, probably, originated, among Christians, the custom of burying in churches, or adjoining cemeteries. Such impressions, however, are soon obliterated by habit; and, whatever may be their effect in awakening the pious affections, it is insufficient to sanction a practice, which, from local circumstances, may be not only inconvenient, but dangerous. St. Mary's parish contains 16,654 souls, and its church-yard about 32,000 square feet: hence the proportion for each inhabitant is not two square feet; and it is a fact, which I have witnessed, that, in order to make room for others, bodies, in that cemetery, have been taken up in an absolute state of putrefaction, to the great and very dangerous annoyance of the vicinity. In some other cemeteries the evil is not so great; but in that of St. Anne's, it is, I am informed, if possible, more distressing. In the removal of this nuisance, opposition may be expected from prejudice and superstition; but these have already began to give way, and particularly in that class where they usually are most powerful. The Liberty poor, from the difficulty of finding room in

their

their parish church-yards, and the desire of
evading the payment of burial fees, have
been of late years, almost universally, interred
in the Hospital-fields, and other country cemeteries. Even the imaginary sanctity of the
church-yard of St. James's parish* seems to
have declined in the estimation of the lower
class, and the numbers interred there are
gradually diminishing. Thus, necessity, and,
perhaps, common sense, have commenced a
reform in this particular, which a wise legislature, it is hoped, may be able to complete.

Why brothels, soap manufactories, slaugh-
ter-houses, glass-houses, lime-kilns, distilleries, &c. are suffered to exist in the midst
of a crowded population, I shall not presume to enquire. Their deleterious effects
are abundantly known, and, I trust, will be
remedied. On the subject of dram-shops,
however, the most alarming of all nuisances, I will take the liberty of stating
one simple, but authentic fact. Thomas-
street, the termination of the great southern

and

* The Pope, it is affirmed, offers up prayers, on St. James's
day, for the rest of the souls of those who are interred in this
church-yard.

and western roads, and the link of connection between the disaffected of country and
city, contains 190 houses; and of these, in
1798, and probably at this day, no less
than fifty-two were licensed to vend raw
spirits; a poison, productive of vice, riot,
and disease; hostile to all habits of decency,
honesty, and industry; and, in short, de-
structive to the souls and bodies of our fel-
low-creatures. These houses, open at all
hours, by day and by night, are scenes of
unceasing profaneness and intemperance,
which even the sanctity of the Sabbath cannot suspend; and it is an undoubted fact,
that, on that day, sacred among Christians
to piety and peace, more deeds of profaneness, immorality, and disorder, are perpe-
trated in this vicinity, than in the other six.
Intemperance, idleness, and irreligion, afford
excellent materials for the designing and disaffected to work on; and, accordingly, here
was found the focus of rebellion. That, in
northern climates, a moderate quantity of
spirits may be necessary to the labouring
poor, to counteract the effects of cold and
damp, is admitted: but the abuse of it has
become

become not only distressing to humanity, but frightful to reflection; and every good man must, with an aching heart, lament that necessity, which obliges a Christian government to derive a revenue from the temporal and eternal misery of thousands of its subjects.

It is a circumstance, perhaps, not generally known, that not one house of ill-fame exists in the Liberty. This circumstance I wish I could attribute to its superior virtue, not its poverty. But where intoxication is almost universal, chastity cannot exist: and I found, on enquiry, that, of the nocturnal street-walkers, that infest the more opulent parts of the city, a very large proportion issues from the Liberty.

For these painful, and often disgusting details, I should, perhaps, apologize to the reader: but he will have the candour to reflect, that my sole and anxious object is, to have evils of such serious magnitude alleviated, or, if possible, removed; that, to be removed, they must be first known; and that, to persons of elevated rank and station, who alone possess influence sufficient for a work so truly humane, faithful description

is

is the only means by which they can learn the existence of such evils. As pastor of a parish, that embraces so large a portion of, what we may emphatically call, the region of filth and misery, I am, in some degree, entitled to the melancholy office of being the historian of its wretchedness; and feel it my duty to bring forward to the public eye, the lot of so many thousand neglected, but not useless beings, with the chearing hope of its being ameliorated. The very liberal part which Government has taken, in establishing a Fever Hospital, in this quarter of the city, convinces me, that this hope is not vain; and I trust that this admirable institution is only a prelude to further exertions of humanity. Such efforts, in favour of the neglected and the forgotten, become the followers of our Divine Master, and are every way worthy of a Nobleman, who, like the great and good Prince he represents, glories in being a Christian.

These few hints will, I hope, awaken enquiry, and not be deemed impertinent or ill-timed, at a moment, when, under the immediate auspices of our Chief Governor,

K          a Bill

a Bill is preparing, for the better regulation of the wretched police of this city; and when his Excellency's feelings are alive to this work of mercy, that embraces at once the tranquillity, cleanliness, health, and comfort, of the second city of the British Empire.

It remains, only, that I express my grateful sense of the notice with which his Excellency has honoured this work, from the moment he was informed of its existence. The purity of the motive was sufficient to conciliate his attention. Happy shall I be, should its execution merit his approbation, and justify, in any degree, that liberality, which induced him to make it the property of the State.

FINIS.

# POPULATION TABLES

OF THE

## NINETEEN PARISHES

AND

## TWO DEANERIES

OF THE

## *CITY OF DUBLIN,*

A. D. 1798.

Shewing what Streets, and parts of Streets, &c. are comprehended in each
Parish; with the number of Inhabitants, whether Male or Female; and
of Houses, whether Inhabited or Waste.

———⤜∘∘∘⊕∘∘⤛———

☞ *Where a Street, Lane, Alley, Square, &c. extends into more than one Parish,
the Alphabetical List, annexed to this work, refers to the number of the Parochial
Tables, in which its several parts will be found.*

Republished in 1974 by Gregg International Publishers Limited
Westmead, Farnborough, Hants., England

# No. I.

## Parish of Saint James.

| NAMES OF STREETS, &c. | POPULATION. | | | HOUSES. | |
|---|---|---|---|---|---|
| | Males. | Females. | TOTAL. | Inhabited. | Waste. |
| Watling-street, E. side from No. 1 to 30; W. side entire, . . . | 193 | 201 | 394 | 46 | 6 |
| Lord Galway's-walk, | 13 | 26 | 39 | 3 | 1 |
| Cook's-lane, . . . | 27 | 32 | 59 | 5 | 0 |
| St. James's-street, . . | 1139 | 1197 | 2336 | 181 | 12 |
| Conoly's-lane, . . | 17 | 17 | 34 | 5 | 0 |
| Glannan's-lane, . . | 4 | 5 | 9 | 1 | 0 |
| Sherlock's-yard, . . | 3 | 5 | 8 | 2 | 0 |
| Bason-lane, . . . . | 17 | 23 | 40 | 3 | 0 |
| Pig-town, . . . | 50 | 39 | 89 | 12 | 1 |
| Bason-place, from No. 1 to 7, . . . . . | 30 | 31 | 61 | 7 | 0 |
| Echlin's-lane, . . . . | 47 | 58 | 105 | 11 | 1 |
| Cherrytree-lane, . . . | 48 | 55 | 103 | 5 | 0 |
| Stevens's-lane, . . . | 18 | 19 | 37 | 3 | 0 |
| Bow-lane, . . . . . | 407 | 528 | 935 | 63 | 4 |
| Irwin-street, . . . . | 179 | 199 | 378 | 21 | 0 |
| Rope-walk, . . , | 22 | 21 | 43 | 10 | 0 |
| Bow-bridge, . . . . | 137 | 209 | 346 | 26 | 1 |
| Kilmainham-road & town, | 237 | 255 | 492 | 68 | 5 |
| Commons-lane, . . | 5 | 12 | 17 | 4 | 1 |
| Dolphin's-barn-lane, . | 269 | 281 | 550 | 57 | 0 |
| Rehoboth-lane, . . | 9 | 20 | 29 | 5 | 0 |
| **TOTAL** . . | 2871 | 3233 | 6104 | 538 | 32 |

## No. II.

### Parish of Saint Catharine.

| NAMES OF STREETS, &c. | POPULATION. | | | HOUSES. | |
|---|---|---|---|---|---|
| | Males. | Females. | TOTAL. | Inhabited. | Waste. |
| Coomb, N. side, from No. 40 to 69, to Pimlico, . . . . | 232 | 374 | 606 | 33 | 4 |
| Ardee-street, or Crooked Staff, W. side only, | 75 | 86 | 161 | 11 | 0 |
| Francis street, part of W. side, from No. 150 to 159, to Thomas-street, . . . . | 40 | 56 | 96 | 10 | 1 |
| Cut-purse-row, N. side, | 1 | 2 | 3 | 2 | 6 |
| Sweeny's-gate and Tenter-lane, . . . . | 15 | 29 | 44 | 6 | 0 |
| Stirling-street, . . . | 13 | 32 | 45 | 2 | 1 |
| Corn-market, N. side, Nos. 17 and 18, . . | 3 | 7 | 10 | 2 | 0 |
| Thomas-street, . . . | 1154 | 1300 | 2454 | 181 | 9 |
| Molyneux's - yard, off Thomas-str. | 11 | 23 | 34 | 5 | 0 |
| Black-horse-yard, do. | 24 | 22 | 46 | 3 | 0 |
| Talbot-inn-yard, do. | 14 | 11 | 25 | 1 | 0 |
| Reily's-court, do. . | 3 | 3 | 6 | 1 | 0 |
| New-sun-inn-yard, do. . . . | 17 | 11 | 28 | 3 | 0 |
| Churn-inn-yard, do. | 8 | 9 | 17 | 2 | 0 |
| Cherry - tree - inn - yard, do. . . | 4 | 3 | 7 | 1 | 0 |
| Yellow - lyon - inn - yard, do. . . | 5 | 5 | 10 | 1 | 0 |
| White-horse-lane, do. | 38 | 58 | 96 | 5 | 0 |
| Brown's-alley, do. | 14 | 27 | 41 | 6 | 0 |
| White - bull - inn - yard, do. . . | 6 | 6 | 12 | 1 | 0 |
| Lime-kiln-yard, do. | 34 | 58 | 92 | 3 | 0 |
| New-row, Thomas-street, | 167 | 188 | 355 | 40 | 2 |
| Wormwood-gate, . . | 22 | 25 | 47 | 6 | 0 |
| M'Cracken's-alley, . . | 49 | 80 | 129 | 13 | 0 |
| Croaker's-alley, or Meeting-house-lane, . . | 65 | 106 | 171 | 8 | 1 |

# Parish of Saint Catharine, continued.

| NAMES OF STREETS, &c. | POPULATION. | | | HOUSES. | |
|---|---|---|---|---|---|
| | Males. | Females. | TOTAL. | Inhabited. | Waste. |
| John-street, . . . . | 78 | 72 | 150 | 9 | 3 |
| John's-lane, . . . . | 24 | 48 | 72 | 5 | 0 |
| Mullinahack, . . . . | 87 | 70 | 157 | 9 | 0 |
| Dirty-lane, or Bridge-foot-street, from No. 1 to 14, E. side; from No. 52¼ to 69, W. side, . . . . . | 200 | 225 | 425 | 32 | 3 |
| M'Cormick's-court off Dirty-lane, | 18 | 28 | 46 | 3 | 0 |
| Collison's Fields, or Black-ditch, do. . . . . | 11 | 18 | 29 | 4 | 0 |
| Bonham-street, . . . | 59 | 49 | 108 | 11 | 3 |
| Marshallsea-lane, . . | 13 | 16 | 29 | 4 | 0 |
| Mass-lane, no population. . . . | | | | | |
| Meath-street, . . . | 525 | 619 | 1144 | 81 | 3 |
| Vicar-street, . . . . | 217 | 222 | 439 | 33 | 2 |
| Engine-alley, . . . | 200 | 206 | 406 | 27 | 0 |
| Catharine-street, . . . | 42 | 46 | 88 | 6 | 0 |
| Crosstick-alley, entire, except No. 4. . . | 48 | 70 | 118 | 10 | 3 |
| Flag-alley, . . . . | 11 | 23 | 34 | 5 | 0 |
| Pimlico, . . . . . | 231 | 281 | 512 | 45 | 3 |
| Delany's-court, off Pimlico, . . | 5 | 6 | 11 | 1 | 0 |
| Jackson's-alley, do. | 34 | 94 | 128 | 8 | 1 |
| Tripilo, . . . . . | 138 | 213 | 351 | 22 | 0 |
| Thomas-court, . . . | 370 | 539 | 909 | 54 | 4 |
| Miller's-alley, off Thomas-court, | 53 | 85 | 138 | 7 | 0 |
| Gilbert's-alley, do. | 8 | 19 | 27 | 3 | 1 |
| Meath-row, . . . . | 77 | 71 | 148 | 9 | 3 |
| Cole's-lane, . . . . | 7 | 5 | 12 | 2 | 1 |
| Swan-alley, . . . | 21 | 30 | 51 | 5 | 0 |
| Little Thomas-court, . | 68 | 119 | 187 | 11 | 0 |
| Hanbury-lane, . . . | 126 | 130 | 256 | 20 | 4 |
| Scanlon's-court, off Hanbury-lane, | 25 | 45 | 70 | 3 | 0 |
| Meath-market, . . . | 58 | 63 | 121 | 31 | 8 |
| Earl-street, . . . . | 223 | 262 | 485 | 36 | 5 |

## Parish of Saint Catharine, continued.

| NAMES OF STREETS, &c. | POPULATION. | | | HOUSES. | |
|---|---|---|---|---|---|
| | Males. | Females. | TOTAL. | Inhabited. | Waste. |
| Cole's-alley, . . . . | 283 | 408 | 691 | 40 | 5 |
| Gill's - square, off Cole's-alley, . | 56 | 86 | 142 | 8 | 0 |
| Cambden-court, do. | 4 | 7 | 11 | 2 | 0 |
| Elbow-lane, . . . . | 264 | 370 | 634 | 36 | 0 |
| Gibraltar, off Elbow-lane, . . | 35 | 58 | 93 | 6 | 2 |
| Little Elbow-lane, . . | 42 | 45 | 87 | 6 | 1 |
| Cork street, . . . . | 752 | 868 | 1620 | 126 | 15 |
| Love-lane, . . . . | 21 | 20 | 41 | 5 | 0 |
| Chamber-street, . . . | 167 | 176 | 343 | 34 | 9 |
| Weaver's-square, . . | 112 | 149 | 261 | 19 | 1 |
| Ormond-street, . . . | 122 | 143 | 265 | 14 | 4 |
| Brown-street, . . . | 135 | 173 | 308 | 20 | 3 |
| Marybonne-lane, . . . | 607 | 797 | 1404 | 90 | 5 |
| John-street, . . . . | 91 | 101 | 192 | 13 | 0 |
| Braithwaite-street, . . | 161 | 206 | 367 | 30 | 1 |
| Pool-street, . . . . | 160 | 220 | 380 | 26 | 1 |
| Summer-street, . . . | 48 | 59 | 107 | 9 | 0 |
| Robert-street, . . . | 79 | 78 | 157 | 15 | 0 |
| White-hall, . . . . | 18 | 26 | 44 | 6 | 0 |
| Water-row or Russel's-lane | 34 | 52 | 86 | 6 | 0 |
| Bowes's-lane, . . . . | 15 | 17 | 32 | 4 | 3 |
| Taylor's-lane.—No population. | | | | | |
| Bell-view, . . . . . | 36 | 41 | 77 | 6 | 0 |
| Crawley's - yard, now School street, . | 27 | 47 | 74 | 7 | 6 |
| Ransford-street, . . . | 395 | 500 | 895 | 46 | 2 |
| Bardon's-yard, off Ransford-street, | 20 | 25 | 45 | 3 | 0 |
| Davis's Coal-yard, do. | 15 | 16 | 31 | 3 | 0 |
| Sugar-house-lane, . . | 37 | 25 | 62 | 7 | 0 |
| Crane-street, . . . . | 80 | 86 | 166 | 14 | 5 |
| Rope walk, . . . . | 39 | 36 | 75 | 8 | 2 |
| Portland-street, . . . | 27 | 23 | 50 | 6 | 0 |
| Canal-place, . . . . | 40 | 55 | 95 | 6 | 2 |
| Canal Stores, . . . | 22 | 21 | 43 | 5 | 0 |
| Washerwoman's-lane, . | 33 | 57 | 90 | 10 | 0 |
| Bason-place, No. 8, 9, & 10 | 9 | 13 | 22 | 3 | 0 |
| TOTAL . . . | 8977 | 11199 | 20176 | 1481 | 140 |

# No. III.

## Parish of Saint Luke.

| NAMES OF STREETS, &c. | POPULATION. | | | HOUSES. | |
|---|---|---|---|---|---|
| | Males. | Females. | TOTAL. | Inhabited. | Waste. |
| Coomb, S. side entire, . | 525 | 614 | 1139 | 73 | 8 |
| Cain's-alley, . . . | 56 | 72 | 128 | 6 | 0 |
| Green's-alley, . . | 8 | 16 | 24 | 4 | 0 |
| Daniel's-alley, . . | 56 | 120 | 176 | 11 | 0 |
| Three-nun-alley, . | 23 | 32 | 55 | 5 | 0 |
| Stillas's-court, . . | 58 | 74 | 132 | 7 | 0 |
| Poddle, S. side, from } No. 13 to No. 17, } | 40 | 58 | 98 | 8 | 0 |
| New-market, . . . . | 432 | 614 | 1046 | 62 | 6 |
| Ardee-street, or Crook- } ed-staff, . . . . } | 151 | 177 | 328 | 12 | 2 |
| Ardee-row, or Mutton- } lane, . . . . } | 95 | 167 | 262 | 16 | 1 |
| Atkinson's-alley, . . | 18 | 29 | 47 | 4 | 0 |
| Brabazon's - street, or } Truck-street, . . } | 122 | 160 | 282 | 18 | 3 |
| Brabazon's - row, or } Cuckold's-row, . } | 75 | 94 | 169 | 13 | 5 |
| Hunt's-alley, . . | 31 | 58 | 89 | 5 | 0 |
| Fordam's-alley, . . . | 328 | 570 | 898 | 53 | 1 |
| Skinner's-alley, . . . | 322 | 491 | 813 | 52 | 1 |
| New-row-on-the-Poddle, | 359 | 453 | 812 | 52 | 7 |
| Ward's-hill, . . . . | 28 | 24 | 52 | 6 | 2 |
| Mill-street, . . . . | 139 | 206 | 345 | 25 | 4 |
| Warren's-mount, . . | 25 | 15 | 40 | 3 | 0 |
| Mill-lane, . . . . . | 19 | 42 | 61 | 4 | 1 |
| Sweeny's-lane, . . . | 54 | 64 | 118 | 6 | 0 |
| Black-pitts, W. side, . | 64 | 63 | 127 | 9 | 0 |
| TOTAL . . | 3028 | 4213 | 7241 | 454 | 41 |

# No. IV.

## Parish of Saint Nicholas Without.

| NAMES OF STREETS, &c. | POPULATION. | | | HOUSES. | |
|---|---|---|---|---|---|
| | Males. | Females. | TOTAL. | Inhabited. | Waste. |
| St. Francis-street, E. side entire; W. side, from the Coomb to No. 149 inclusive, . . . | 853 | 1078 | 1931 | 154 | 13 |
| Handkerchief-alley, off Francis-street, | 16 | 15 | 31 | 4 | 0 |
| Binns's-court, do. . | 56 | 69 | 125 | 8 | 3 |
| O'Brian's-alley, do. | 10 | 14 | 24 | 3 | 3 |
| Francis's-court, do. | 19 | 1 | 20 | 2 | 0 |
| Chapel-alley, do. . | 18 | 26 | 44 | 4 | 0 |
| Sun-inn-yard, do. . | 7 | 11 | 18 | 1 | 0 |
| Red - cow - gate - yard, do. . | 5 | 6 | 11 | 2 | 0 |
| Calender-yard, do | 19 | 28 | 47 | 3 | 0 |
| Churn - inn - yard, do. . . . . | 4 | 5 | 9 | 1 | 0 |
| Infirmary-yard, do. | 69 | 92 | 161 | 6 | 0 |
| Plunket-street, . . . | 701 | 1103 | 1804 | 92 | 0 |
| Hanover-lane, . . . | 192 | 246 | 438 | 35 | 1 |
| Hanover-square, . . . | 28 | 19 | 47 | 9 | 0 |
| Limerick-alley, . . . | 2 | 5 | 7 | 2 | 0 |
| Ash-street, . . . . | 140 | 186 | 326 | 30 | 0 |
| Swift's-alley, . . . . | 41 | 107 | 148 | 9 | 1 |
| Garden-lane, . . | 272 | 380 | 652 | 39 | 1 |
| Carman's-hall, . . . | 81 | 101 | 182 | 16 | 1 |
| Pye-alley, . . . | 1 | 13 | 14 | 1 | 0 |
| Park-street, . . . . | 84 | 123 | 207 | 13 | 3 |
| Hanover-street, . . . | 27 | 47 | 74 | 9 | 1 |
| Mark's-alley, . . . . | 82 | 115 | 197 | 23 | 3 |
| Spittle-field, . . . . | 173 | 173 | 346 | 25 | 1 |
| Wall's-lane, . . . . | 57 | 66 | 123 | 12 | 1 |
| St. Patrick's-street, W. side, from No. 1 to 32, and from 36 to 49; E. side, from 50 to 56, and from Walker's-alley to Nicholas-street, . . . . | 510 | 722 | 1232 | 92 | 4 |

## Parish of Saint Nicholas Without, continued.

| NAMES OF STREETS, &c. | POPULATION. | | | HOUSES. | |
|---|---|---|---|---|---|
| | Males. | Females. | TOTAL. | Inhabited. | Waste. |
| Poddle, North side, from No. 1 to 10; S. side, No. 1, 11 and 12, | 38 | 62 | 100 | 12 | 1 |
| Upper St. Kevin's-street, S. side, from New-st. to the Poddle, . . | 48 | 49 | 97 | 6 | 0 |
| Coomb, North side, from No. 1 to 39, . . . | 277 | 372 | 649 | 45 | 0 |
| Crosstick-al. one House, viz. No. 4. . . | 6 | 9 | 15 | 1 | 0 |
| New-street, E. side, from No. 14 to 31; W. side entire, . . . . | 694 | 929 | 1623 | 114 | 10 |
| Three-stone-alley, . . | 36 | 44 | 80 | 8 | 0 |
| Fumbally's-lane, . . . | 73 | 71 | 144 | 13 | 0 |
| Malpas-street, . . . . | 31 | 50 | 81 | 9 | 2 |
| Bonny's-lane, . . . . | 35 | 43 | 78 | 10 | 0 |
| Ducker's-lane, . . . | 2 | 14 | 16 | 3 | 0 |
| Fatal-alley, . . . . | 20 | 23 | 43 | 7 | 0 |
| Donovan's-lane, . . . | 11 | 9 | 20 | 4 | 0 |
| Black-pits, E. side, . . | 121 | 166 | 287 | 26 | 0 |
| Bride's-al. S. side, from No. 1 to 9; N. side, from No. 28 to 34, | 43 | 63 | 106 | 26 | 0 |
| Mill-yd. off Bride's-alley, . . . | 18 | 30 | 48 | 3 | 0 |
| Draper's-court, do. | 62 | 82 | 144 | 8 | 0 |
| Bull-alley, S. side, from No. 1 to 9; N. side, from No. 31 to 38, | 72 | 85 | 157 | 15 | 2 |
| Walker's-alley, N. side, | 36 | 79 | 115 | 6 | 0 |
| City-market, from No. 1 to 43, . . . . . | 147 | 185 | 332 | 41 | 2 |
| Cutpurse-row, S. side, . | 11 | 17 | 28 | 5 | 2 |
| Lamb-alley, . . . . | 10 | 15 | 25 | 3 | 0 |
| TOTAL . . | 5258 | 7048 | 12306 | 950 | 55 |

# No. V.

## Parish of Saint Nicholas Within.

| NAMES OF STREETS, &c. | POPULATION | | | HOUSES | |
|---|---|---|---|---|---|
| | Males. | Females. | TOTAL. | Inhabited. | Waſte. |
| High-street, No. 70 only, the corner house of Nicholas-street, . | 0 | 0 | 0 | 0 | 1 |
| Skinner's-row, from the Tholsel to No. 5, S. side, . . . . . | 23 | 29 | 52 | 7 | 0 |
| Prince of Wales-court, | 27 | 23 | 50 | 5 | 0 |
| Nicholas-street, entire, No. 19½ and 25 excepted, . . . . | 173 | 228 | 401 | 35 | 3 |
| Kennedy's-lane, . . . | 52 | 65 | 117 | 15 | 1 |
| Back-lane, { N.side,from Nich.-street, to No. 18, S.side, from No. 49, to Nicholas-street, | 202 | 242 | 444 | 34 | 5 |
| City-row, part of City-market, from No. 44, to 52, as correct, . | 31 | 19 | 50 | 9 | 0 |
| Angel-alley, No. 3 and 4, as correctly numbered, . . . . . | 6 | 1 | 7 | 2 | 0 |
| M'Cullough's - alley, in part, no inhabited houses. Ram-alley, no inhabited houses. | | | | | |
| TOTAL . . | 514 | 607 | 1121 | 107 | 10 |

# No. VI.

## Parish of Saint Audeon.

| NAMES OF STREETS, &c. | POPULATION. | | | HOUSES. | |
|---|---|---|---|---|---|
| | Males. | Females. | TOTAL. | Inhabited. | Waste. |
| Watling-street, E. side, from No 31 to 42, and Usher's-island, | 39 | 50 | 89 | 8 | 2 |
| Usher's-island, . . . | 80 | 114 | 194 | 23 | 3 |
| Usher's-quay, . . . | 184 | 173 | 357 | 41 | 3 |
| Usher's-street, . . . | 33 | 57 | 90 | 11 | 1 |
| Usher's-lane, . . . . | 30 | 38 | 68 | 10 | 1 |
| Island street, . . . . | 111 | 109 | 220 | 11 | 1 |
| Dog-and-duck-yard, . . | 32 | 39 | 71 | 7 | 0 |
| Usher's-court, or Meeting-house-yard, . | 69 | 86 | 155 | 16 | 1 |
| Bridge-street, . . . . | 216 | 224 | 440 | 48 | 2 |
| Chapel-alley, . . | 22 | 15 | 37 | 5 | 0 |
| Wolfe's alley, . . | 7 | 19 | 26 | 3 | 0 |
| Brazen - head - inn-yard, . . . | 9 | 15 | 24 | 2 | 0 |
| Minor's-alley, . . | 4 | 7 | 11 | 1 | 0 |
| Upper Bridge-street, . | 19 | 25 | 44 | 9 | 17 |
| Merchant's-quay, from No. 10 to 24, . . | 121 | 81 | 202 | 22 | 5 |
| Cook-street, from No. 16 to 85, . . . | 427 | 480 | 907 | 56 | 5 |
| Swan alley, . . . | 4 | 3 | 7 | 1 | 0 |
| Archibold's-court, . | 9 | 11 | 20 | 3 | 0 |
| Keizar's-lane, . . | 31 | 53 | 84 | 3 | 0 |
| St. Audeon's arch, . | 37 | 67 | 104 | 9 | 1 |
| Hope's-yard, . . | 36 | 49 | 85 | 7 | 0 |
| Schoolhouse - lane, W. side, . . | 55 | 77 | 132 | 3 | 3 |
| Bethel's-court, off Schoolhouse-lane, | 8 | 27 | 35 | 2 | 0 |
| Corn-market entire, No. 17 and 18 excepted, | 137 | 215 | 352 | 33 | 2 |
| Purcell's court, . . | 73 | 134 | 207 | 10 | 4 |
| Bear's-court, . . | 11 | 12 | 23 | 3 | 0 |
| High-street, from No. 17 to 43, and Gorely's-alley, . . . | 208 | 247 | 455 | 27 | 3 |
| Back-lane, from No. 19 to 48, . . . . | 301 | 367 | 668 | 33 | 2 |
| Byrne's-court . . | 40 | 44 | 84 | 5 | 0 |
| Skipper's-alley, W. side, no inhabited house. | | | | | |
| TOTAL . . | 2353 | 2838 | 5191 | 415 | 53 |

D

# No. VII.

## Parish of Saint Michael.

| NAMES OF STREETS, &c. | POPULATION | | | HOUSES | |
|---|---|---|---|---|---|
| | Males. | Females. | TOTAL. | Inhabited. | Waste. |
| Merchant's-quay, from Rosemary - lane to Skipper's-alley, . | 40 | 48 | 88 | 7 | 1 |
| Cook-street, { N. side, from Rosemary-lane to Skipper's-alley, S. side, from Schoolhouse-lane to Michael's-lane,' . | 96 | 137 | 233 | 21 | 2 |
| Rosemary-lane, W. side, | 24 | 21 | 45 | 5 | 1 |
| Chapel-yard, . . . . | 6 | 2 | 8 | 1 | 0 |
| Skipper's-alley, E. side, no inhabited houses. | | | | | |
| Schoolhouse-lane, E. side, | 102 | 122 | 224 | 9 | 1 |
| Michael's-lane, . . . | 321 | 323 | 644 | 24 | 1 |
| Crosby's-court, . . | 27 | 30 | 57 | 2 | 0 |
| Cox's-court, . . | 43 | 43 | 86 | 6 | 0 |
| Borr's-court, . . . . | 55 | 77 | 132 | 6 | 1 |
| Cock-hill, from No. 5 to 12, . . . . | 51 | 60 | 111 | 9 | 1 |
| Christ-church-lane, W. side, . . . . . | 53 | 57 | 110 | 8 | 1 |
| Chapter-court, . | 6 | 9 | 15 | 2 | 1 |
| High-street, { N. side, from Christ-church - lane to Schoolhouse-lane, S. side, from Gorely's-alley to No. 69, . . . . | 302 | 398 | 700 | 45 | 6 |
| Jones's-court, . . | 23 | 27 | 50 | 5 | 0 |
| Gorely's-alley, part of E. side, no inhabited houses. | | | | | |
| M'Cullough's - alley, in part, . | 13 | 12 | 25 | 2 | 0 |
| Angel-court, . . | 18 | 10 | 28 | 3 | 2 |
| Angel-alley, in part, viz. No. 1, 2, 5, 6, 7, correct, | 7 | 16 | 23 | 5 | 0 |
| Skinner's-row, N. side, from No. 32 to 37, | 11 | 9 | 20 | 3 | 2 |
| TOTAL . . | 1198 | 1401 | 2599 | 163 | 20 |

# No. VIII.

## Parish of Saint John.

| NAMES OF STREETS, &c. | POPULATION. | | | HOUSES. | |
|---|---|---|---|---|---|
| | Males. | Females. | TOTAL. | Inhabited. | Waste. |
| Essex-bridge-street, . . | 32 | 35 | 67 | 9 | 0 |
| Essex-quay, . . . . . | 110 | 154 | 264 | 23 | 1 |
| Wood-quay, . . . . . | 244 | 300 | 544 | 27 | 1 |
| Fisher's-alley, . . | 11 | 9 | 20 | 4 | 0 |
| Johnston's-court, . | 46 | 74 | 120 | 8 | 0 |
| Redmond's-alley, . | 18 | 26 | 44 | 3 | 0 |
| Rose-alley, . . . | 41 | 41 | 82 | 4 | 0 |
| Merchant's-quay, No. 1 on the S. side, and 35, 36, 37, on the N. side, | 9 | 7 | 16 | 4 | 0 |
| Lower Exchange-street, | 142 | 157 | 299 | 24 | 10 |
| Upp. Exchange-st. from No. 12 to 17, W. side, | 32 | 36 | 68 | 6 | 0 |
| Smock-alley, . . . . | 88 | 97 | 185 | 16 | 6 |
| Copper-al. { No. 1, 2, 3, 4, 5, on the S. side, No. 35, 36, on the N. side, . . | 10 | 14 | 24 | 4 | 3 |
| Fishamble-str. from No. 2 to 55, properly 57, | 423 | 468 | 891 | 55 | 3 |
| John's-court, . . | 31 | 19 | 50 | 3 | 0 |
| Sall's-court, . . . | 5 | 7 | 12 | 1 | 1 |
| Virgine-court, . . | 11 | 21 | 32 | 2 | 0 |
| Molesworth-court, . | 9 | 19 | 28 | 4 | 2 |
| Fleece-alley, . . | 40 | 25 | 65 | 7 | 0 |
| Deanery-court, . . | 5 | 2 | 7 | 1 | 0 |
| Medcalf's-court, . | 14 | 15 | 29 | 3 | 0 |
| Winetavern-street, . . | 449 | 457 | 906 | 51 | 2 |
| Brazil-court, . . | 10 | 15 | 25 | 2 | 0 |
| John's-lane, . . . . | 44 | 63 | 107 | 13 | 0 |
| Ball-court-yard, . | 9 | 7 | 16 | 3 | 0 |
| Plowman's-court, . | 9 | 7 | 16 | 2 | 0 |
| Cock-hill, No. 1, 2, 3, 4, and a back house, | 49 | 57 | 106 | 5 | 0 |
| Rosemary-lane, E. side, | 11 | 29 | 40 | 3 | 1 |
| Howard's-lane, . . . | 2 | 3 | 5 | 1 | 0 |
| Cook-street, { N. side, from Wine tavern-street to Rosemary-lane, S. side, from Michael's-lane to Winetavern-str. | 35 | 39 | 74 | 7 | 1 |
| TOTAL . . | 1939 | 2203 | 4142 | 295 | 31 |

# No. IX.

## Parish of Saint Werburgh.

| NAMES OF STREETS, &c. | POPULATION. | | | HOUSES. | |
|---|---|---|---|---|---|
| | Males. | Females. | TOTAL. | Inhabited. | Waste. |
| Werburgh-street, . . . | 191 | 207 | 398 | 23 | 3 |
| Hoey's-court, . . | 103 | 118 | 221 | 18 | 0 |
| Darby's-fquare, No. ⎫ 1,5,6,7,8, as cor-⎬ rectly numbered, ⎭ | 27 | 36 | 63 | 4 | 1 |
| Skinner's-row, from No. ⎫ 6 to 31, . . . . ⎭ | 103 | 134 | 237 | 27 | 1 |
| Bolton-court, . . | 19 | 16 | 35 | 2 | 1 |
| Wilme's-court, . . | 12 | 12 | 34 | 3 | 0 |
| Caftle-street, . . . . | 237 | 299 | 536 | 59 | 1 |
| Garter-court, . . | 10 | 9 | 19 | 3 | 1 |
| Cole's-alley, . . . | 87 | 110 | 197 | 22 | 3 |
| Silver-court, . . . | 3 | 5 | 8 | 2 | 1 |
| Pembroke-court, . | 67 | 75 | 142 | 11 | 0 |
| Temple-court, . . | 26 | 20 | 46 | 3 | 0 |
| Fifhamble-street, ⎰ No. 1, E. side ; ⎱ ⎰ No. 58,59,60, ⎱ ⎰ W. side, . ⎱ | 32 | 36 | 68 | 4 | 0 |
| Copper-alley, from No. ⎫ 6 to 34, . . . . ⎭ | 207 | 254 | 461 | 20 | 9 |
| Orpin's-court, . . | 15 | 30 | 45 | 4 | 0 |
| Cork-hill, . . . . . | 70 | 70 | 140 | 14 | 2 |
| Upper Exchange street, ⎰ E. side, entire ; ⎱ ⎰ W. side, No. 18, ⎱ ⎰ 19, 20, . . ⎱ | 70 | 104 | 174 | 9 | 2 |
| Parliament-street, . . | 119 | 105 | 224 | 27 | 2 |
| Essex-gate, S. side, . . | 7 | 6 | 13 | 2 | 0 |
| Essex-street, ⎰ N. side, from ⎱ ⎰ No. 2 to 10, . ⎱ ⎰ S. side, from No. ⎱ ⎰ 42 to 53, . ⎱ | 114 | 142 | 256 | 18 | 3 |
| Crane-lane, . . . . | 74 | 123 | 197 | 13 | 1 |
| Crampton-court, No. 1, ⎫ 2, 3, 18, 19 . . . ⎭ | 2 | 12 | 14 | 4 | 1 |
| Dame-street, ⎰ S. side, No. 1, 2, ⎱ ⎰ and half No. 3, ⎱ ⎰ a double houfe, ⎱ ⎰ N. side, No. 90, ⎱ ⎰ 91, 92, 93, ⎱ | 31 | 35 | 66 | 6 | 1 |
| Exchange-court, . . . | 22 | 23 | 45 | 7 | 0 |
| TOTAL . . | 1648 | 1981 | 3629 | 305 | 33 |

# No. X.

## Deanery of Christ Church.

| NAMES OF STREETS, &c. | POPULATION. | | | HOUSES. | |
|---|---|---|---|---|---|
| | Males. | Females. | TOTAL. | Inhabited. | Waſte. |
| Christ-church-lane, E. side, | 17 | 12 | 29 | 4 | 0 |
| Hell, . . . . . . | 16 | 26 | 42 | 3 | 1 |
| Christ-church-yard, . . | 58 | 78 | 136 | 14 | 1 |
| Fishamble-street, { Two Houses on each side of the entrance into Christ-church-yard, both numbered 57, . . | 17 | 9 | 26 | 2 | 0 |
| TOTAL . . | 108 | 125 | 233 | 23 | 2 |

# No. XI.

## Deanery of Saint Patrick.

| NAMES OF STREETS, &c. | POPULATION. | | | HOUSES. | |
|---|---|---|---|---|---|
| | Males. | Females. | TOTAL. | Inhabited. | Waste. |
| Bride-st. W. side, from No. 29 to 44, . . | 85 | 80 | 165 | 16 | 1 |
| Canon-street, . . . . | 130 | 150 | 280 | 15 | 0 |
| Patrick's-close, . . . | 131 | 176 | 307 | 24 | 2 |
| Myler's-alley, . . . | 78 | 91 | 169 | 15 | 3 |
| Goodman's-alley, . . | 30 | 33 | 63 | 5 | 1 |
| Walker's-alley, S. side, . | 14 | 20 | 34 | 5 | 0 |
| Bull-alley, one house, viz. that next Bride-street on the S. side, . . | 3 | 2 | 5 | 1 | 0 |
| Patrick-st. W. side, from No. 33 to 35; E. side, from the Cathedral to Walker's-alley, . . | 35 | 44 | 79 | 11 | 2 |
| Patrick's back-close, . | 30 | 57 | 87 | 8 | 2 |
| Mitre-alley, . . . . | 54 | 74 | 128 | 11 | 2 |
| Upper Kevin's-street, N. side, from No. 1 to 12; S. side, from New-st. to Edge's-court, . . | 193 | 229 | 422 | 28 | 0 |
| New-st. No. 1, 2, and a B. H. on the E. side, | 13 | 18 | 31 | 3 | 0 |
| Edge's-court, . . . . | 55 | 100 | 155 | 8 | 0 |
| Cathedral-lane, W. side, | 37 | 41 | 78 | 5 | 0 |
| Corbaly's-row, . . . | 25 | 38 | 63 | 5 | 0 |
| Poddle, two houses between Patrick-st. and upper Kevin's-street, | 9 | 6 | 15 | 2 | 0 |
| TOTAL . . | 922 | 1159 | 2081 | 162 | 11 |

# No. XII.

## Parish of Saint Bridget.

| NAMES OF STREETS, &c. | POPULATION. | | | HOUSES. | |
|---|---|---|---|---|---|
| | Males. | Females. | TOTAL. | Inhabited. | Waste. |
| St. Bride-street, E. side entire; W. side, from No. 1 to 28, . . | 448 | 504 | 952 | 83 | 3 |
| Cummin's-court, . | 1 | 1 | 2 | 1 | 1 |
| Sherry's-court, . . | 10 | 13 | 23 | 2 | 1 |
| Derby's-square, off Werburgh-street, Nos. 2, 3, 4, as correct, . . | 25 | 21 | 46 | 3 | 0 |
| Rofs-lane, . . . . | 75 | 71 | 146 | 12 | 4 |
| Bride's-alley, S. side, from No. 10 to 15; N. side, from No. 16 to 27, . . . . | 48 | 53 | 101 | 17 | 0 |
| Bull-alley, S. side, from No. 10 to 17; N. side, from No. 22 to 30, | 113 | 119 | 232 | 16 | 3 |
| Bishop-street, N. side, . | 81 | 176 | 257 | 27 | 1 |
| Peter's-street, . . . | 101 | 147 | 248 | 32 | 2 |
| Wood-street, . . . . | 198 | 276 | 474 | 41 | 2 |
| Golden-lane, . . . . | 342 | 423 | 765 | 61 | 1 |
| Dobbin's-court, . | 3 | 3 | 6 | 1 | 0 |
| Maiden-lane, . . . . | 70 | 87 | 157 | 14 | 0 |
| Oliver's-alley, . . . | 8 | 2 | 10 | 1 | 0 |
| Peter's-row, W. side, . | 28 | 54 | 82 | 12 | 0 |
| Whitefriar's-st. W. side, | 86 | 112 | 198 | 15 | 0 |
| Chancery-lane, . . . | 194 | 254 | 448 | 40 | 1 |
| Great-ship-street, . . | 199 | 247 | 446 | 48 | 3 |
| Clarke's-court, . . | 14 | 19 | 33 | 4 | 0 |
| Michael-a-Pole, . . | 24 | 24 | 48 | 1 | 0 |
| White's-court, . . | 19 | 80 | 49 | 7 | 0 |
| Buckridge's-court, . | 20 | 29 | 49 | 5 | 0 |
| Little-ship-street, . . | 178 | 237 | 415 | 31 | 0 |
| St. Stephen's-st. N. side, | 161 | 226 | 387 | 40 | 0 |
| Great-George's-st. S. W. side, from No. 47 to 61; E. side, from No. 22 to 46, . . | 271 | 304 | 575 | 59 | 1 |

# Parish of Saint Bridget, continued.

| NAMES OF STREETS, &c. | POPULATION. | | | HOUSES. | |
|---|---|---|---|---|---|
| | Males. | Females. | TOTAL. | Inhabited. | Waste. |
| Tinkler's-court, . . | 4 | 5 | 9 | 1 | 1 |
| Rothery's-yard, . . | 8 | 22 | 30 | 2 | 0 |
| George's-court, . . | 15 | 19 | 34 | 4 | 1 |
| Fade-street, . . . . | 95 | 135 | 230 | 18 | 0 |
| Joseph's-lane, . . . . | 62 | 79 | 141 | 14 | 1 |
| Drury-lane, . . . . | 231 | 299 | 530 | 43 | 0 |
| Castle-market and its dependencies, . . | 54 | 48 | 102 | 18 | 0 |
| Exchequer-street, { South side, from Great George's-street, to William-street, - | 193 | 204 | 397 | 29 | 1 |
| Clarke's-court, . . | 13 | 16 | 29 | 2 | 0 |
| William-street, W. side, . | 144 | 214 | 358 | 40 | 0 |
| TOTAL . . | 3536 | 4473 | 8009 | 744 | 27 |

# No. XIII.

## Parish of Saint Peter.

| NAMES OF STREETS, &c. | POPULATION. | | | HOUSES. | |
|---|---|---|---|---|---|
| | Males. | Females. | TOTAL. | Inhabited. | Waste. |
| Grand-canal-street, S. side, no inhabited houses. | | | | | |
| Wentworth-place S. side, | 35 | 37 | 72 | 6 | 1 |
| Denzille-street, S. side, | 68 | 57 | 143 | 19 | 1 |
| Hamilton's-row, S. side, no inhabited houses. | | | | | |
| Harcourt - place, one house, viz. S. side, . | 3 | 7 | 10 | 1 | 0 |
| Lower Merion-st. E. side, | 15 | 16 | 31 | 3 | 0 |
| Upper Merion-st. E. side, | 64 | 83 | 147 | 12 | 0 |
| Merion-square, entire, . | 400 | 459 | 859 | 69 | 2 |
| Holles-street, . . . . | 135 | 171 | 306 | 32 | 1 |
| Lower Mount-street, . | 40 | 54 | 94 | 13 | 9 |
| Grant's-row, . . . | 36 | 55 | 91 | 9 | 1 |
| Holles-row, . . . | 42 | 34 | 76 | 4 | 0 |
| Wilson's-place, . . | 19 | 29 | 48 | 3 | 0 |
| Kelly's-place, . . | 21 | 32 | 53 | 3 | 0 |
| M'Clean's-lane, . . | 30 | 27 | 57 | 6 | 0 |
| Upper Mount-street, . | 5 | 15 | 20 | 4 | 2 |
| Fitzwilliam-street, . . | 10 | 26 | 36 | 6 | 4 |
| Fitzwilliam-lane, . | 35 | 42 | 77 | 6 | 0 |
| Fitzwilliam-square, . . | 19 | 22 | 41 | 4 | 0 |
| Baggot-street, . . . . | 153 | 195 | 348 | 38 | 9 |
| Baggot-court, . . | 13 | 10 | 23 | 4 | 0 |
| Chancellor's-lane, . | 6 | 9 | 15 | 1 | 0 |
| Merion-row, S. side, . | 8 | 22 | 30 | 5 | 0 |
| Hume-street, . . . . | 53 | 73 | 126 | 15 | 2 |
| Ely-Place, . . . . . | 99 | 103 | 202 | 20 | 1 |
| Ely-lane, . . . | 13 | 9 | 22 | 1 | 0 |
| Leeson-street, (not including the Magdalen Asylum), . . . . | 157 | 234 | 391 | 43 | 6 |
| Leeson - place, and Quinn's-lane, . | 135 | 184 | 319 | 23 | 7 |
| St. Stephen's-green, E. S. and W. side, . | 373 | 545 | 918 | 88 | 6 |
| Proud's-lane, . . | 7 | 13 | 20 | 2 | 0 |
| Glover's-alley, . . | 47 | 39 | 86 | 5 | 0 |

F

# Parish of Saint Peter, continued.

| NAMES OF STREETS, &c. | POPULATION. | | | HOUSES. | |
|---|---|---|---|---|---|
| | Males. | Females. | TOTAL. | Inhabited. | Waste. |
| King's-st. South, S. side, | 261 | 305 | 566 | 35 | 0 |
| King's-court, . . | 65 | 70 | 135 | 10 | 0 |
| St. Stephen's-st. S. side, | 149 | 224 | 373 | 33 | 2 |
| Whitefriar's-st. E. side, | 32 | 74 | 106 | 12 | 1 |
| Peter's-row, E. side, . | 6 | 6 | 12 | 2 | 0 |
| York-street, . . . . | 225 | 282 | 507 | 57 | 0 |
| Aungier-street, . . . | 344 | 489 | 833 | 80 | 3 |
| Whitefriar's-lane, . | 43 | 62 | 105 | 5 | 0 |
| Longford-street, . . . | 74 | 104 | 178 | 18 | 0 |
| Longford-lane, . . | 32 | 51 | 83 | 3 | 0 |
| Little Longford-street, . | 41 | 53 | 94 | 12 | 2 |
| Mercer-street, . . . | 70 | 85 | 155 | 19 | 0 |
| Bow-lane, . . . | 56 | 52 | 108 | 9 | 2 |
| Digges's-lane, . . | 157 | 180 | 337 | 18 | 1 |
| Digges's-court, . . | 42 | 42 | 84 | 5 | 0 |
| French-street, . . . . | 127 | 195 | 322 | 27 | 1 |
| Little Digges's-street, | 9 | 11 | 20 | 3 | 0 |
| Cheater's-alley, . . | 14 | 11 | 25 | 4 | 0 |
| Digges's-street . . . | 49 | 127 | 176 | 19 | 2 |
| Cuffe-street, . . . . | 196 | 297 | 493 | 46 | 5 |
| Cuffe-lane, . . . | 31 | 33 | 64 | 5 | 0 |
| Montague-court, . | 24 | 30 | 54 | 9 | 0 |
| Harcourt-street, . . . | 155 | 190 | 345 | 36 | 7 |
| Harcourt-road, . . . | 9 | 12 | 21 | 3 | 0 |
| Montague-street, . . . | 34 | 59 | 93 | 14 | 1 |
| Kevin's port, . . . | 225 | 324 | 549 | 38 | 1 |
| Protestant-row, . . | 3 | 2 | 5 | 1 | 0 |
| Cambden Market, . | 13 | 20 | 33 | 5 | 0 |
| Long-lane, . . . | 12 | 19 | 31 | 4 | 0 |
| Cambden-street, . . . | 239 | 351 | 590 | 74 | 1 |
| Gunpowder - office } yard, . . . } | 23 | 27 | 50 | 3 | 0 |
| Charlotte-street, . . . | 85 | 93 | 178 | 23 | 2 |
| Charlemont-street, . . | 220 | 369 | 589 | 65 | 5 |
| Charlemont-row, . | 5 | 6 | 11 | 2 | 0 |
| Gordon's lane, . . | 20 | 43 | 63 | 9 | 1 |
| Clarke's-lane, . . | 10 | 21 | 31 | 6 | 0 |
| Fennell's-lane, . . | 13 | 17 | 30 | 5 | 0 |
| Canal-quay, W of } Charlemont bridge, } | 8 | 7 | 15 | 2 | 1 |
| Charlemont-place, . | 27 | 31 | 58 | 7 | 0 |
| Peter-place, . . . | 26 | 32 | 58 | 8 | 2 |

## Parish of Saint Peter, continued.

| NAMES OF STREETS, &c. | POPULATION. | | | HOUSES. | |
|---|---|---|---|---|---|
| | Males. | Females. | TOTAL. | Inhabited. | Waste. |
| Porto-Bello, . . . . | 105 | 156 | 261 | 30 | 1 |
| Old Porto-Bello, . . | 37 | 58 | 95 | 13 | 0 |
| Redmond's-hill, . . . | 45 | 76 | 121 | 12 | 3 |
| Bishop's-street, S. side, | 94 | 110 | 204 | 24 | 2 |
| Lower Kevin's-street, . | 552 | 700 | 1252 | 83 | 3 |
| Liberty-lane, . . | 132 | 144 | 276 | 24 | 0 |
| Church-lane, . . | 33 | 41 | 74 | 6 | 0 |
| Tool's-lane, . . . | 11 | 16 | 27 | 3 | 0 |
| Ferns's-court, . . | 34 | 40 | 74 | 4 | 0 |
| Bride-street, from Upper Kevin's-street to No. 45, . . . . | 72 | 94 | 166 | 13 | 2 |
| Grogan's-court, . | 15 | 21 | 36 | 4 | 0 |
| Faucett's-court, . | 10 | 8 | 18 | 3 | 1 |
| Up. Kevin's-st. { N. side, from No. 16 correct, to Bride-street; S. side, from Lower Kevin's-street to Edge's-court, | 287 | 335 | 622 | 40 | 0 |
| Cathedral-lane, E. side, . . . | 61 | 84 | 145 | 11 | 1 |
| Leinster-row, . . | 28 | 21 | 49 | 4 | 2 |
| New-str. { E. side, from No. 3 to 13, and from No. 32 to the Circular-road, . | 134 | 176 | 310 | 35 | 4 |
| Williams's-lane, . | 8 | 12 | 20 | 5 | 5 |
| Circular-road, E. of New-street, | 11 | 18 | 29 | 5 | 0 |
| St. Patrick's Library, . | 7 | 4 | 11 | 1 | 0 |
| Magdalen Asylum, Leeson-street, . . . | 0 | 32 | 32 | 1 | 0 |
| TOTAL . . | 6890 | 9173 | 16063 | 1512 | 116 |

# No. XIV.

## Parish of Saint Anne.

| NAMES OF STREETS, &c. | POPULATION. | | | HOUSES. | |
|---|---|---|---|---|---|
| | Males. | Females. | TOTAL. | Inhabited. | Waste. |
| Lower Merion-st. W. side, | 12 | 16 | 28 | 7 | 0 |
| Upper Merion-st. W. side, | 108 | 145 | 253 | 21 | 2 |
| Lacy's-lane, . . . | 27 | 41 | 68 | 4 | 0 |
| Merion-row, N. side, . | 28 | 31 | 59 | 7 | 3 |
| St. Stephen's-green, N. | 139 | 213 | 352 | 31 | 2 |
| King's-st South, N. side, | 110 | 191 | 301 | 28 | 0 |
| Lime-kiln-yard, . | 7 | 5 | 12 | 3 | 0 |
| Johnston's-place, . . | 13 | 27 | 40 | 6 | 0 |
| William-street, E. side, | 127 | 153 | 280 | 29 | 2 |
| Exchequer-st. S. side, from William-street to Grafton-street, . . | 72 | 104 | 176 | 19 | 1 |
| Wilson's-yard, . . | 8 | 7 | 15 | 3 | 0 |
| Clarendon-street, . . | 211 | 306 | 517 | 55 | 3 |
| Clarendon-market, in 5 stalls, . . . . . | 6 | 11 | 17 | 5 | 0 |
| Clarendon-row, . . . | 63 | 76 | 139 | 4 | 0 |
| Chatham-row, . . . | 25 | 27 | 52 | 3 | 1 |
| Coppinger's-row, . . . | 11 | 18 | 29 | 3 | 1 |
| Grafton-street, E. side entire ; W. side, from King - street to Exchequer-street, . . | 438 | 497 | 935 | 92 | 4 |
| Adam-court, . . | 37 | 43 | 80 | 8 | 0 |
| Grafton or Spann's-lane, . . . | 97 | 126 | 223 | 10 | 0 |
| Tangier-lane, . . | 18 | 20 | 38 | 3 | 0 |
| Chatham-street, . . . | 67 | 91 | 158 | 18 | 3 |
| Pitt-street, . . . . | 41 | 48 | 89 | 13 | 0 |
| Harry-street, . . . . | 23 | 30 | 53 | 7 | 0 |
| Johnston's-court, . . | 51 | 49 | 100 | 8 | 4 |
| Dawson-street, . . . | 269 | 373 | 642 | 60 | 3 |
| Duke-street, . . . . | 119 | 150 | 269 | 23 | 0 |
| Anne-street, . . . . | 113 | 168 | 281 | 30 | 0 |
| Molesworth-street, . . | 160 | 233 | 393 | 37 | 0 |
| Frederick-street, . . . | 110 | 169 | 279 | 35 | 3 |
| Kildare-street, . . . | 170 | 232 | 402 | 46 | 0 |
| Schoolhouse-lane, . | 36 | 63 | 99 | 4 | 0 |
| Nassau-street, S. side, . | 119 | 168 | 287 | 34 | 1 |
| Nassau-lane, . . . | 8 | 6 | 14 | 1 | 0 |
| Leinster-street, S. side, | 65 | 85 | 150 | 13 | 0 |
| Clare-street, . . . . | 82 | 141 | 223 | 26 | 1 |
| Clare-lane, . . . | 34 | 29 | 63 | 4 | 0 |
| Park-st. E. side & S. side, | 47 | 65 | 112 | 11 | 2 |
| TOTAL . . | 3071 | 4157 | 7228 | 711 | 36 |

# No. XV.

## Parish of Saint Andrew.

| NAMES OF STREETS, &c. | POPULATION. | | | HOUSES. | |
|---|---|---|---|---|---|
| | Males. | Females. | TOTAL. | Inhabited. | Waste. |
| Great-George's-street, E. side, from Dame-street to Exchequer-street; W. side, from No. 62 to Dame-st. | 266 | 297 | 563 | 44 | 3 |
| Exchequer-street, N. side, | 206 | 244 | 450 | 44 | 3 |
| Grafton-street, from Exchequer-street to College-green, . . . | 102 | 131 | 233 | 23 | 1 |
| Fleet-lane, W. side, . | 27 | 43 | 70 | 4 | 0 |
| Fleet-alley, W. side, . | 13 | 18 | 31 | 1 | 0 |
| Dame-street, from the center of No. 3 to No. 89, . . . . . | 304 | 302 | 606 | 70 | 5 |
| Coghill's-court, . . | 25 | 21 | 46 | 4 | 1 |
| Palace-street, . . . . | 16 | 21 | 37 | 5 | 0 |
| Dame-lane, . . . | 21 | 24 | 45 | 4 | 0 |
| Dame-court, . . | 57 | 54 | 111 | 14 | 1 |
| King's-head-court, . | 26 | 32 | 58 | 6 | 0 |
| Trinity-place, . . | 93 | 79 | 172 | 20 | 1 |
| St. Andrew's-lane, . | 55 | 74 | 129 | 7 | 0 |
| Trinity-street, . . | 77 | 83 | 160 | 17 | 0 |
| St. Andrew's-street, formerly Hog-hill, . | 85 | 115 | 200 | 25 | 1 |
| Church-lane, . . . . | 29 | 35 | 64 | 6 | 1 |
| Suffolk-street, . . . | 76 | 123 | 199 | 25 | 0 |
| Essex-street, from No. 11 to 41, . . . | 195 | 260 | 455 | 33 | 5 |
| Crampton-court, from No. 4 to 17, . . | 22 | 30 | 52 | 10 | 4 |
| Sycamore-alley, . . . | 116 | 110 | 226 | 16 | 3 |
| Eustace-street, . . . | 81 | 100 | 181 | 24 | 1 |
| Temple-lane, . . . . | 30 | 38 | 58 | 10 | 2 |
| Crow-street, . . . . | 70 | 100 | 1 | 19 | 2 |
| Fownes's-street, . . . | 59 | 58 | 11 | 18 | 5 |
| St. Cecilia-street, . . | 30 | 24 | 54 | 4 | 0 |
| Cope-street, . . . . | 48 | 54 | 102 | 14 | 2 |
| Northumberland court | 12 | 20 | 32 | 2 | 0 |

G

# Parish of Saint Andrew, continued.

| NAMES OF STREETS, &c. | POPULATION. | | | HOUSES. | |
|---|---|---|---|---|---|
| | Males. | Females. | TOTAL. | Inhabited. | Waste. |
| Crown-alley, . . . | 15 | 17 | 32 | 3 | 0 |
| College-green, . . . | 170 | 169 | 339 | 33 | 6 |
| Forster-place, . . | 11 | 21 | 32 | 3 | 0 |
| Parliament-h. { No Inhabitants resident, except during the sitting of Parliament. | 0 | 0 | 0 | 0 | 0 |
| Anglesea-street, . . . | 154 | 188 | 342 | 35 | 2 |
| Temple-bar, . . . . | 391 | 493 | 884 | 58 | 2 |
| Bagnio-slip, . . . | 6 | 7 | 13 | 2 | 3 |
| Hatter's-lane, or } Arsdell's-row, . | 16 | 20 | 36 | 2 | 0 |
| Bedford-row, . . . . | 58 | 68 | 126 | 9 | 1 |
| Fleet-street, { N. side, from Bedford-row to Fleet-alley; S. side, from Anglesea-street to Fleet-lane, . . . . | 266 | 333 | 599 | 50 | 5 |
| Crampton-quay, . . . | 39 | 45 | 84 | 6 | 2 |
| Aston-quay, from Fleet-} alley to Bedford-row, | 171 | 210 | 381 | 25 | 0 |
| New-passage to Carlisle-bridge, no houses in 1798, . . . . | 0 | 0 | 0 | 0 | 0 |
| Price's-lane, . . . . | 55 | 71 | 126 | 9 | 1 |
| Lee's-lane, . . . . | 21 | 24 | 45 | 4 | 0 |
| College-street, one house, } viz. No. 12, . . | 2 | 10 | 12 | 1 | 0 |
| TOTAL . . | 3516 | 4166 | 7682 | 709 | 63 |

# No. XVI.

## Parish of Saint Mark.

| NAMES OF STREETS, &c. | POPULATION. | | | HOUSES. | |
|---|---|---|---|---|---|
| | Males. | Females. | TOTAL. | Inhabited. | Waste. |
| College-st. entire, No.12 excepted, . . . | 90 | 106 | 196 | 15 | 2 |
| Fleet-lane, E. side, . . | 33 | 54 | 87 | 5 | 0 |
| Fleet-alley, E. side, no inhabited houses. . | 0 | 0 | 0 | 0 | 0 |
| Fleet-street, E. of Fleet-lane and Fleet-alley, | 218 | 310 | 528 | 40 | 3 |
| Townsend-street, . . | 764 | 1012 | 1776 | 136 | 20 |
| Fleet-market, . . | 43 | 66 | 109 | 11 | 0 |
| Tucker's-yard, . . | 35 | 31 | 66 | 6 | 2 |
| Spring-garden-lane, . | 23 | 18 | 41 | 3 | 1 |
| Tennis-court, . . | 72 | 57 | 129 | 6 | 0 |
| Park-place, or Carter's-alley, . | 127 | 218 | 345 | 13 | 0 |
| Sandwith-street, . . . | 11 | 8 | 19 | 2 | 1 |
| Hawkins-street, . . . | 148 | 181 | 329 | 29 | 3 |
| Sugar-house-lane, . | 2 | 1 | 3 | 1 | 0 |
| Aston's-quay, E. of Fleet-al. | 157 | 177 | 334 | 17 | 1 |
| Stewart's-court, . . | 7 | 10 | 17 | 3 | 0 |
| George's quay, . . . | 303 | 375 | 678 | 30 | 0 |
| City-quay, . . . . . | 269 | 315 | 584 | 41 | 0 |
| Banfield's-lane, . . | 6 | 9 | 15 | 3 | 0 |
| Sir John Rogerson's-quay, | 284 | 233 | 517 | 28 | 0 |
| Hanover-street, . . | 2 | 8 | 10 | 1 | 0 |
| Nowland's-lane, . | 8 | 6 | 14 | 2 | 0 |
| Lime-street, . . . | 2 | 2 | 4 | 1 | 0 |
| Poolbeg-street, . . . | 224 | 293 | 517 | 42 | 4 |
| Stocking-lane, . . . | 129 | 189 | 318 | 20 | 0 |
| Luke-street, . . . . | 69 | 76 | 145 | 14 | 3 |
| White's-lane, . . . . | 52 | 53 | 105 | 11 | 2 |
| George's-street, E. . . | 44 | 57 | 101 | 12 | 0 |
| Moss-street, . . . . | 205 | 263 | 468 | 34 | 4 |
| Prince's-street, . . . | 13 | 15 | 28 | 3 | 1 |
| Gloster-street, S. . . | 79 | 80 | 159 | 11 | 0 |
| Mark-street, . . . . | 30 | 65 | 95 | 13 | 2 |
| Nassau-street, N. side, . | 10 | 17 | 27 | 5 | 1 |
| Leinster-street, N. side, | 30 | 20 | 50 | 2 | 0 |
| Park-street, W. side, . | 20 | 29 | 49 | 4 | 0 |
| Harcourt-place, N. side, | 17 | 17 | 34 | 5 | 0 |
| Hamilton's-row, N. side, | 16 | 39 | 55 | 8 | 1 |
| Denzille-street, N. side, | 13 | 36 | 49 | 7 | 2 |

## Parish of Saint Mark, continued.

| NAMES OF STREETS, &c. | POPULATION. | | | HOUSES. | |
|---|---|---|---|---|---|
| | Males. | Females. | TOTAL. | Inhabited. | Waste. |
| Wentworth-place, N. side, | 29 | 46 | 75 | 9 | 0 |
| Grand-canal-street, N. side, no houses as yet. | 0 | 0 | 0 | 0 | 0 |
| Westland-row, . . . | 18 | 49 | 67 | 4 | 0 |
| Cumberland-street, S. . | 55 | 71 | 126 | 21 | 5 |
| Boyne-street, rere of do. and Boyne-lane, . | 190 | 231 | 421 | 27 | 0 |
| Erne-street, . . . . | 0 | 2 | 2 | 1 | 2 |
| Great Clarence - street, no inhabited houses, | 0 | 0 | 0 | 0 | 1 |
| TOTAL . . | 3847 | 4845 | 8692 | 646 | 62 |

## Parish of Saint Paul.

| NAMES OF STREETS, &c | POPULATION. | | | HOUSES. | |
|---|---|---|---|---|---|
| | Males. | Females. | TOTAL. | Inhabited. | Waste. |
| Park-gate-street, . . . | 120 | 190 | 310 | 36 | 3 |
| Barrack-street, . . . | 587 | 858 | 1445 | 99 | 3 |
| Granby-court, . . | 18 | 17 | 35 | 6 | 0 |
| Featherbed-lane, . | 6 | 17 | 23 | 2 | 0 |
| Boot-yard, . . . | 25 | 53 | 78 | 6 | 0 |
| Dawson's-yard, . . | 44 | 98 | 142 | 7 | 0 |
| Silver-street, . . . . | 62 | 81 | 143 | 11 | 1 |
| Liffey-street, . . , . | 42 | 51 | 93 | 8 | 2 |
| Flood-street, . . . . | 83 | 122 | 205 | 15 | 4 |
| Kane's-court, . . | 18 | 20 | 38 | 3 | 0 |
| Pembroke, or Sand-quay, | 21 | 38 | 59 | 5 | 2 |
| Tighe-st. or Gravel-walk, | 329 | 466 | 795 | 51 | 4 |
| Browne's-alley, . . | 11 | 12 | 23 | 2 | 0 |
| Ellis's-quay, . . . . | 34 | 51 | 85 | 9 | 0 |
| John-street, . . . . | 18 | 22 | 40 | 3 | 1 |
| Queen-street, . . . . | 339 | 438 | 777 | 79 | 4 |
| Queen's-court, . . | 5 | 3 | 8 | 2 | 5 |
| Burges's-lane, . . . | 16 | 16 | 32 | 1 | 1 |
| Bridewell-lane, . . . | 11 | 14 | 25 | 2 | 0 |
| Hendrick-s reet, . . | 58 | 90 | 148 | 19 | 1 |
| Hendrick-lane, . . | 16 | 28 | 44 | 4 | 0 |
| Black-hall-street, . . | 59 | 66 | 125 | 15 | 6 |
| Blue-coat-hospital, . . | 134 | 24 | 158 | 1 | 0 |
| Parade at St Paul's-church | 4 | 5 | 9 | 2 | 1 |
| Temple-street, . . . | 41 | 59 | 100 | 13 | 1 |
| Mountpelier, . . . . | 56 | 77 | 133 | 19 | 0 |
| Arbour-hill, . . . . | 119 | 158 | 277 | 42 | 9 |
| Stony-batter, . . . . | 219 | 188 | 407 | 52 | 3 |
| Chicken-lane, . . | 17 | 28 | 45 | 10 | 5 |
| Manor-street, . . . . | 429 | 534 | 963 | 127 | 7 |
| Daly's-court, . . | 13 | 12 | 25 | 7 | 2 |
| Swan's-lane, . . . | 15 | 12 | 27 | 6 | 0 |
| Garden-lane, . . | 51 | 62 | 113 | 22 | 2 |
| Prussia-street, . . . | 183 | 237 | 410 | 64 | 5 |
| Aughrim-street, . . . | 116 | 163 | 279 | 46 | 5 |
| Brunswick-st. N. side, from No. 17 to Stony-batter ; S. side, from Stony-batter to No. 49, | 103 | 178 | 281 | 24 | 3 |

H

## Parish of Saint Paul, continued.

| NAMES OF STREETS, &c. | POPULATION. | | | HOUSES. | |
|---|---|---|---|---|---|
| | Males. | Females. | TOTAL. | Inhabited. | Waste. |
| George's-lane, . . | 20 | 29 | 49 | 3 | 1 |
| Red-cow-lane, . . | 45 | 46 | 91 | 8 | 2 |
| Smith's - court, off } Red-cow-lane, } | 22 | 34 | 56 | 6 | 0 |
| Grange-Gorman-lane, . | 191 | 240 | 431 | 76 | 18 |
| Fitzwilliam-place, . | 8 | 16 | 24 | 3 | 0 |
| Love-lane, . . . | 6 | 10 | 16 | 3 | 0 |
| Stanhope-street, . . . | 13 | 23 | 36 | 5 | 2 |
| King-street, North, N. side, from Red-cow-lane to Stony-batter; S. side, from Stony-batter to Smithfield, | 156 | 240 | 396 | 40 | 7 |
| Smithfield, W. side only, | 185 | 225 | 410 | 26 | 0 |
| Hay-market, . . . . | 84 | 96 | 180 | 13 | 3 |
| Arran-quay, from No. 19 to Queen-street, | 88 | 110 | 198 | 26 | 0 |
| West-Arran-street, E. side, from Arran-quay to Phœnix-street; W. side entire, . . . | 48 | 69 | 117 | 11 | 3 |
| TOTAL . . | 4288 | 5616 | 9904 | 1050 | 116 |

# No. XVIII.

## Parish of Saint Michan.

| NAMES OF STREETS, &c. | POPULATION. | | | HOUSES. | |
|---|---|---|---|---|---|
| | Males. | Females. | TOTAL. | Inhabited. | Waste. |
| West - Arran - street, from Phœnix - street to Smithfield, · · | 25 | 38 | 63 | 4 | 0 |
| Smithfield, E. side only, | 205 | 253 | 458 | 30 | 2 |
| Duck-lane, · · · | 3 | 4 | 7 | 2 | 0 |
| Carter's-alley, · · | 35 | 58 | 93 | 6 | 0 |
| Factory-lane, · · | 28 | 34 | 62 | 5 | 0 |
| King-str. N. { N. side, from Bolton-street to Redcow-lane; S. side, from Smithfield to Capel-street, | 647 | 836 | 1483 | 122 | 8 |
| Whitehall-court, · | 19 | 28 | 47 | 5 | 1 |
| Brunswick-str. { N. side, from Upper Church-street to No. 16; S. side, from No. 50 to Upper Church-street, · · · | 131 | 168 | 299 | 34 | 3 |
| Snugborough, · · | 13 | 11 | 24 | 3 | 0 |
| Arran-q. from Church-street to No. 18, · | 54 | 78 | 132 | 18 | 0 |
| Phœnix-street, · · · | 206 | 287 | 493 | 27 | 2 |
| Lincoln-lane, · · · | 37 | 50 | 87 | 13 | 0 |
| Ball-yard, · · · | 16 | 16 | 32 | 6 | 4 |
| Bow-lane, · · · · | 111 | 108 | 219 | 14 | 2 |
| Hammond-lane, · · · | 182 | 206 | 388 | 29 | 5 |
| Church-street, · · · | 1293 | 1517 | 2810 | 189 | 24 |
| Field's-court, · · | 9 | 10 | 19 | 3 | 4 |
| Townley-court, · | 18 | 18 | 36 | 5 | 1 |
| Cole's-court, · · | 38 | 48 | 86 | 4 | 0 |
| Russell's-court, · | 10 | 12 | 22 | 2 | 1 |
| George-inn-yard, · | 11 | 14 | 25 | 2 | 3 |
| Byrne's-court, · · | 23 | 31 | 54 | 3 | 0 |
| Catherine's-lane, · | 18 | 26 | 44 | 4 | 3 |
| New Church-street, · · | 142 | 169 | 311 | 17 | 0 |
| Bow-street, · · · · | 339 | 429 | 768 | 46 | 9 |
| Bedford-street, · · · | 26 | 36 | 62 | 6 | 0 |

# Parish of Saint Michan, continued.

| NAMES OF STREETS, &c. | POPULATION. | | | HOUSES. | |
|---|---|---|---|---|---|
| | Males. | Females. | TOTAL. | Inhabited. | Waste. |
| Browne-street, between King-st. and Bow-st. | 36 | 61 | 97 | 8 | 0 |
| Kavanagh's-court, off do. | 13 | 16 | 29 | 4 | 1 |
| May-lane, . . . . . | 119 | 139 | 258 | 18 | 0 |
| King's-inns-quay, . . | 51 | 55 | 106 | 13 | 1 |
| Upper Ormond-quay, . | 147 | 158 | 305 | 35 | 1 |
| Pill-lane, . . . . . | 507 | 626 | 1133 | 97 | 12 |
| Blue-hand-court, off Pill-lane, . . | 30 | 24 | 54 | 5 | 1 |
| Arran-street, . . . . | 128 | 159 | 287 | 26 | 1 |
| L. Strand-st. { S. side, from Arran-st. to No. 6; N. side, from No 17 to Arran-st | 116 | 140 | 256 | 18 | 0 |
| Johnston's - alley.— No population. | | | | | |
| Charles-street, . . . | 304 | 390 | 694 | 40 | 0 |
| Ormond-market, . . . | 0 | 0 | 0 | 0 | 0 |
| Mountrath-street, . . | 102 | 124 | 226 | 19 | 3 |
| Toshe's-court, . . | 9 | 15 | 24 | 2 | 0 |
| Mass-lane, . . . . | 10 | 21 | 31 | 4 | 0 |
| Morgan-place, . . . | 0 | 3 | 3 | 1 | 3 |
| Mary's-lane, . . . . | 451 | 517 | 968 | 67 | 4 |
| Boot-lane entire, except No. 1, belonging to Bank of Ireland, and in Mary's parish, . | 207 | 231 | 438 | 34 | 0 |
| Fisher's-lane, . . . | 179 | 193 | 372 | 30 | 1 |
| Bradogue-alley, . | 15 | 27 | 42 | 3 | 0 |
| Bull-lane, . . . . . | 129 | 164 | 293 | 19 | 0 |
| Greek street, . . . . | 97 | 138 | 235 | 30 | 3 |
| Lattin's-court, . . | 36 | 59 | 95 | 7 | 9 |
| Anderson's-court, . | 24 | 32 | 56 | 5 | 2 |
| Beresford-street, . . . | 202 | 279 | 481 | 42 | 6 |
| Stirrup-lane, . . | 53 | 68 | 121 | 8 | 1 |
| Kelche's yard, . . | 2 | 9 | 11 | 3 | 0 |
| Simpson's-court, . | 8 | 15 | 23 | 4 | 2 |
| Anne-street, North, . | 85 | 129 | 214 | 27 | 3 |
| George's-hill, . . . | 49 | 42 | 91 | 12 | 0 |
| Halston-street, . . . | 77 | 108 | 185 | 14 | 2 |
| Ball's-lane, . . . . | 9 | 17 | 26 | 3 | 1 |
| Cuckow-lane, . . . | 17 | 17 | 34 | 4 | 0 |

## Parish of Saint Michan, continued.

| NAMES OF STREETS, &c | POPULATION. | | | HOUSES. | |
|---|---|---|---|---|---|
| | Males. | Females. | TOTAL. | Inhabited. | Waste. |
| Petticoat-lane, . . . | 24 | 32 | 56 | 4 | 1 |
| Lit. Britain-str. { N. side, from No. 5 to Green-street; S. side, from Petticoat-lane to Stable-lane, . . . . | 53 | 66 | 119 | 12 | 1 |
| Green-street, . . . . | 94 | 122 | 216 | 16 | 2 |
| Coleraine-street, . . . | 58 | 87 | 145 | 15 | 1 |
| Linen-hall-street, . . | 52 | 56 | 108 | 14 | 0 |
| Lurgan-street, . . . | 27 | 30 | 57 | 9 | 0 |
| Lisburn-street, . . . | 10 | 21 | 31 | 4 | 0 |
| Linen-hall, . . . . | 12 | 22 | 34 | 1 | 0 |
| Constitution - hill, or } Glasmanoge, . . | 236 | 287 | 523 | 45 | 4 |
| Townsend-st. off do. | 27 | 30 | 57 | 4 | 0 |
| Broad-stone, . . . . | 230 | 322 | 552 | 112 | 11 |
| Monk's-place, . . | 30 | 39 | 69 | 11 | 1 |
| Phibbsborough-lane, | 45 | 73 | 118 | 22 | 1 |
| Yarn-hall.—No Population. | | | | | |
| Henrietta-str. { N.E. side, except the house next Bolton-street; S.W. side, except the house next Bolton-street, | 100 | 106 | 206 | 13 | 0 |
| Henrietta-place, . | 16 | 29 | 45 | 4 | 0 |
| Stable-lane, off Henrietta-street.—No Population. | | | | | |
| TOTAL . . | 7865 | 9783 | 17648 | 1487 | 141 |

# No. XIX.

## Parish of Saint Mary.

| NAMES OF STREETS, &c. | POPULATION. | | | HOUSES. | |
|---|---|---|---|---|---|
| | Males. | Females. | TOTAL. | Inhabited. | Waste. |
| Capel-street, . . . . | 612 | 767 | 1379 | 162 | 4 |
| Little Strand st. S. side, from No. 7 to Capel-street ; N. side, from Capel-st. to No. 16, | 76 | 81 | 157 | 10 | 0 |
| Mary's-abbey, . . . | 146 | 136 | 282 | 36 | 2 |
| Meeting-house-lane, | 26 | 4 | 30 | 4 | 0 |
| Little Mary-street, . . | 233 | 230 | 463 | 30 | 0 |
| Stable-lane, . . . | 16 | 22 | 38 | 2 | 0 |
| Little Britain-street, N. side, from Capel-st. to No. 4 ; S. side, from Stable-lane to Capel-st. | 21 | 25 | 46 | 6 | 0 |
| Lower Ormond-quay, . | 160 | 185 | 345 | 34 | 4 |
| Batchelor's-walk, from Lower Liffey - street to Sackville-street, . | 121 | 147 | 268 | 32 | 0 |
| Abbey-st. S. side, from Capel-st. to No. 53 ; N. side, from Williams's-lane to Capel-st. | 492 | 632 | 1124 | 109 | 11 |
| Great Strand-street, . | 192 | 191 | 383 | 39 | 2 |
| The Lots, N. side, West of the rere of No. 54 Abbey-street ; S. side entire, . . . . . | 14 | 15 | 29 | 4 | 1 |
| Murry - court, off Strand-street, . | 12 | 29 | 41 | 4 | 0 |
| Prince's-street, West of Williams's-lane, . | 21 | 22 | 43 | 4 | 0 |
| Mary-street, . . . . | 210 | 318 | 528 | 52 | 2 |
| Henry-st. S. side, from Middle Liffey-street to No. 22; N. side, from Off-lane to Denmark-street, . . . . | 248 | 323 | 571 | 50 | 2 |

## Parish of Saint Mary, continued.

| NAMES OF STREETS, &c. | POPULATION. | | | HOUSES. | |
|---|---|---|---|---|---|
| | Males. | Females. | TOTAL. | Inhabited. | Waste. |
| Great Britain-st. S. side, from Capel-street to Moore-lane ; N. side, from Cavendish - row to Capel-street, | 512 | 655 | 1167 | 127 | 0 |
| Stafford-street, . . . | 156 | 224 | 380 | 41 | 4 |
| Jervis-street, . . . . | 185 | 371 | 556 | 62 | 3 |
| Swift's-row, . . . . | 83 | 95 | 178 | 11 | 1 |
| Lower Liffey-street, . | 131 | 144 | 275 | 31 | 0 |
| Middle Liffey-street, . | 287 | 318 | 605 | 34 | 1 |
| Denmark-street, . . . | 273 | 404 | 677 | 39 | 0 |
| Cole's-lane, . . . . | 243 | 254 | 497 | 33 | 2 |
| Moore-street, . . . | 274 | 349 | 623 | 56 | 0 |
| Chapel-lane, . . . . | 34 | 52 | 86 | 6 | 0 |
| Wheeler's-alley, . . . | 15 | 18 | 33 | 3 | 0 |
| M'Cann's-lane, . . . | 19 | 21 | 40 | 3 | 0 |
| Cross-lane, off Cole's-lane, | 16 | 20 | 36 | 3 | 0 |
| Sampson's-lane, . . . | 77 | 85 | 162 | 16 | 0 |
| Benneting's - lane, now Cole's-lane market, | 99 | 125 | 224 | 28 | 0 |
| Stable-lane, off middle Liffey-street, . . | 10 | 11 | 21 | 2 | 0 |
| Moore-lane, . . . . | 27 | 30 | 57 | 5 | 0 |
| Sackville-lane, . . . | 66 | 73 | 139 | 12 | 0 |
| Off-lane, . . . . . | 81 | 88 | 169 | 8 | 0 |
| Back-yard, off Moore-st. | 22 | 21 | 43 | 4 | 1 |
| Bolton-street, . . . . | 295 | 426 | 721 | 64 | 0 |
| M'Manus-court, . | 13 | 17 | 30 | 5 | 0 |
| Bryner's-alley, . . | 6 | 6 | 12 | 1 | 0 |
| Ryder's-row, . . . . | 31 | 49 | 80 | 7 | 0 |
| Britain-lane, . . . . | 62 | 86 | 148 | 10 | 0 |
| Loftus-lane, . . . . | 111 | 149 | 260 | 20 | 0 |
| Cross-lane, . . . . | 117 | 176 | 293 | 23 | 0 |
| Cherry-lane, . , . . | 47 | 94 | 141 | 10 | 0 |
| Turn-again-lane, . . . | 36 | 48 | 84 | 11 | 0 |
| Dominick-street, . . . | 243 | 344 | 587 | 59 | 0 |
| Granby-row, . . . . | 174 | 245 | 419 | 44 | 0 |
| Granby-place, . . | 26 | 30 | 56 | 4 | 0 |

# Parish of Saint Mary, continued.

| NAMES OF STREETS, &c. | POPULATION. | | | HOUSES. | |
|---|---|---|---|---|---|
| | Males. | Females. | TOTAL. | Inhabited. | Waste. |
| Palace-row, (N. B. This is extra-parochial, as also Mrs. Dean's house in Granby-row.) . | 91 | 110 | 201 | 12 | 0 |
| Frederick-street, North, the S. W. side only, | 23 | 26 | 49 | 6 | 1 |
| Yarn-hall-street, . . . | 6 | 6 | 12 | 1 | 0 |
| Henrietta-st. 2 houses next Bolton-street, | 6 | 5 | 11 | 2 | 0 |
| Stable-lane off Henrietta street, . | 14 | 24 | 38 | 3 | 0 |
| Dorset-street, S. E. side, from Dominick-st. to Frederick-st.; N. W. side, from White's-lane to Bolton-street, | 484 | 611 | 1095 | 99 | 0 |
| Gilshenan's-lane, . | 18 | 25 | 43 | 7 | 0 |
| Gooding's-yard, . | 44 | 58 | 102 | 8 | 0 |
| King's-lane, . . . | 51 | 69 | 120 | 21 | 2 |
| Kelly's-lane, . . | 20 | 38 | 58 | 7 | 0 |
| Bishop's-yard, . . | 10 | 14 | 24 | 5 | 0 |
| Blessington-street, no population in 1798. | | | | | |
| Paradise-row, . . . | 117 | 178 | 295 | 45 | 0 |
| Graham's-row, . . | 24 | 29 | 53 | 10 | 0 |
| Lane from Paradise-row to the Royal Circus, . . . | 11 | 16 | 27 | 6 | 0 |
| TOTAL . . | 7290 | 9364 | 16654 | 1590 | 43 |

## Parish of Saint Thomas.

| NAMES OF STREETS, &c. | POPULATION. | | | HOUSES. | |
|---|---|---|---|---|---|
| | Males. | Females. | TOTAL. | Inhabited. | Waste. |
| Lower Sackville-street, . | 104 | 141 | 245 | 25 | 6 |
| Upper Sackville-street, . | 275 | 341 | 616 | 59 | 1 |
| The Lotts, { N. side, E. of the rere of No. 54, Abbey-street, | 9 | 7 | 16 | 3 | 0 |
| Abbey-street, { S. side, from No. 54 to Lower Sackville-st.; N. side, from Lower Sackville-street to Williams's-lane, . | 76 | 92 | 168 | 25 | 5 |
| Prince's str. E. of Williams's-lane, . . | 20 | 25 | 45 | 4 | 0 |
| Henry-street, { S. side, from No. 23 to Lower Sackville-st.; N. side, from Upper Sackville-street to Off-lane, . . . | 40 | 57 | 97 | 8 | 2 |
| Batchelor's-walk, from Sackville - street to Union-street, . . | 72 | 73 | 145 | 7 | 0 |
| Lower Abbey-street, . | 352 | 482 | 834 | 54 | 3 |
| Custom-house, . . . | 20 | 38 | 58 | 1 | 0 |
| Beresford-place, . . . | 3 | 4 | 7 | 1 | 4 |
| Union-street, . . . . | 57 | 57 | 114 | 6 | 0 |
| Marlborough-street, . . | 426 | 520 | 946 | 99 | 5 |
| Tucker's-row, . . . | 98 | 92 | 190 | 13 | 0 |
| Stable-lane, between Tucker's-row and Earl-street, . | 53 | 59 | 112 | 8 | 0 |
| Back yard, off do. . | 11 | 18 | 29 | 2 | 0 |
| Roach's-lane, off Marlborough-st. | 7 | 12 | 19 | 2 | 0 |
| Earl-street, North, . . | 95 | 149 | 244 | 25 | 2 |
| Elephant lane, . . . | 24 | 32 | 56 | 4 | 0 |
| Gregg's-lane, . . . | 34 | 42 | 76 | 6 | 0 |

# Parish of Saint Thomas, continued.

| NAMES OF STREETS, &c. | POPULATION. | | | HOUSES. | |
|---|---|---|---|---|---|
| | Males. | Females. | TOTAL. | Inhabited. | Waste. |
| Potter's-alley, . . . | 33 | 39 | 72 | 6 | 1 |
| Entrance to Marlbo-rough-green, . . | 19 | 18 | 37 | 3 | 0 |
| Cope-street, North, . . | 25 | 33 | 58 | 8 | 0 |
| Great Britain-st. S. side, from Moore-lane to Summer-hill, . . | 186 | 275 | 461 | 46 | 4 |
| Summer-hill, S. side only | 152 | 251 | 403 | 51 | 3 |
| Rutland-street, . . . | 19 | 13 | 32 | 6 | 2 |
| Morgan's-lane, . . . | 12 | 14 | 26 | 5 | 3 |
| Portland-row, . . . | 13 | 13 | 26 | 3 | 3 |
| Buckingham-street, . . | 36 | 45 | 81 | 10 | 0 |
| Meredith-place, . . . | 3 | 4 | 7 | 1 | 0 |
| Washington-row, . . | 3 | 3 | 6 | 2 | 4 |
| Caroline-row, without the Circular-road, . | 0 | 0 | 0 | 0 | 0 |
| Stratford-row, . . . | 12 | 19 | 31 | 5 | 0 |
| Gloucester-street, . . | 139 | 197 | 336 | 41 | 0 |
| Lower Gloucester-street, | 41 | 39 | 80 | 10 | 1 |
| Cumberland-street, North, | 144 | 200 | 344 | 41 | 1 |
| Cumberland-lane, . | 37 | 51 | 88 | 6 | 0 |
| Stable-lane, off Cumberland-st., between No. 4 and 5, . . | 2 | 3 | 5 | 1 | 0 |
| Stable-lane, off Cumberland-st. between No. 38 and 39. . . | 7 | 8 | 15 | 2 | 0 |
| Lower Gardiner-street, | 47 | 64 | 111 | 15 | 10 |
| Gloucester-place, . . | 18 | 20 | 38 | 6 | 1 |
| Upper Gloucester-place, | 0 | 0 | 0 | 0 | 0 |
| Mecklenburgh-street, . | 272 | 397 | 669 | 78 | 7 |
| Mecklenburgh-lane, No. 1, . . | 18 | 21 | 39 | 5 | 0 |
| Mecklenburgh-lane, No. 2, . . | 23 | 37 | 60 | 3 | 0 |

## Parish of Saint Thomas, continued.

| NAMES OF STREETS, &c. | POPULATION. | | | HOUSES. | |
|---|---|---|---|---|---|
| | Males. | Females. | TOTAL. | Inhabited. | Waste. |
| Mabbot-street, . . . | 137 | 150 | 287 | 31 | 5 |
| Back yard, off Mabbot-street, | 8 | 9 | 17 | 3 | 0 |
| Mabbot-lane, No. 1, | 15 | 11 | 26 | 4 | 0 |
| Do. No. 2, . . . | 34 | 39 | 73 | 11 | 0 |
| Montgomery-street, . . | 296 | 320 | 616 | 72 | 3 |
| Barlow's-square, . . . | 17 | 20 | 37 | 7 | 0 |
| Martin's-lane, . . . | 7 | 5 | 12 | 3 | 0 |
| North Strand, . . . | 134 | 179 | 313 | 39 | 3 |
| Mayor-street, . . . | 34 | 28 | 62 | 5 | 2 |
| North Wall, . . . . | 34 | 43 | 77 | 11 | 1 |
| TOTAL . . | 3753 | 4809 | 8562 | 892 | 82 |

# No. XXI.

## Parish of Saint George.

| NAMES OF STREETS, &c. | POPULATION. | | | HOUSES. | |
|---|---|---|---|---|---|
| | Males. | Females. | TOTAL. | Inhabited. | Waste. |
| Great Britain-st. North side, from Cavendish-row to Summer-hill, | 243 | 353 | 596 | 59 | 0 |
| Johnston's-court, . | 31 | 58 | 89 | 7 | 4 |
| Summer-hill, N. W. side, | 135 | 196 | 331 | 48 | 2 |
| Lane's-lane, . . | 29 | 39 | 68 | 14 | 1 |
| Cavendish-row, . . . | 126 | 142 | 268 | 24 | 0 |
| Frederick-street North, North-East side only, | 9 | 10 | 19 | 3 | 0 |
| Dorset-street, { S. E. side, from Frederick-street to Lower Dorset-st. N. W. side, one house only, . . | 17 | 27 | 44 | 5 | 0 |
| White's-lane, . . | 12 | 34 | 46 | 8 | 0 |
| Lower Dorset-street, . | 257 | 335 | 592 | 78 | 5 |
| Kelly's-row, . . | 35 | 43 | 78 | 14 | 0 |
| Synnot's-place, . . | 16 | 28 | 44 | 6 | 2 |
| Great George's-street, N. | 237 | 273 | 510 | 48 | 2 |
| George's-court, . | 10 | 14 | 24 | 2 | 0 |
| Upper Temple-street, . | 90 | 121 | 211 | 23 | 2 |
| Lower Temple-street, | 56 | 89 | 145 | 14 | 6 |
| Stable-lane, off Upper Temple-st. | 16 | 23 | 39 | 6 | 0 |
| Temple-court, off Lower Temple-st. | 43 | 53 | 96 | 9 | 0 |
| Gardiner's-row, . . . | 44 | 48 | 92 | 8 | 0 |
| Great Denmark-street, | 62 | 55 | 117 | 11 | 1 |
| Gardiner's-place, . . | 94 | 153 | 247 | 28 | 3 |
| Stable-lane, . . . | 12 | 22 | 34 | 4 | 0 |
| Grenville-street, . . . | 49 | 48 | 97 | 11 | 7 |
| Stable-lane, . . . | 5 | 9 | 14 | 3 | 3 |
| Mountjoy-square, N. side, | 50 | 50 | 100 | 10 | 3 |
| Mountjoy-square, W. side, | 37 | 30 | 67 | 9 | 6 |
| Mountjoy-square, S. side, | 91 | 99 | 190 | 16 | 2 |
| Mountjoy - square, East side, no population in 1798, . . . . . | 0 | 0 | 0 | 0 | 0 |

## Parish of Saint George, continued.

| NAMES OF STREETS, &c. | POPULATION. | | | HOUSES. | |
|---|---|---|---|---|---|
| | Males. | Females. | TOTAL. | Inhabited. | Waste. |
| Middle Gardiner-street, | 72 | 87 | 159 | 21 | 7 |
| Russel's-lane, . . | 24 | 19 | 43 | 4 | 0 |
| Belmont-place, . . | 10 | 10 | 20 | 2 | 1 |
| Mountjoy-place, . . . | 11 | 18 | 29 | 5 | 7 |
| Great Charles-street, . | 15 | 14 | 29 | 4 | 7 |
| Stable-lane, . . . | 15 | 10 | 25 | 3 | 0 |
| Mountjoy-court, off ⎱ ditto, . . . ⎰ | 8 | 14 | 22 | 4 | 4 |
| Fitzgibbon-street, . . | 4 | 3 | 7 | 1 | 1 |
| Belvidere-place, . . . | 40 | 54 | 94 | 10 | 5 |
| Upper Gardiner-street, . | 36 | 54 | 90 | 12 | 8 |
| Eccles-street, . . . | 163 | 246 | 409 | 51 | 0 |
| Eccles-lane, . . . | 7 | 4 | 11 | 2 | 0 |
| TOTAL . . | 2211 | 2885 | 5096 | 587 | 89 |

*An* ALPHABETICAL. LIST *of the Streets, Squares, Lanes, Alleys, Quays, Courts, Yards, &c. in the City of* DUBLIN, *in* 1798; *mentioning the next principal adjoining Street: with a reference to the Parochial Table, in which the Population of each Street, Lane, &c. is to be found.*

———

## A.

Abbey-street, Upper, XIX. and XX.

Abbey-street, Lower, XX.

Adam-court, *Grafton-street*, XIV.

Adam-and-Eve-lane, } or Chapel-yard, } *Merchant's-quay*, VII.

Aldborough-place, *Circular-road.*

Anderson's-court, *Greek-street*, XVIII.

Andrew's-lane, *Exchequer-street*, XV.

Andrew's-street, XV.

Angel-alley, *High-street*, V. and VII.

Angel-court, *High-street*, VII.

Anglesea-street, *College-green*, XV.

Anne-street, North, *Linen-hall*, XVIII.

Anne-street, South, *Dawson-street*, XIV.

Arbour-hill, *Barracks*, XVII.

Archibold's-court, VI.

Ardee-street, *New-market*, II. and III.

Ardee-row, *New-market*, III.

Arran-quay, XVII. and XVIII.

Arran-street, East, *Ormond-quay*, XVIII.

Arran-street, West, *Arran-quay*, XVII. and XVIII.

Ash-street, *Coombe*, IV.

Aston's-

Aston's-quay, XV. and XVI.
Atkinson's-alley, *Coombe,* III.
Audeon's-arch, *Corn-market,* VI.
Aughrim-street, *Manor-street,* XVII.
Aungier-street, XIII.

**B.**

Back-yard, *Moore-street,* XIX.
Bason-lane, *James's-street,* I.
Bason-place, *Bason-lane,* I. and II.
Batchelor's-walk, XIX. and XX.
Back-lane, *Nicholas-street,* V. and VI.
Baggot-street, *Merrion-street,* XIII.
Baggot-court, *Baggot-street,* XIII.
Bagnio-slip, *Temple-bar,* XV.
Ball-court-yard, *John's-lane,* VIII.
Ball's-lane, *Anne-street, North,* XVIII.
Bell-yard, *Lincoln-lane,* XVIII.
Banfield's-lane, XVI.
Bardon's-yard, *Ransford-street,* II.
Barlow's-square, *Montgomery-street,* XX.
Barrack-street, XVII.
Bedford-row, *Fleet-street,* XV.
Bedford-street, *Bow-street,* XVIII.
Belmont-place, *Gardiner's-street,* XXI.
Bell-view, *Crane-lane,* II.
Belvidere-place, *Mountjoy-square,* XXI.
Benneting's-lane, *Moore-street,* XIX.
Bear's-court, *Corn-market,* VI.
Beresford-place, *Abbey-street,* XX.
Beresford-street, *King-street, North,* XVIII.
Bethesda-lane, *Dorset-street.*
Binns's-court, *Francis-street,* IV.
Bishop's-street, *Kevin's-street,* XII. and XIII.

Bishop's-

Britain.

Britain-lane, *Great Britain-street*, XIX.
Britain-street, Great, *Capel-street,*. XIX. and XX.
Britain-street, Little, *Capel-street,* XVIII. and XIX.
Broad-stone, *Constitution-hill*, XVIII.
Browne's-alley, *Tighe-street*, XVII.
Browne's-alley, *Thomas-street*, II.
Browne's-street, *King's-street, North*, XVIII.
Browne's-street, *Weaver's-square*, II.
Brunswick-street, *Church-street*, XVII. and XVIII.
Bryner's-alley, *Bolton-street*, XIX.
Buckingham-street, *Summer-hill*, XX.
Buckridge's-court, *Great Ship-street*, XII.
Bull-alley, *Patrick-street*, XII. and IV.
Bull-lane, *Pill-lane*, XVIII.
Burges's-lane, XVII.
Byrne's-hill, *Ardee-street*, II.
Byrne's-court, *Back-lane*, VI.
Byr's-court, *Church-street*, XVIII.

### C.

Cain's-alley, *Coombe*, III.
Calender-yard, *Francis-street*, IV.
Camden-street, *Kevin's-port*, XIII.
Camden-market, *Camden-street*, XIII.
Canal-street, Grand, *Denzile-street*, XIII.
Canal-place, stores, and harbour, *James's-street*, II.
Canal-quay, W. of *Charlemont-bridge*, XIII.
Canon-street, *Bride-street*, XI.
Capel-street, XIX.
Carman's-hall, *Francis-street*, IV.
Caroline-row, *Summer-hill*, XX.
Carrion-row, or Meath-row, *Thomas-street*, II.
Carter's-alley, *Smithfield*, XVIII.
Castle-market, *South Great George's-street*, XII.
Castle-street, *Cork-hill*, IX.
Cathedral-lane, *Kevin's-street*, XI. and XIII.

Catherine's-

L

Circular-

Cork-street, *Ardee-street*, II.
Cork-hill, *Dame-street*, IX.
Corn-market, *High-street*, II. and VI.
Cow-parlour, *Brown-street*, II.
Cox's-court, *Michael's-lane*, VII.
Crampton-court, *Dame-street*, XV. and IX.
Crampton-quay, *Aston's-quay*, XV.
Crane-lane, E. *Dame-street*, IX.
Crane-street, *Thomas-street*, II.
Crawley's-yard, *Gt. Thomas-court*, II.
Crosbie-court, *Michael's-lane*, VII.
Croaker's-alley, *Mulinahack*, II.
Cross-lane, *Bolton-street*, XIX.
Cross-lane, *Cole's-lane*, XIX.
Crosstick-alley, *Meath-street*, II. and IV.
Crown-alley, *Temple-bar*, XV.
Crow-street, *Dame-street*, XV.
Cuckoo-lane, *N. Anne-street*, XVIII.
Cuffe-street, *Stephen's-green*, XIII.
Cuffe-lane, *Cuffe-street*, XIII.
Cumberland-street, S. *Hamilton-row*, XVI.
Cumberland-street, N. *Mecklenburgh-street*, XX.
Cummin's-court, *Bride-street*, XII.
Custom-house, XX.
Cutpurse-row, *Corn-market*, II. and IV.

### D.

Daly's-court, *Manor-street*, XVII.
Dame-court, *Dame-lane*, XV.
Dame-lane, *Palace-street*, XV.
Dame-street, *College-green*, IX. and XV.
Daniel's alley, *Coombe*, III.
Darby-square, *Werburgh-street*, IX. and XII.
Davis's Coal-yard, *Ransford-street*, II.
Dawson-street, *Stephen's-green*, XIV.

Dawson-

8

Dawson-yard, *Barrack-street*, XVII.
Deanery-court, *Fishamble-street*, VIII.
Delany's-court, *Pimlico*, II.
Denmark-street, North, *Gardiner's-row*, XXI.
Denmark-street, South, *Great Britain-street*, XIX.
Denzille-street, *Hamilton's-row*, XVI. and XII.
Digges-court, *Digges-lane*, XIII.
Digges-lane, *Stephen-street*, XIII.
Digges-street, *French-street*, XIII.
Dirty-lane, *see Bridgefoot-street*, II. and VI.
Dobbin's-court, *Golden-lane*, XII.
Dog-and-Duck-yard, *Usher's-quay*, VI.
Dolphin's-barn-lane, *Cork-street*, I.
Dominick-street, *Great Britain-street*, XIX.
Dorset-street, *Bolton-street*, XIX. and XX.
Ducker's-lane, *New-street*, IV.
Draper's-court, *Nicholas-street*, IV.
Drury-lane, *Stephen-street*, XII.
Duck-lane, *Smithfield*, XVIII.
Duke-lane, *Duke-street*, XIV.
Duke-row, *Summer-hill, included in ditto.*
Duke-street, *Grafton-street*, XIV.

E.

Earl-street, North, *Henry-street*, XX.
Earl-street, South, *Meath-street*, II.
Eccles-street, *Dorset-street*, XXI.
Eccles-lane, *Eccles-street*, XXI.
Echlin's-lane, *James's-street*, I.
Edge-court, *Kevin's-street*, XI.
Elbow-lane, Great, *Pimlico*, II.
Elbow-lane, Little, *Upper Coombe*, II.
Elephant-lane, *Sackville-street*, XX.
Ellis's-quay, *Queen-street*, XVII.
Ely-place, *Hume-street*, XIII.
Ely-lane, *Ely-place*, XIII.

Engine-

Engine-alley, *Meath-street*, II.
Erne-street, *Holles-street*, XVI.
Essex-bridge-street, VIII.
Essex-gate, *Parliament-street*, IX.
Essex-quay, *Essex-bridge*, VIII.
Essex-street, *Temple-bar*, IX. XV.
Eustace-street, *Dame-street*, XV.
Exchange-court, *Cork-hill*, IX.
Exchange-street, Upper, *Cork-hill*, VIII. IX.
Exchange-street, Lower, *Essex-gate*, VIII.
Exchequer-street, *Grafton-street*, XII. XIV. XV.

## F.

Factory-lane, *Smithfield*, XVIII.
Fade-street, *South Great George's-street*, XII.
Fatal-alley, *New-street*, IV.
Faucet's-court, *Bride-street*, XIII.
Featherbed-lane, *Barrack-street*, XVII.
Fennel's-lane, *Charlemont-street*, XIII.
Fern's-court, *Lower Kevin's-street*, XIII.
Fishamble-street, *Castle-street*, IX. and VIII.
Field's-court, *Church-street*, XVIII.
Fisher's-alley, *Winetavern-street*, VIII.
Fisher's-lane, *Pill-lane*, XVIII.
Fitzgibbon-street, *Mountjoy-square*, XXI.
Fitzwilliam-lane, *Fitzwilliam-street*, XIII.
Fitzwilliam-place, XVII.
Fitzwilliam-street, *Merion-square*, XIII.
Fitzwilliam-square, *Baggot-street*, XIII.
Flag-alley, *Meath-street*, II. and IV.
Fleece-alley, *Fishamble-street*, VIII.
Fleet-lane, *Fleet-street*, XV. and XVI.
Fleet-market, *Townsend-street*, XVI.
Fleet-alley, *Fleet-street*, XV. and XVI.
Fleet-street, *Temple-bar*, XV. and XVI.
Flood-street, *Silver-street*, XVII.

ᴊrdam's-

10

Fordam's-alley, *Coombe*, III.
Forster's-place, *College-green*, XV.
Fownes's-street, *Dame-street*, XV.
Francis-street, *Lower Coombe*, II. and IV.
Francis-court, *Francis-street*, IV.
Frederick-street, North, *Rutland-square*, XIX. and XXI.
Frederick-street, South, *Molesworth-street*, XIV.
French-street, *York-street*, XIII.
Fumbaly's-lane, *New street*, IV.

## G.

Galway-walk, *Watling-street*, I.
Garden-lane, *Manor-street*, XVII.
Garden-lane, *Francis-street*, IV.
Gardiner-place, *Mountjoy-square*, XXI.
Gardiner-row, *Palace-row*, XXI.
Gardiner-street, Upper, *Dorset-street*, XXI.
Gardiner-street, Lower, *Beresford-place*, XX.
Garter-court, *Castle-street*, IX.
George's-court, *North Great George's-street*, XXI.
George's-hill, *Mary's-lane*, XVIII.
George's-inn-yard, *Church-street*, XVIII.
George's-lane, *Brunswick-street*, XVII.
George's-quay, *George's-street*, XVI.
George's-street, East, *George's quay*, XVI.
George's-street, Great, North, *Great Britain-street*, XXI.
George's-street, Great, South, *Dame-street*, XII. and XV.
George's-court, *South Great George's-street*, XII.
Gibraltar, *Elbow-lane*, II.
Gilbert's-alley, *Thomas-court*, II.
Gillshenan's-lane, *Dorset-street*, XIX.
Gill-square, *Cole-alley*, II.
Glannan's-lane, *James's-street*, I.
Gloster-street, South, *Moss-street*, XVI.
Gloucester-place, *Gloucester-street*, XX.
Gloucester-street, *Marlborough-street*, XX.

Glover's-

Glover's-alley, *Mercer's-street*, XIII.
Golden-lane, *Stephen's-street*, XII.
Goodin's-yard, *Dorset-street*, XIX.
Goodman's-alley, *Patrick-street*, XI.
Gordon's-lane, *Charlemont-street*, XIII.
Goreley's-alley, *High-street*, V. and VII.
Grafton-lane, *Grafton-street*, XIV.
Grafton-street, *College-green*, XIV. and XV.
Graham's-row, *Paradise-row*, XIX.
Granby-court, *Barrack-street*, XVII.
Granby-place, *Granby-row*, XIX.
Granby-row, *Rutland-square*, XIX.
Grand Canal-street, *Denzille-street*, XIII. and XVI.
Grange-gorman-lane, *Brunswick-street*, XVII.
Grant's-row, *Upper Mount-street*, XIII.
Gravel-walk, *Barrack-street*, XVII.
Greek-street, *Mary's-lane*, XVIII.
Green's-alley, *Coombe*, III.
Green-street, *Little Britain-street*, XVIII.
Greg's-lane, *Marlborough-street*, XX.
Grenville-street, *Mountjoy-square*, XXI.
Grogan's-court, *Bride-street*, XIII.
Gunpowder-office-yard, *Camden-street*, XIII.

### H.

Halston-street, *Mary's-lane*, XVIII.
Hamilton's-row, *Park-street*, XVI. and XIII.
Hammond-lane, *Old Church-street*, XVIII.
Hanbury-lane, *Meath-street*, II.
Handkerchief-alley, *Francis-street*, IV.
Hanover-lane, *Francis-street*, IV.
Hanover-street, *Townsend-street*, XVI.
Hanover-street, *Lower Coombe*, IV.
Harcourt-place, *Park-street*, XVI. and XIII.
Harcourt-street, *Cuffe-street*, XIII.
Harcourt-road, *Harcourt-street*, XIII.

Harry-

Harry-street, *Grafton-street*, **XIV.**
Hatter's-lane, *Temple-bar*, **XV.**
Hawkins's-street, *Townsend-street*, **XVI.**
Hay-market, *Smithfield*, **XVII.**
Hell, *Christ-church-lane*, **X.**
Hendrick-street, *Queen-street*, **XVII.**
Hendrick-lane, *Hendrick-street*, **XVII.**
Henrietta-place, *Henrietta-street*, **XVIII.**
Henrietta-street, *Bolton-street*, **XVIII.** and **XIX.**
Henry-street, *Mary-street*, **XIX.** and **XX.**
High-street, *Skinner-row*, **V. VI.** and **VII.**
Hoey's-court, *Werburgh-street*, **IX.**
Holles-street, *Merrion-square*, **XIII.**
Holles-row, *Holles-street*, **XIII.**
Hope's-yard, *Cook-street*, **VI.**
Hume-street, *Stephen's-green*, **XIII.**
Hunt's-alley, *Brabazon's-row*, **III.**

### I. and J.

Jackson's-alley, *Pimlico*, **II.**
James's-gate, *James's-street*, **II.**
James's-street, *Thomas-street*, **I.**
Jervis-lane, *Mary-street*, **XIX.**
Jervis-street, *Great Britain-street*, **XIX.**
Infirmary-yard, *Francis-street*, **IV.**
John's-lane, *Fishamble-street*, **VIII.**
John's-lane, *Thomas-street*, **II.**
John's-street, *Thomas-street*, **II.**
John's-street, *Tighe-street*, **XVII.**
John's-street, *Pimlico*, **II.**
Johnston's-alley, *Little Strand-street*, **XVIII**
Johnson's-court, *Grafton-street*, **XIV.**
Johnston's-court, *Fishamble-street*, **VIII.**
Johnston's-court, *Wood-quay*, **VIII.**
Johnston's-court, *Great Britain-street*, **XXI.**
Johnson's-place, *William-street*, **XIV.**

Johnson's-

Johnson's-alley, *Arran-street*, XVIII.
Jones's-court, *High-street*, VII.
Joseph's-lane, *Castle-market*, XII.
Irwin-street, *Bow-bridge*, I.
Island-street, *Bridgefoot-street*, VI.

K.

Kane's-court, *Flood-street*, XVII.
Keizar's-lane, *Cook-street*, VI.
Kelche's-yard, *Beresford-street*, XVIII.
Kelly's-lane, *Dorset-street*. XIX.
Kelly's-place, *Lower Mount-street*, XIII.
Kelly's-row, *Dorset-street*, XXI.
Kennedy's-lane, *Nicholas-street*, V.
Kevin's-street, Lower, *Great Cuffe-street*, XIII.
Kevin's-street, Upper, *Poddle*, XI. and XIII.
Kevin's-port, *Redmond's-hill*, XIII.
Kildare-place, *Kildare-street*, XIV.
Kildare-street, *Stephen's-green*, XIV.
Kilmainham, *Mount-Browne*, I.
King's-head-court, *Exchequer-street*, XV.
King's-inns-street, *Dorset-street*, not built in 1798.
King's-inns-quay, *Ormond-quay*, XVIII.
King's-lane, *Dorset-street*, XIX.
King's-street, North, *Bolton-street*, XVII. and XVIII.
King's-street, South, *Stephen's-green*, XIII. and XIV.
King's-court, *King's-street, South*, XIII.

L.

Lacy's-lane, *Merion-square*, XIV.
Lane's-lane, *Summer-hill*, XXI.
Lamb-alley, *Cutpurse-row*, IV.
Latin-court, *Greek-street*, XVIII.
Lee's-lane, *Fleet-street*, XV.
Leeson-street, *Stephen's-green*, XIII.
Leeson-place, *Leeson-street*, XIII.

M

Leinster-

Leinster-street, *Nassau-street*, XIV.
Leinster-row, *Cathedral-lane*, XIII.
Liberty-lane, *Kevin's-street*, XIII.
Liffey-street, *Barrack-street*, XVII.
Liffey-street, Upper, *Abbey-street*, XIX.
Liffey-street, Lower, *Ormond-quay*, XIX.
Lime-kiln-yard, *King-street, South*, XIV.
Lime-kiln-yard, *Thomas-street*, II.
Limerick-alley, *Francis-street*, IV.
Lincoln-lane, *Arran-quay*, XVIII.
Linen-hall, XVIII.
Linen-hall-street, *King-street, North*, XVIII.
Lisburn-street, *Linen-hall-street*, XVIII.
Loftus-lane, *Capel-street*, XIX.
Long-lane, *New-street*, XIII.
Longford-lane, *Great Longford-street*, XIII.
Longford-street, Great, *Aungier-street*, XIII.
Longford-street, Little, *Aungier-street*, XIII.
Lots, *Sackville-street*, XIX. and XX.
Love-lane, *Brown-street*, II.
Luke-street, *Townsend-street*, XVI.
Lurgan-street. *Linen-hall-street*, XVIII.

### M.

Mabbot-lane, *Mabbot-street*, XX.
Mabbot-street, *Beresford-place*, XX.
M'Clean's-lane, *Lower Mount-street*, XIII.
Magdalen Asylum, *Leeson-street*, XIII.
Maiden-lane, *Wood-street*, XII.
Malpas-street, *New-street*, IV.
Manor-street, *Stony-batter*, XVII.
Mark's-alley, *Francis-street*, IV.
Mark's-street, *Townsend-street*, XVI.
Marlborough-green, *Marlborough-street*, XX.
Marlborough-street, *Abbey-street*, XX.
Marybonne-lane, *Thomas-court*, II.

Marshalsea-

Marshalsea-lane, *Thomas-street*, II.
Martin's-lane, *Montgomery-street*, XX.
Mary's-abbey, *Capel-street*, XIX.
Mary's-street, Great, *Capel-street*, XIX.
Mary's-lane, *Church-street*, XVIII.
Mass-lane, North, *King's-inns-quay*, XVIII.
Mass-lane, West, *Bridge-foot-street*, II.
May-lane, *Bow-street*, XVIII.
Mayor-street, *North Strand*, XX.
M'Cracken's-alley, *New-row*, II.
M'Cormick's-court, *Dirty-lane*, II.
M'Cullogh's-alley, *High-street*, V. and VII.
M'Manus's-court, *Bolton-street*, XIX.
Meath-street, *Thomas-street*, II.
Meath-market, *Hanbury-lane*, II.
Meath-row, *Thomas-street*, II.
Mecklenburgh-lane, *Mecklenburgh-street*, XX.
Medcalf's-court, *Fishamble-street*, VIII.
Meeting-house-lane, *Mary's-abbey*, XIX.
Meeting-house-lane, or Croker's-alley, *Mullinahack*, II.
Mercer s-street, *York-street*, XIII.
Merchant's-quay, *Usher's-quay*, VI. VII. and VIII.
Meredith-place, *Buckingham-street*, XX.
Merion-row, *Baggot-street*, XIII. and XIV.
Merion-square, *Merion-street*, XIII.
Merion-street, Lower, *Merion-square*, XIII. and XIV.
Merion-street, Upper, *Merion-square*, XIII. and XIV.
Michael-a-Pole-court, *Great Ship-street*, XII.
Michael's-lane, *High-street*, VII.
Miller's-alley, *Thomas-court*, II.
Mill-lane, *Mill-street*, III.
Mill-street, *Ardee-street*, III.
Minor's-alley, *Bridge-street*, VI.
Mitre-alley, *Kevin's-street*, XI.
Molesworth-court, *Fishamble-street*, VIII.
Molesworth-street, *Dawson-street*, XIV.

Molyneaux's-

Molyneaux's-yard, *Thomas-street*, II.
Monk-place, *Phipsborough*, XVII.
Montague-court, *Great Cuffe-street*, XIII.
Montague-street, *Camden-street*, XIII.
Montgomery-street, *Mabbot-street*, XX.
Montpelier-hill, *Arbour-hill*, XVII.
Moore-lane, *Great Britain-street*, XIX.
Moore-street, *Great Britain-street*, XIX.
Morgan's-place, *Summer-hill*, XX.
Morgan-place, *King's-inns-quay*, XVIII.
Moss-street, *Townsend-street*, XVI.
Mount-Browne, *James's-street*, I.
Mountjoy-court, *Great Charles-street*, XXI.
Mountjoy-square, *Gardiner-street*, XXI.
Mountjoy-place, *Mountjoy-square*, XXI.
Mountrath-street, *Pill-lane*, XVIII.
Mount-street, Lower, *Merion-square*, XIII.
Mount-street, Upper, *Merion-square*, XIII.
Mullinahack, *John's-street*, II.
Murry's-court, *Strand-street*, XIX.
Mutton-lane, *Ardee-street*, III.
Myler's-alley, *Bride-street*, XI.

### N.

Nassau-street, *Grafton-street*, XIV. and XVI.
Nassau-lane, *Nassau-street*, XIV.
New-market, *Chamber-street*, III.
New-row, *Poddle*, III.
New-row, *Thomas-street*, II.
New-street, *Kevin's street*, IV. XI. and XIII.
New-sun-inn-yard, *Thomas-street*, II.
Nicholas-street, *Patrick's-street*,
Northumberland-court, *Cope-street*, XV.

North-

North-wall, *North-strand*, XX.
Nowland's-lane, *Rogerson's-quay*, XVI.

O.

Off-lane, *Moore-street*, XIX.
Oliver-alley, *Wood-street*, XII.
Ormond-market, *Ormond-quay*, XVIII.
Ormond-quay, Upper, *Essex-bridge*, XVIII.
Ormond-street, *Weaver's-square*, II.
Orpin's-court, *Copper-alley*, IX.
Oxmantown-green, *N. King's-street*, XVII.

P.

Palace-row, *Rutland-square*, XIX.
Palace-street, *Dame-street*, XV.
Parade, *Paul's-church*, XVII.
Paradise-row, *Dorset-street*, XIX.
Parkgate-street, *Barrack-street*, XVII.
Park-place, *Townsend-street*, XVI.
Park-street, *Leinster-street*, XIV. and XVI.
Park-street, *Ash-street*, IV.
Parliament-row, *Fleet-street*.
Parliament-street, *Cork-hill*, IX.
Patrick's-close, *Patrick's-street*, XI.
Patrick's-back-close, *Mitre-alley*, XI.
Patrick's-library, *Bride-street*, XIII.
Patrick's-street, *Nicholas-street*, IV. and XI.
Pembroke-court, *Castle-street*, IX.
Pembroke-street, *Leeson-street*.
Pembroke-quay, *Ellis's-quay*, XVII.
Peter's-place, *Charlemont-street*, XIII.
Peter's-row, *Peter's-street*, XII. and XIII.
Peter's-street, *Bride-street*, XII.

Petticoat-

Petticoat-lane, *Little Britain-street*, XVIII.
Phœnix-street, *Hammond-lane*, XVIII.
Phipsborough, *Broad-stone*, XVII.
Pig-town, *James's-street*, I.
Pill-lane, *Old Church-street*, XVIII.
Pimlico, *Ardee-street*, II.
Pipe-office-yard, *Barrack-street*, XVII.
Pitt-street, *Harry-street*, XIV.
Plowman's-court, *John's-lane*, VIII.
Plunket-street, *Francis-street*, IV.
Poddle, *Patrick's-street*, III. IV. and XI.
Pool-street, *Braithwaite-street*, II.
Poolbeg-street, *Hawkins's-street*, XVI.
Portland-street, *Ransford-street*, II.
Portland-row, *Summer-hill*, XX.
Potter's-alley, *Marlborough-street*, XX.
Portobello, *Camden-street*, XIII.
Proud's-lane, *Stephen's-green*, XIII.
Price's-lane, *Fleet-street*, XV.
Prince of Wales's-court, *Skinner-row*, V.
Prince's-street, *Sackville-street*, XIX. and XX.
Prince's-street, *City-quay*, XVI.
Protestant-row, *Camden-street*, XIII.
Prussia-street, *Manor-street*, XVII.
Pudding-row, *Winetavern-street*, VIII.
Purcell's-court, *Corn-market*, VI.
Pye-alley, *Garden-lane*, IV.

## Q.

Queen's-court, *Queen-street*, XVII.
Queen-street, *Arran-quay*, XVII.
Quinn's-lane, *Leeson-place*, XIII.

Ram-

## R.

Ram-alley, *Skinner-row*, V.
Ransford-street, *Thomas-court*, II.
Red-cow-inn-yard, *Francis-street*, IV.
Red-cow-lane, *Brunswick-street*, XVII.
Redmond's-alley, *Wood-quay*, VIII.
Redmond's-hill, *Kevin's-port*, XIII.
Reilly's-court, *Thomas-street*, II.
Rehoboth-lane, *Dolphin's-barn-lane*, I.
Roache's-lane, *Marlborough-street*, XX.
Robert-street, *Marybonne-lane*, II.
Robinson's-alley, *Lower Coombe*.
Rogerson's-quay, *City-quay*, XVI.
Rope-walk, *Ransford-street*, II.
Rope-walk, *Irwin-street*, I.
Rothery's-yard, *Great George's-street, S.* XII.
Rose-alley, *Wood-quay*, VIII.
Rosemary-lane, *Merchant's-quay*, VII. and VIII.
Ross-lane, *Bride-street*, XII.
Russel's-court, *Old Church-street*, XVIII.
Russel's-lane, *Gardiner's-street*, XXI.
Russel-place, *Summer-hill*.
Rutland-square, *Great Britain-street*, XIX. and XXI.
Rutland-street, Lower, *Summer-hill*, XX.
Ryder's-row, *Capel-street*, XIX.

## S.

Sackville-lane, *Moore-street*, XIX.
Sackville-street, *Great Britain-street*, XX.
St. George's-place, Lower, *Dorset-street*.
Sampson's-lane, *Moore-street*, XIX.
Sandwith-street, *Townsend-street*, XVI.
Sall's-court, *Fishamble-street*, VIII.
School-house-lane, *High-street*, VI. and VII.
School-street, *Earl-street*, II.

Sherlock's-

Sherlock's-yard, *James's-street*, I.
Sherry-court, *Bride-street*, XII.
Ship-street, Great, *Stephen's-street*, XII.
Ship-street, Little, *Bride-street*, XII.
Silver-street, *Barrack-street*, XVII.
Silver-court, *Castle-street*, IX.
Simpson's-court, *Beresford-street*, XVIII.
Skinner's-row, *Castle-street*, VII. IX.
Skinner's-alley, *New-market*, III.
Skipper's-alley, *Cook-street*, VI. VII.
Smith's-court, *Red-cow-lane*, XVII.
Smithfield, *King's-street*, XVII. XVIII.
Smock-alley, *Fishamble-street*, VIII.
Snugborough, *Brunswick-street*, XVIII.
Span-lane, *Grafton-street*, XIV.
Spittlefields, *Mark's-alley*, IV.
Spring-garden-lane, *Townsend-street*, XVI.
Spring-gardens, *Summer-hill*, XX. XXI.
Stafford-street, *Abbey-street*, XIX.
Stable-lane, *Upper Temple-street*, XXI.
Stable-lane, *Gardiner's-place*, XXI.
Stable-lane, *Grenville-street*, XXI.
Stable-lane, *Great Charles-street*, XXI.
Stable-lane, *Cumberland-street*, North, XX.
Stable-lane, *Earl-street*, North, XX.
Stable-lane, *Little Mary-street*, XIX.
Stable-lane, *Liffey-street*, XIX.
Stable-lane, *Henrietta-street*, XIX.
Stanhope-street, *Grange-gorman-lane*, XVII.
Stanley's-street, *Brunswick-street*, XVII.
Stephens's-lane, *James's-street*, I.
Stephen's-green, *York-street*, XIII. XIV.
Stephen's-street, *Great George's-street*, South, XII. XIII.
Sterling-street, *Mill-street*, II.
Stewart's-court, *Aston's-quay*, XVI.
Stillas's-court, *Coombs*, III.

Stirrup-

Tenter-

## U. and V.

## W.

Ward's-

Ward's-hill, *Mill-street*, III.

Warren-mount, *Mill-street*, III.

Washer-woman's-lane, *Bason-place*, II.

Washington-row, *Summer-hill*, XX.

Water-row, part of Ormond-market, XVIII.

Water, or Russel's-lane, *Robert-street*, II.

Watling-street, *James's-street*, I. and VI.

Weaver's-square, *Chamber-street*, II.

Werburgh-street, *Castle-street*, IX.

Westland-row, *Park-street*, XVI.

Westmoreland-street, *Fleet-street*, (built since 1798.)

Wentworth-place, *Holles-street*, XIII. and XVI.

Wheeler's-alley, *Cole's-lane*, XIX.

Whit.-bull-inn-yard, *Thomas-street*, II.

White's-lane, *George's-quay*, XVI.

White's-lane, *Upper Dorset-street*, XXI.

White's-court, *Great Ship-street*, XII.

Whitefriar's-street, *Stephen's-street*, XII. and XIII.

Whitefriar's-lane, *Aungier's-street*, XIII.

White's-hall, *Marybonne-lane*, XII.

White's-hall-court, *King-street*, North, XVIII.

White-horse-lane, *Thomas-street*, II.

William's-lane, *Abbey-street*, XIX. and XX.

William's-lane, *New-street*, XIII.

William's-street, *Stephen's-street*, XII. XIV.

Wilme's-court, *Skinner's-row*, IX.

Wilson's-yard, *Exchequer-street*, XIV.

Wilson's-place, *Lower Mount-street*, XIII.

Winetavern-street, *Merchant's-quay*, VIII.

Wolfe's-alley, *Bridge-street*, VI.

Wood-quay, *Winetavern-street*, VIII.

Wood-street, *Whitefriar's-street*, XII.

Wormwood-gate, *Cook-street*, II.

Yarn-

# Y.

# JOURNAL

OF THE

# STATISTICAL SOCIETY

OF

# LONDON.

# VOL. XI.

LONDON:

JOHN WILLIAM PARKER, 445, WEST STRAND.

Republished in 1974 by Gregg International Publishers Limited
Westmead, Farnborough, Hants., England

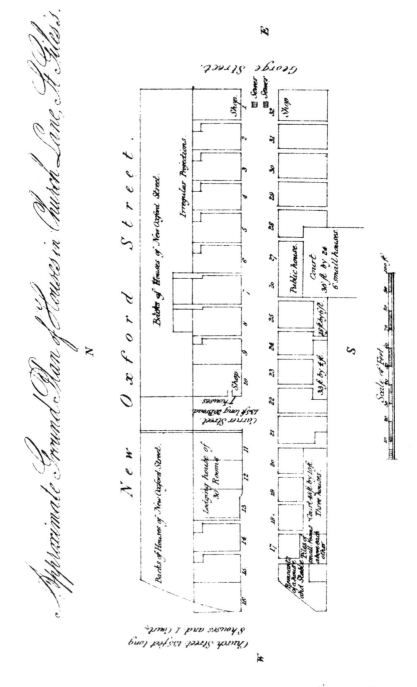

# QUARTERLY JOURNAL

OF THE

# STATISTICAL SOCIETY OF LONDON.

*MARCH*, 1848.

*Report of a Committee of the Council of the Statistical Society of London, consisting of* LIEUT.-COLONEL W. H. SYKES, V.P.R.S., DR. GUY, *and* F. G. P. NEISON, ESQ., *to investigate the State of the Inhabitants and their Dwellings in Church Lane, St. Giles's.*

[Read before the Statistical Society of London, 17th January, 1848.]

IT is only necessary to premise, that the inquiry of the Committee is consequent upon communications made to the Council by one of its members, respecting the state of the houses and their inhabitants in Church Lane, St. Giles's, which involved such startling circumstances, that the Council deemed it a duty to have them verified and attested, not less for the sake of the public, than to add to those stores of information for the collection of which the Statistical Society was founded.

Your Committee, pursuant to their appointment on the 18th of December, met in Church Lane, on Thursday, the 23rd December, at 1 P.M. :—Present—Colonel Sykes and Dr. Guy, and Mr. Balfour, Agent of the Committee.

Church Lane is situated in the Parish of St. Giles; it is 290 ft. long, 20 ft. wide, and contains 32 houses. It runs parallel with New Oxford Street, and is bounded at the west end by the backs of the new houses in Broad Street, and opens at the east end into George Street. There are several back courts, one of which measures 48 ft. long by 10 ft. broad, and contains seven small houses, the entrance to this court being by a narrow passage 2 ft. broad and 20 ft. long. These houses are of wood, and contain two rooms. Another court is 36 ft. by 24 ft., and contains six small houses. The houses in Church Lane consist of a parlour or ground-floor, of two rooms, a first floor, of one or two rooms, and a second floor, of one room. To the first landing on the stairs of some of the houses, one or two small wooden rooms are attached behind, occasioning considerable risk from fire. The houses have cellars under the ground-floor, but as there is no drainage whatever from them, they are not tenanted, with the exception of two; but some of them are used as day-rooms. The narrow entrance passage into each house terminates in a back yard 5 or 6 ft. square.

The lane is lighted by three gas-lights. Water is supplied three times a week, but there is neither pump, tank, cistern, nor water-butt, so that the tenants of all the houses, with the exception of one lodg-ing-house, three shops, and a public-house, are compelled to save the water in their respective rooms, in such vessels as they can command; but as the water does not continue on for a sufficient length of time to enable all the inhabitants of the street to secure enough, supposing they had vessels to hold it, they are compelled to deal with the shops or public-house to obtain a pitcherful now and then; and they some-times are compelled to filch the water from each other.

The back yards are 5 or 6 ft. squ i re, with broken pavement, and most of them have accumulations of filth and night-soil, and the drainage from them (which is superficial) runs through the passage of the houses into the street. The back rooms, most of which are lighted by only one small window, patched with paper and rags, open by low doors into this pestiferous area. These yards are, in most instances, without privies, and in the few cases where they do exist, they are in a most dilapidated condition. In the houses furnished with a water-butt, this vessel is to be found in the yard.

The under landlords, renting the houses, examined by your Com-mittee, on the north side, are Mr. Conroy, marine-store dealer, George Street; Mr. FitzGerald, general dealer; and Mr. Mason, the keeper of the public-house in the street. The superior landlords on the south side, are Lady Hanmer and Mr. Grout, and on the north-side, the Buckeredge Estate.

As the value of your Committee's Report would much depend upon the detailed and graphic pictures which it might supply, your Committee resolved to inspect personally every room in every house; but as such an examination of every room in the street would swell the Report to an inconvenient length, your Committee determined upon taking a portion of the houses; and that there might not be the slightest imputation of selection, your Committee resolved to examine the houses in the order of their numbers. No. 1, of Church Lane, being .. shop and a corner house, belonging rather to George Street than to Church Lane, your Committee commenced with the house No. 2.

The rooms are let either unfurnished or, if it be not a misnomer, fur-nished. In the first instance, the walls and floor are bare; and for such rooms, on the 1st and 2nd floor, 3s. weekly are paid. In the second instance, the furniture consists of a small deal table, two rickety or broken deal chairs, a bedstead, without hangings of any kind, flock mat-tress, two blankets, and one pair of coarse sheets, one bolster, and one quilt, a tub or pail, a pot or pan, and a kettle, and in some cases, a saucepan. These articles constitute the furniture. Crockery, knives and forks, &c, are provided by the tenant. The rent of such a room varies from 3s. 3d. to 5s. 6d., according to size.

*House, No. 2.—Parlour or Ground Floor.*

Size of room, 14 ft. long, 13 ft. broad, 6 ft. high; size of window, 5 ft. 3 in. by 5 ft.; rent paid, 8s. weekly for two rooms; under-rent paid, 3d. per night for each adult; time occupied, 28 years by landlady. Number of families, 3; consisting of 8 males above 20, 5 females above 20, 4 males under 20, 5 females under 20, total 22 souls. Number of persons ill, 2, fever and measles; deaths in 1847, 1, measles. Country, 7 English, 15 Irish; trade, dealers and mendicants. State of rooms, filthy; state of furniture, bad and dirty; state of windows, 21 whole and 9 broken panes. Number of beds, 6 ; number of bedsteads, 6, in two rooms.

A man and his wife and children, occupying a bed for a week, pay 3s., but 12 adults, at 3d. per night, Sunday not counting, give the landlady 18s. a week for the 8s. she pays, or a profit of 10s.

The rent paid for the ground-floor of this house is 3s. above the ground-floor of other houses in the street.

1,092 cubic feet of air, 1st room, 815 cubic feet of air, 2nd room ; total, 1,907 cubic feet of air for 22 persons.

### No. 2.—Back Room, Ground Floor.

Size of room, 11 ft. 4 in. long, 11 ft. 3 in. broad, 6 ft. 5 in. high ; size of window, 3 ft. 4 in. by 3 ft. 3 in.

The yard of this house, 6 ft. square, in a very bad state. The privy has no seat or door; night-soil scattered about the yard. Liquid filth under the broken pavement.

This room is rented with the preceding, and may be said to form part of it; the twenty-two tenants being common to the two rooms.

### The Cellar of this House

Was found occupied. 3 beds, 3 bedsteads, dirty. 1 male above 20, 3 females above 20, 4 males under 20, 3 females under 20; total 11 persons : adults pay 3d. per night.

This is the only cellar found with beds in the houses examined.

### No. 2.—First Floor.

Only one room. Size of room, 17 ft. 6 in. long, 13 ft. 9 in. broad, 8 ft. 3 in. high; size of window, 5 ft. 9 in. by 4 ft. 4 in. ; rent paid, 3s. weekly; under-rent paid, 1s. 6d. and 1s. 2d. each family; time occupied, 3 months. Number of families, 3, and 1 widow with 4 children; comprising 3 males above 20, 3 females above 20, 4 males under 20, 6 females under 20; total 16. Number of persons ill, ——*; deaths in 1847, ——. Country, Irish ; trade, dealers. State of rooms, dirty ; state of furniture, bad, dirty; state of windows, 24 whole, 6 broken. Number of beds, 3 ; number of bedsteads, 3.

### No. 2.—Second Floor.

Size of room, 17 ft. long, 13 ft. broad, 8 ft. 3 in. high ; size of window, 5 ft. 4 in. by 3 ft. 3 in. ; rent paid, 3s. weekly; under-rent paid, 2s.; time occupied, 2 years. Number of families, 2 ; consisting of 3 males above 20, 2 females above 20, 3 males under 20, 4 females under 20; total 12. Number of persons ill, 1, asthma ; deaths in 1847, none. Country, Irish; trade, dealers. State of rooms, dirty; state of furniture, bad, dirty; state of windows, 21 whole, 8 broken. Number of beds, 3; number of bedsteads, 2.

Three females sleep in one bed. A son, aged 22, sleeps with his mother.

* As a general rule, the blanks in the Report may be understood to indicate that the particulars specified were not ascertained. It was deemed right to print the agent's notes with only such corrections as were indicated by the memoranda taken on the spot by the reporters, and such slight verbal alterations as were necessary to clearness and accuracy.

*Tuesday,* 28*th December,* 1847.

Present—Col. Sykes, Dr. Guy, F. G. P. Neison, Esq., and the Agent.

The Committee proceeded to inspect the houses next in order.

### *House, No.* 3.—*Two Parlours on Ground Floor.*

Size of rooms:—front room, 17 ft. 6 in. long, 13 ft. 9 in. broad, 8 ft. high; size of windows, 5 ft. 4 in. by 4 ft.; back room, 11 ft. 4 in. square; rent paid, 5*s.* weekly; under-rent paid, 1*s.* 6*d.* each adult; time occupied, 5 years. Number of families, 4; consisting of 5 males above 20, 5 females above 20, 3 males under 20, and 4 females under 20; total 17. Number of persons ill, ——; deaths in 1847, ——. Country, Irish; trade, dealers and mendicants. State of rooms, dirty; state of furniture, bad and dirty; state of windows, 8 panes whole, 8 broken. Number of beds, 6; number of bedsteads, 5, of which 3 in front room 2 in back. Yard filthy, covered with night soil; no privy, no water.

These are nightly lodging-rooms, and the landlady frequently accommodates four or five more persons at 3*d.* per night. The entrance to the back room is by a door 4 ft. 2 in. by 3 ft., the room itself being a kind of black-hole.

### *No.* 3.—*First Floor,—One Room.*

Size of room, 17 ft. long, 13 ft. broad, 9 ft. high; size of only window, 5 ft. 4 in. by 2 ft. 2 in.; rent paid, 3*s.* weekly; under-rent paid, 1*s.* each family; time occupied, 3 months. Three males above 20, 5 females above 20, 5 males under 20, and 4 females under 20; total 17. Number of persons ill, 1 low fever; number of deaths in 1847, ——. Country, Irish; trade, labourers and dealers. State of rooms, dirty; furniture, only 1 chair and table; state of windows, 9 whole panes, 3 broken. Number of beds, 3, made of shavings; number of bedsteads, 1.

### *No.* 3.—*Second Floor,—One Room.*

Size of room, 17 ft. long, 13 ft. broad, 9 ft. high; size of window, 5 ft. 4 in. by 2 ft. 2 in.; rent paid, 3*s.* weekly; under-rent paid, ——; time occupied, 7 years. Number of families, 1; comprising 1 male above 20, 1 female above 20, 3 males under 20, and 3 females under 20; total 8. The eldest boy 15 years of age. Number of persons ill, 1, cold and fever; deaths in, 1847 ——. Country, Irish; trade, dealer. State of rooms, dirty; state of furniture, bad; state of windows, 7 whole panes, 5 broken. Number of beds, 2; number of bedsteads, 2.

### *No.* 3.—*Back Room opening from Stair Landing.*

Size of room, 11 ft. 2 in. long, 9 ft. 4 in. broad, 6 ft. high; size of windows, 3 ft. 9 in. by 2 ft. 11 in.; rent paid, 3*s.* weekly, furnished; under-rent paid, ——; time occupied, 3 years. Number of families, 1; comprising 1 male above 20, 2 females above 20, 2 males under 20, and 2 females under 20; total 8. Number of persons ill, 1; deaths in 1847, ——. Country, Irish; trade, blind beggar. State of rooms, dirty; state of furniture, bad, dirty; state of windows, 5 whole, 7 broken. Number of beds, 3; number of bedsteads, 1.

The beds and coverings were composed of rags and shavings.

The eldest girl is 16, and the 2 females above 20, are the blind man's wife and her sister.

### House, No. 4.—*Two Parlours, on Ground Floor.*

Size of front room, 14 ft. long, 13 ft. broad, 6 ft. high; size of windows, 3 ft. 4 in. by 2 ft. 2 in. Size of back-room, 11 ft. 2 in. long, 9 ft. 4 in. broad, less than 6 feet in height; 1 window with 4 whole panes; rent paid, 5s. 6d. weekly for 2 rooms; under-rent paid, 3d. per night each adult; time occupied, 2 years; number of families, 5; comprising 4 males above 20, 9 females above 20, three of them single, 2 males under 20, 4 females under 20; total 19. Number of persons ill, 2; deaths in 1847, 1, measles. Country, Irish; trade, dealers and mendicants. State of rooms and furniture, bad, dirty; state of windows, 6 whole panes, and 10 broken. Number of beds, 6; number of bedsteads, 6.

The door of this room opens into the yard, 6 feet square, which is covered over with night soil; no privy, but there is a tub for the accommodation of the inmates; the tub was full of night soil. These are nightly lodging-rooms. In the front room one girl, 7 years old, lay dead, and another was in bed with its mother, ill of the measles.

### No. 4.—*First Floor.*

Size of room, 17 ft. long, 13 ft. broad, 8 ft. high; size of window, 5 ft. 4 in. by 3 ft. 2 in.; rent paid, 3s weekly; under-rent paid, ——; time occupied, 1 month. Number of families, 4; consisting of 5 males above 20, 5 females above 20, 4 males under 20, 2 females under 20; total 16. Number of persons ill, 2, one man dying; deaths in 1847, ——. Country, Irish; trade, mendicants and dealers. State of rooms, filthy; state of furniture, bad, dirty, only 1 table and 2 chairs; state of windows, 8 broken panes. Number of beds, 1 bed and a quantity of shavings; number of bedsteads, 1.

*Particulars of the above Families.*—1. Man, wife, and 2 children, pay 1s. per week; 2. Man and 1 daughter, 10d.; 3. Two females, single, 10d.; 4. Man, wife, and 3 children (landlord); 5. Man, wife, and 1 child, 1s.

Two of the single women were 25, and 1 of the boys was 18. Here were 16 persons with only one bedstead! The landlord covered his rent, and made 8d. weekly.

### No. 4.—*Second Floor.*

Size of room, 17 ft. long, 13 ft. broad, 8 ft. high; size of windows, 5 ft. 4 in. by 3 ft. 8 in.; rent paid, 3s. weekly; under-rent paid, ——; time occupied, 1 month. Number of families, 5, besides single persons; comprising 5 males above 20, 6 females above 20, 9 males under 20, 3 females under 20; total 23. Number of persons ill, fever, 1 man and 2 children; deaths in 1847, 1 child. Country, Irish; trade, beggars. State of rooms, filthy; state of furniture, bad, dirty, 1 old table, stool, and chair; state of windows, 8 broken, 4 whole panes. Beds of shavings and rags; no bedsteads.

*Particulars of the above Families,*—1. Man, 2 boys, and girl, (landlord); 2. Three boys, (sons of landlord); 3. Man, wife, and 1 boy,

1*s.* 2*d* ; 4. Man, wife, and 4 children, 1*s.* 2*d.*; 5. Man, wife, and 1 child, 10*d.*; man, wife, and child, 10*d.*; 1 single female, 6*d.* Profit on room, 1*s.* 6*d.*

Amongst the children was a girl of 18 and a boy of 13.

Extreme wretchedness.

### No. 4.—*Back Room on the Stairs.*

Size of room, 12 ft, long, 12 ft. broad, 5 ft. 6 in. high; size of window, 3 ft. 9 in. by 2 ft. 11 in.; rent paid 3*s.* weekly, furnished; under-rent paid, ——— ; time occupied, 4 months. Number of families, 1; consisting of 1 male above 20, 1 female above 20, no males under 20, 1 female under 20; total 3. Number of persons ill, none; deaths in 1847, ———. Country, Irish, 19 years in London; trade, market labourer. State of rooms, comparatively clean, state of furniture, decent; state of windows, all whole. Number of beds, 2; number of bedsteads, 2.

The tenant makes his livelihood as a labourer in Covent-garden market. Although the members of the Committee could not stand upright in the room, it was on the whole decent, and comparatively comfortable.

### House, No. 5.—*Two Parlours on Ground Floor.*

Size of front room, 14 ft. long, 13 ft. broad, 6 ft. high; size of window, 5 ft. 4 in by 3 ft. 8 in.; rent paid, 5*s.* weekly, no lodgers; under-rent paid, ——— ; time occupied, 8 months. Number of families, 1, and 1 single woman; comprising 1 male above 20, 2 females above 20, 1 male under 20, no females under 20; total 4. Number of persons ill, 1, the wife; deaths in 1847, ———. Country, English; trade, dealers. State of rooms, clean; state of furniture, tidy; state of windows, whole. Number of beds, 2; number of bedsteads, 2.

The drain from the yard runs through the passage superficially.

No privy and no water to the house.

### No. 5.—*First Floor.*

Size of room, 17 ft. long, 13 ft. broad, 8 ft. high; size of window, 2 ft. 4 in., two windows; rent paid, 3*s.* weekly; under-rent paid, ——— ; time occupied, ———. Number of families, 2; comprising 2 males above 20, 2 females above 20, 4 males under 20, 6 females under 20; total 14. Number of persons ill, 4 of fever; deaths in 1847, ———. Country, ——— trade, ———. State of rooms, bad; state of furniture, bad; state of windows, ———. Number of beds, 3; number of bedsteads, 3.

*Particulars of the Families.*—1. Husband, wife, and 6 children, eldest girl 16; 2. Husband, wife, and 4 children, eldest boy 17: they pay 1*s.* 6*d.*, and all sleep together.

### No. 5.—*Back Room on Stairs:*

Size of room, 12 ft. long, 12 ft. broad, 5 ft. 6 in. high; one small window; rent paid, 2*s.* weekly; under-rent paid, ——— ; time occupied, 6 weeks. Number of families, 2, and 2 single men; consisting of 3 males above 20, 2 females above 20, 1 male under 20, 1 female under 20; total 7. Number of persons ill, ——— ; deaths in 1847, ———. Country, Irish; trade, mendicants. State of rooms, dirty; state of furniture,

bad; state of windows, broken.  Beds of rags and shavings; bedsteads, ——.

No bedstead or furniture in this room, and the bedding consists of
shavings and dirty rags.

The members of the Committee could not stand upright in the
room, and its cubic contents were only 792 feet; room dark.

### No. 5.—Second Floor.

Size of room, 17 ft. long, 13 ft. broad, 8 ft. high ; two windows, size
5 ft. 4 in. ; rent paid, 3s. weekly; under-rent paid, 1s. each family;
time occupied, ——.  Number of families, 6; comprising 6 males above
20, 6 females above 20, 5 males under 20, 5 females under 20; total
22.  Number of persons ill, 2 children of measles; deaths in 1847,
——.  Country, Irish; trade, dealers.  State of rooms, dirty; state of
furniture, bad, 1 table and 2 chairs; state of windows, broken.  Number of beds, 1, all the rest rags; number of bedsteads, 1.

*Particulars of the above.*—1. Man, wife, and boy (landlord); 2.
Man, wife, and 3 children, 1s.; 3. Man, wife, and 1 child, 1s.; 4.
Man, wife, and 3 children, 1s.; 5. Man and wife, 1s.; 6. Man, wife,
and 2 children, 1s.

The landlord in this room lives free, and clears 2s. weekly, but finds
firing.

### House, No. 6.—Parlour,—One Room.

Size of room, 17 ft. long, 13 ft. broad, 8 ft. high; size of window,
5 ft. 4 in. by 3 ft. 8 in.; rent paid, 3s. weekly; under-rent paid, ——;
time occupied, 3 years.  Number of families, 1; comprising 1 male
above 20, 2 females above 20, no males under 20, no females under 20;
total 3.  Number of persons ill, ——; deaths in 1847, ——.  Country,
Irish; trade, dealer.  State of rooms, rather clean; state of furniture,
fair; state of windows, fair.  Number of beds, 2; number of bedsteads, 2.

This family consists of man, wife, and sister.

Although there is a comparative state of cleanliness and comfort,
with lengthened occupancy, the family have neither privy nor water.

### No. 6.—First Floor.

Size of room, 17 ft. long, 13 ft. broad, 8 ft. high; size of window,
5 ft. 4 in. ; rent paid, 3s. weekly; under-rent paid, ——; time occupied,
2 months.  Number of families, 3; consisting of 1 male above 20, 3
females above 20, 2 males under 20, and 1 female under 20; total 7.
Number of persons ill, ——; deaths in 1847, ——.  Country, Irish;
trade, dealers.  State of rooms, dirty; state of furniture, dirty;
state of window, 11 panes remaining.  Number of beds, 3; number of
bedsteads, 2.

The family consists of husband, wife, and 4 children, and a widow
woman who pays 3d. per night.  No privy nor water.

### No. 6.—Second Floor.

Size of room, 17 ft. long, 13 ft. broad, 8 ft. high; size of window,
5 ft. by 4 ft. 3 in.; rent paid, 3s. weekly, under-rent paid, ——; time
occupied, ——.  Number of families, 2, and 3 single men; consisting of

4 males above 20, 5 females above 20, 2 males under 20, and 1 female under 20; total 12. Number of persons ill, ——; deaths in 1847, ——. Country, Irish; trade, dealers. State of rooms, dirty; state of furniture, bad; state of windows, broken. Number of beds, 3; number of bedsteads, ——.

*Particulars of Families.*—1. Widow and 4 children; son 19, daughters 20, 22, and 24; 2. Husband, wife, and 2 children; pay 1*s.* 6*d.*; 3 single men, pay 1*s.*; 2 have resided 2 months. Great wretchedness. No bedstead. Single men and single women herded together.

### *No. 6.—First Room on Stairs, Back of House.*

Size of room, 10 ft. 3 in. long, 9 ft. 10 in broad, 6 ft. 8 in. high; size of window, 3 ft. 6 in. by 4 ft.; rent paid, 2*s.* weekly; under-rent paid, 2*s.*; time occupied, 1 month. Number of families, 1; comprising 1 male above 20, 1 female above 20, 1 male under 20, and 1 female under 20; total 4. Number of persons ill, ——; deaths in 1847, ——. Country, Irish; trade, mat-makers. State of room, tidy; state of furniture, bad; state of window, 27 whole panes, 3 broken. Number of beds, 1; number of bedsteads, 1.

### *No. 6.—Second Room on Stairs at Back of House.*

Size of room, 13 ft. long, 11 ft. 7 in. broad, 7 ft. high; size of window, 3 ft. 4 in. by 2 ft. 2 in.; rent paid, 2*s.* 3*d.* weekly, furnished; under-rent paid, ——; time occupied, ——. Number of families, 1; comprising 1 male above 20, 2 females above 20, 2 males under 20, and 1 female under 20; total 6. Number of persons ill, ——; deaths in 1847, ——. Country, Irish: trade, dealers. State of rooms, dirty; State of furniture, bad; state of windows, broken. Number of beds, 2; number of bedsteads, 2.

Of these 6 persons in a closet, occupying 2 beds, one daughter was 24 years old and one son 20; the closet having 1054 cubic feet of air.

### *Thursday, 30th December,* 1847.

Present—Colonel Sykes and F. G. P. Neison, Esq., and the Agent.

The Committee proceeded to inspect the house next in order.

### *House, No. 7.—Two Parlours on Ground-Floor.*

Size of 1st room, 14 ft. 6 in. long, 13 ft. broad, 6 ft. 3 in. high; size of windows, ——; rent paid, 5*s.* weekly for two rooms; time occupied, 4 months. Number of families, 3, and two single men; comprising 7 males above 20, 5 females above 20, 7 males under 20, 3 females under 20; total 22. Number of persons ill, 1; deaths in 1847, ——. Country, Irish; trade, dealers. State of rooms, dirty; state of furniture, bad; state of windows, broken and quite open. Number of beds, 7; number of bedsteads, 4.

The landlord has been 4 months here, but 5 years at No. 21.

This is a common lodging-room, but nightly lodgers *not taken in.* No privy or water.

*Particulars of the Families.*—In the front room, 1. Man and wife and 9 children, three grown up; 2. Man and wife, pay 1*s.* 3*d.*; 3. Man and wife, pay 1*s.*; 4. Single woman, pays 1*s.*; total 16; 2 bedsteads.

In the back closet, 11 feet square, 2 men and their wives, and two single men, who pay 2s. ; total 6 ; 2 bedsteads only.

The population in these two rooms herd together like brutes.

### No. 7.—*Rooms in Yard.*

Size of rooms, 12 ft. long, 11 ft. broad, 6 ft. high ; size of window, 2 ft. 10 in. by 2 ft. 2 in.; rent paid, 2s. weekly; under-rent paid, ——; time occupied, ——. Number of families, 1, and a single female; comprising 1 male above 20, 1 female above 20, 4 males under 20; total 6. Number of persons ill, 1 ; deaths in 1847, ——. Country, Irish ; trade, paper-maker. State of rooms, dirty; state of furniture; bad ; state of windows, 7 whole, 6 broken. Number of beds, 2, number of bedsteads, 1.

Another small room in this yard, empty. Rooms built of wood ; filthy. No privy or water.

### No. 7.—*First Floor.*

Size of room, 14 ft. 6 in. long; 13 ft. broad, 6 ft. 5 in. high ; size of window, 5 ft. 4 in. by 3 ft. 3 in. ; rent paid, 3s. weekly; under-rent paid, —— ; time occupied, 9 years. Number of families, 1 ; comprising 1 male above 20, 2 females above 20, 3 males under 20, females under 20, none; total 6. Number of persons ill, 1, cold ; deaths in 1847, ——. Country, Irish ; trade, labourers. State of rooms, tidy; state of furniture, bad ; state of windows, 11 panes whole, 5 blocked up. Number of beds, 2 ; number of bedsteads, 2.

The daughter, 15 years of age, takes out about 5s. worth of oranges (200) daily; and supposing she sold the whole, at rates averaging from 2 to 3 a penny, which she rarely does, she makes 1s. 6d., or 9s. a week.

### No. 7.—*Second Floor.*

Size of room, 14 ft. 6 in. long, 31 ft. broad, 6 ft. 5 in. high ; size of window, 5 ft. 4 in. by 3 ft. 3 in. ; rent paid, 3s. weekly; under-rent paid, 1s. 6d. ; time occupied, 3 years. Number of families 2, and 2 boys, of 16 and 17; comprising 2 males above 20, 2 females above 20, 6 males under 20, 2 females under 20; total 12. Number of persons ill, —— ; deaths in 1847, ——. Country, Irish ; trade, shoemaker, works at home. State of rooms, tidy; state of furniture, tidy; state of windows, 12 whole, 4 broken. Number of beds, 5 ; number of bedsteads, 5.

The landlord of this room has been 27 years in the parish.

*Particulars of the Families.*—1. Husband and wife and 4 children, a girl of 14; 2. Husband and wife and 2 children : 3. Two lads of 17 and 16, unconnected with the families, who pay for their bed between them 1s. 6d. weekly, and calculate that they earn 1s. daily, as market-porters.

### No. 7.—*Back Room, No. 1, First Floor.*

Size of room, 11 ft. 2 in. long, 9 ft. 4 in. broad, 6 ft. high ; size of windows, 2 ft. 10 in. by 2 ft. 3 in. ; rent paid, 2s. weekly; under rent paid, —— ; time occupied, 7 months. Number of families, 1 ; comprising 1 male above 20, 1 female above 20, 2 males under 20 ; total 4.

Number of persons ill, 1; deaths in 1847, 1, fever. Country, Irish: trade, mendicants. State of rooms, dirty; state of furniture, bad; state of windows, broken. Beds of shavings; number of bedsteads, 1.

The whole of this family were in the workhouse some time since with the fever. A daughter died three weeks ago from fever, and the mother was ill of fever. The family has been 16 years in this street. All looking wretched.

### *No. 7.—Back Room, No. 2, First Floor.*

Size of room, 11 ft. 2 in. long, 9 ft. 4 in. broad, 6 ft. high; size of window, 3 ft. by 2 ft.; rent paid, 2s. weekly; under-rent paid, 1s. each family; time occupied, 3 weeks. Number of families, 2; comprising 2 males above 20, 2 females above 20, 4 males under 20, 4 females under 20; total 12. Number of persons ill, 3 of fever; deaths in 1847, 1, bowel complaint. Country, Irish; trade, labourer. State of rooms, dirty; state of furniture, bad; state of windows broken. Two bundles of rags for beds; no bedsteads.

The inmates of this room nearly naked; the only things in this room, a few rags and shavings; 4 years from Ireland. Nothing could exceed their squalid misery.

The passage leading to these two rooms is 11 ft. long by 2 ft. 3 in. wide.

### *House, No. 8.—Parlour on Ground-Floor, One Room.*

Size of room, 14 ft. 6 in. long, 13 ft. broad, 6 ft. 5 in. high; size of window, 5 ft. 4 in. by 3 ft. 3 in.; rent paid, 4s. weekly, furnished; under-rent paid, 2s. 3d.; time occupied, 4 months. Number of families, 2; comprising 2 males above 20, 2 females above 20, 2 females under 20; total 6. Number of persons ill, ——; deaths in 1847, ——. Country, Irish; trade, labourer. State of room, clean; state of furniture, tidy; state of windows, whole. Number of beds, 2; number of bedsteads, 1.

Mr. Mason, of the public-house, is landlord of this house, and the tenants must go to his yard opposite to the privy, and are obliged to him for water.

The chief tenant, although only 4 months in this room, has been 14 years in this street.

The families consist of 1. A man and wife and 2 girls, and 2. A man and wife. Only 1 bedstead.

These people say that there is always much fever in the street.

### *No. 8.—First Floor.*

Size of room, 14 ft. 6 in. long, 13 ft. broad, 6 ft. 6 in. high; size of window, 5 ft. 4 in. by 3 ft. 3 in.; rent paid, 4s. 6d. weekly, furnished; under-rent paid, 1s. 6d.; time occupied, 6 months. Number of families 2; comprising 2 males above 20, 3 females above 20, 4 males under 20, 1 female under 20; total 10. Number of persons ill, 2, fever; deaths in 1847, ——. Country, Irish; trade, dealer. State of rooms, dirty; state of furniture, dirty; state of windows, broken. Number of beds, 3; number of bedsteads, 3.

No doubt these persons take other lodgers, as this is a lodging-house.

*Particulars of the Families.*—1. Husband, wife, and 4 children; a daughter of 21. 2. Husband, wife, and 2 children. A son, aged 19, was lying in a dying state.

### No. 8.—Second Floor.

Size of room, 14 ft. 8 in. long, 13 ft. broad, 6 ft. 5 in. high; size of window, 5 ft. 4 in. by 3 ft. 3 in.; rent paid, 3s. weekly; under-rent paid, 1s. 6d.; time occupied, 8 years. Number of families, 2, and 1 single man; comprising 3 males above 20, 2 females above 20, 3 males under 20, 1 female under 20; total 9. Number of persons ill, 1, disease of lungs; deaths in 1847, 1. Country, Irish; trade, mat-makers. State of rooms, dirty; state of furniture, bad; state of windows, broken. Number of beds, 2; number of bedsteads, 1.

One family, consisting of husband and wife, has been 8 years in this room.

The other family consists of husband, wife, and 3 children, and the husband was dying of disease of the lungs.

A single man lived with these two families.

### No. 8.—Back Rooms in Yard.

*No.* 1.—Size of room, 11 ft. 2 in. long, 9 ft. broad, 5 ft. 6 in. high; size of window, 2 ft. 10 in. by 2 ft. 3 in.; rent paid, 3s. 6d. weekly, furnished; under-rent paid, ——; time occupied, 1 week. Number of families, 1; consisting of 1 female above 20, 1 female under 20; total 2. Number of persons ill, ——; deaths in 1847, ——. Country, ——; trade, ——. State of room, dirty; state of furniture, dirty; state of windows, broken. Number of beds, 1; number of bedsteads, 1.

This female, an educated person, aged 40, now apparently an unfortunate female, stated that she was the wife of a commercial traveller, and she came here to hide herself from her friends. Her daughter, 14.

*No.* 2.—Rent 3s. 6d. furnished: occupied by two unfortunate females.

*No* 3.—Rent 3s. 6d. furnished; occupied by 1 female, and a man, wife, and son, aged 18, sick, with only one bed. They are Irish, and have been 10 years in the street.

*No.* 4.—Husband and wife, pay 3s. 6d.

### No. 8.—Third Floor.

Size of room, 14 ft. 6 in. long, 13 ft. broad, 6 ft. 5 in. high; size of window, 5 ft. 4 in. by 3 ft. 3 in.; rent paid, 3s. weekly; under-rent paid, 9d.; time occupied, 10 weeks. Number of families, 3; consisting of 3 males above 20, 5 females above 20, 3 males under 20, 3 females under 20; total 14. Number of persons ill, 3; deaths in 1847, ——. Country, Irish; trade, dealers. State of room, dirty; state of furniture dirty, 1 table, 1 chair; state of windows, broken. Beds of shavings and rags; number of bedsteads, none.

The families consist of, 1. Mother and 7 children, girl aged 20; 2. Husband and wife; 3. Husband, wife, and 2 sons, one aged 20.

The widowed mother and 2 children sick.

Extreme wretchedness.

*House, No. 9.—Ground Floor.*

Size of rooms, 14 ft. 6 in. long, 13 ft. broad, 6 ft. 6 in. high; size of windows, 5 ft. 4 in. by 3 ft. 3 in.; rent paid, 4s. 6d. weekly, furnished; under-rent paid, ——; time occupied, 6 months. Number of families, 1; consisting of 2 males above 20, 2 females above 20, 3 males under 20, 2 females under 20; total 9. Number of persons ill—all; deaths in 1847, 1. Country, Irish; trade, mat-makers. State of rooms, dirty; state of furniture, bad—no chair, 2 stools; state of windows, broken. Number of beds, 2; number of bedsteads, 2.

The family consists of man, wife, and 7 children.

Here were nine human beings, including a grown up girl and a boy of 14, sleeping in two beds.

There were no lodgers.

*No. 9.—Second Floor.*

Size of room, 14 ft. 6 in. long, 13 ft. broad, 6 ft. 6 in. high; size of window, 5 ft. 4 in. by 3 ft. 3 in.; rent paid, 4s. 6d. weekly, furnished; under-rent paid, 1s. 6d.; time occupied, 4 months. Number of families, 2, and a single man; comprising 2 males above 20, 2 females above 20, 3 males under 20, 1 female under 20; total 8. Number of persons ill, 1 child; deaths in 1847, ——. Country, Irish; trade, mat-makers. State of rooms, dirty; state of furniture, bad,—1 table, 1 chair, 3 forms; state of windows, broken. Number of beds, 2; number of bedsteads, 2.

*Particulars of the Families.*—1. Husband, wife, and 3 children; 2. Widow and 1 child; 3. One single man pays 1s. 6d. weekly.

*No. 9.—Third Floor.*

Size of room, 14 ft. 6 in. long, 13 ft. broad, 6 ft. 5 in. high; size of window, 4 ft. 4 in. by 3 ft. 3 in.; rent paid, 4s. weekly, furnished; under-rent paid, ——; time occupied, 6 years. Number of families, 1; consisting of 1 male above 20, 1 female above 20, 4 males under 20, 3 females under 20; total 9. Number of persons ill, 1; deaths in 1847, ——. Country, English; trade, cutler and hawker. State of rooms, clean; state of furniture, clean; state of windows, clean. Number of beds, 2; number of bedsteads, 2.

This family consisted of husband, wife, and 7 children, English, the eldest girl 16. The man made razor-strops and hawked them. They had all taken the temperance pledge, and in spite of their poverty, they, their room and furniture, exhibited a marked contrast to the Irish tenants of other rooms. The mother had not had good health for 16 months.

No privy and no water. The mother obliged to take her infants over to the privy at the public-house and remain with them, because the Irish children beat them. The landlord, when Rogers (the tenant) paid his rent, always offered him a pint of beer, which he did not take.

*House, No. 10.—Second Floor, Three Rooms.*

First floor rooms locked up.

1st room.—Size, 9 ft. long, 6 ft. broad, 6 ft. high; size of windows, small; rent paid, 3s. 6d. weekly, furnished; under-rent paid, ——;

time occupied, 6 weeks. Number of families 1; consisting of 1 male above 20, 1 female above 20; total 2. Number of persons ill, 1 with fever and influenza; deaths in 1847, ——. Country, man English, woman Irish; trade, dealer, make a living by selling shell pin-cushions. State of rooms, dirty; state of furniture, bad; state of windows, fair. Number of beds, 1 ; number of bedsteads, 1.

They have lost 10 children in the last 17 years, 9 of whom are lying in the neighbouring churchyard of St. Giles's, and 1 in a city parish. They all died young, and this affords a melancholy proof of the tenure of infantine life in this locality.

The ground-floor of this house, a huckster's shop.

2nd room.—Size, 13 ft. 7 in. long, 8 ft. broad; size of window, 2 ft. 10 in. by 2 ft. 3 in. ; rent paid, 2s. 3d. weekly, furnished ; under-rent paid, boy 9d. per week ; a family 1s. 3d. ; time occupied, 1 month. Number of families, 2; consisting of 3 males above 20, 2 females above 20, 1 male under 20, 5 females under 20; total 11. Number of persons ill—all, bad eyes; deaths in 1847, ——. Country, Irish ; trade, mendicants. State of rooms, dirty; state of furniture, dirty; state of window, broken. Beds, of shavings ; no bedstead.

3rd room.—Empty.

Families as follows:—1. Husband, wife, and 3 children, son 22 ; 2. Husband, wife, and 3 children, boy 11.

The upper or third floors, empty.

### House, No. 11.—A Lodging House.

This house, with 4 others adjoining, consisting of 30 rooms, is rented by one individual, an Englishman; 25 of the rooms are let out furnished to separate families, at 6d. and 7d. per night each ; and 5 of the rooms, in which are 20 beds, let to males at 3d. per night ; there is also a day room for the use of the night lodgers, with a good fire and cooking utensils. These houses have also a good supply of water from a pump, and other accommodations.

The landlord has occupied it for 12 years.

### House, No. 14.—Two Parlours on Ground Floor.

Occupied by the Irish landlady of the house and one family ; consisting of 3 males above 20, 2 females above 20, and 1 female under 20; total 6. Rent £36 yearly.

These rooms are well furnished and clean, and the landlady is supposed to obtain her living by letting the other parts of the house furnished, and by letting out crockery and pictures; some of the engravings were old and valuable.

There are 7 rooms and a kitchen, but no water or privy.

The landlady calls herself a widow.

### No. 14.—First Floor, Front Room.

Size of room, 9 ft. long, 7 ft. broad, 6 ft. 5 in. high; size of window, 5 ft. by 3 ft. 3 in.; rent paid, 4s. weekly, furnished; under-rent paid, ——; time occupied, 3 months. Number of families, 1 ; consisting of 2 males above 20, 1 female above 20, 1 male under 20, and 1 female under 20; total 5. Number of persons ill, none; deaths in 1847, ——; Country, English ; trade, dealers. State of rooms, very clean ;

state of furniture, good, a remarkable quantity of china; state of window, whole.

Number of beds, 2 ; number of bedsteads, 2.

### No. 14.—First Floor, Back Room.

Size of room, 7 ft. long, 9 ft. broad, 6 ft. 5 in. high; rent, 3s. furnished; family 1, English; consisting of mother and 3 daughters; 1 bed and bedstead, very clean; two females above 20, and 2 under 20; total 4. Room very close.

### No. 14.—Second Floor, Front.

Size of room, 9 ft. long, 7 ft. broad; size of window, 5 ft. by 3 ft. 3 in.; rent paid, 3s. weekly, unfurnished; under-rent paid, ——; time occupied, 12 months. Number of families, 1; consisting of 1 male above 20, 1 female above 20, no male under 20, and 1 female under 20; total 3. Number of persons ill, ——; deaths in 1847, ——. Country, English; trade, dealer. State of rooms, clean.; state of furniture, good, clean; state of window, whole. Number of beds, 1 ; number of bedsteads, 1.

Second floor back, size 10 ft. long, 7 ft. broad; rent 2s. 6d. furnished; 1 man above 20. Country, English; trade, dealer.

A solitary case of single occupancy.

### No. 17.—First Room, in Back Yard of House, No. 18.

Size of room, 10 ft. long, 7 ft. broad, 6 ft. 5 in. high; size of window, 3 ft. by 2 ft. 6 in.; rent paid, 1s. 6d. weekly, furnished; under-rent paid, —— ; time occupied, 2 years. Number of families, 1; consisting of 1 male above 20, 1 female above 20, no male under 20, and 1 female under 20; total 3. Number of persons ill, ——; deaths in 1847, ——. Country, English; trade, grinder. State of rooms, dirty; state of furniture, dirty, bad ; state of window, broken.

No bed or bedstead and no table.

### No. 17.—Second Room.

Size of room, 10 ft. long, 7 ft. broad, 5 ft. 6 in high; size of window, 3 ft. by 2 ft. 6 in.; rent paid, 3s. weekly, furnished; under-rent paid, —— ; time occupied, 12 months. Number of families, 1; consisting of 1 male above 20, 1 female above 20, 1 male under 20, and no female under 20; total 3. Number of persons ill, ——; deaths in 1847, ——. Country, English; trade, sweep. State of rooms, dirty; state of furniture, bad, dirty ; state of window, broken. Number of beds, 1 ; number of bedsteads, 1 broken.

They sleep in their soot-cloths. A mere closet.

### No. 17.—Third Room, in Yard behind House, No. 18.

Size of room, 15 ft. long, 14 ft. broad, 6 ft. high; size of window, 3 ft. by 2 ft. 6 in.; rent paid, 3s. 6d. furnished. Occupied 16 months by one family, consisting of 1 male above 20, 2 females above 20, 1 male under 20, and 2 females under 20; total 6. Persons ill, 1. Country, English; trade, dealers. Beds, 2; bedstead, 1, 2 chairs, and 1 deal table.

The family consists of a mother and 4 children; girl 23, boy 20, and two grandchildren.

### No. 17.—*Fourth Room.*

Size of room, 12 ft. long, 8 ft. broad, 5 ft. 6 in. high ; rent, 1s. 9d. furnished ; under-rent, 6d. Occupied 6 years by one family and 3 widows ; 1 male above 20, 4 females-above 20, and 1 male under 20 ; total 6. Bedsteads, 1 ; beds, 3, very dirty.

Three widows, a single woman, one son grown up, and a girl, 14, huddled together. A tall man could not stand upright in the room.

### No. 17.—*Fifth Room, Back of House, No.* 18.

Size of room, 10 ft. long, 7 ft. broad, 6 ft. high ; size of window, 3 ft. 6 in. by 2 ft. 6 in.; rent paid, 3s. 3d. furnished, weekly ; under-rent, 1s. ; time occupied, 5 years. Occupants consist of, 1. A husband, wife, and 2 children ; 2. Wife's mother; 3. One single female, the landlady, and a son above 20 years of age ; total 7.

The whole of the furniture consists of 1 table, 2 chairs, 2 bedsteads, and 2 beds, very dirty.

### No. 17.—*Sixth Room, joining on to the House, No.* 20.

Size of room, 10 ft. long, 7 ft. broad, 5 ft. 6 in. high ; size of window, 3 ft. 6. in. by 2 ft 6 in.; rent, 2s.; cannot stand up in room ; by one family occupied 1 year and 9 months ; consisting of 1 male above 20, 1 female above 20, and 1 female under 20 ; total 3 ; room in a shocking state.

No privy or water to the house and rooms of No. 17.

### House, No. 18.—*Parlour on Ground Floor.*

Size of room, 15 ft. long, 13 ft. broad, 6 ft. 6 in. high ; size of window, 5 ft. 5 in. by 3 ft. 4 in. ; rent 2s. Families, 1, and 2 females; occupied 7 years; under rent, 10d. and 6d. per week. Country, 1 Irish and 2 English.

No water or privy.

### No. 18.—*First Floor.*

Size of room, 14 ft. long, 14 ft. broad, 6 ft. 6 in. high ; size of window, 5 ft. 4 in. by 3 ft. 3 in.; rent, 3s. 6d. furnished ; occupied 4 years. One family; consisting of 1 male above 20, 1 female above 20, 1 male under 20, and 1 female under 20.; total 4. Country, English ; trade, dealer, bird fancier.

There were 7 birds in the room ; bed and bedsteads, 2 ; room clean.

### No. 18.—*Back Room, First Floor.*

Size of room, 14 ft. long, 14 ft. broad, 6 ft. high ; size of windows, 5 ft. 4 in. by 3 ft. 3 in.; rent, 3s. 6d. furnished. Occupied by 2 females above 20, mendicants ; total 2.

### No. 18.—*Second Floor.*

Size of room, 14 ft. long, 14 ft. broad, 6 ft. 6 in. high ; size of window, 5 ft. 6 in. by 3 ft. 3 in.; rent, 3s. 3d. furnished. One family ; consisting of 1 male above 20, 2 females above 20; total 3. Persons ill, 1. Country, English; trade, cattle-drover. Beds, 1; bedsteads, 1; room, clean.

*No.* 18.—*Back Room, Second Floor.*

Size of room, 13 ft. long, 13 ft. broad; rent, 4*s.* furnished. One family; consisting of 1 male above 20, 1 female above 20, 1 male under 20, and 2 females under 20; total 5. Country, English; cattle-drover; 2 bedsteads and beds; room clean.

List of furniture allowed by the landlords to a furnished room :— 1 deal table, 2 deal chairs, 1 bedstead without hangings, &c., 1. flock bed, 2 old blankets, 1 pair coarse sheets, 1 bolster, 1 quilt, 1 iron pot, 1 tea-kettle, 1 saucepan, and 1 pail.

The Committee did not think it necessary to proceed beyond the eighteenth house, as it would have lengthened the Report very inconveniently; moreover, the houses inspected afforded a just character of the street and its tenants. Nos. 12 and 13 corresponded to No. 11, a common lodging-house, under individual management; it was not, therefore, thought necessary to examine them in detail.

A few words may be said with respect to the OCCUPATION AND CHARACTER of the inhabitants residing in the district visited. They may be classed as follows:—

1st.—Shop-keepers, lodging-house-keepers, publicans, and some of the under-landlords of the houses, who make considerable profit by letting the rooms furnished and unfurnished.

2nd.—Street-dealers in fruit, vegetables, damaged provisions, and sundries, sweeps, knife-grinders, and door-mat makers.

3rd.—Mendicants, crossing-sweepers, street-singers, persons who obtain a precarious subsistence, and country tramps.

4th.—Persons calling themselves dealers, who are probably thieves, and the occupants of houses of ill fame.

5th.—Young men and lads, of ages varying from 11 to 30, known as pickpockets and thieves of various degrees.

About one-half of the inhabitants are Irish, chiefly natives of Cork, who, for the most part, have been long resident in London. About one-eighth are of Irish descent, born in England; the remainder consist of English, some of whom have been in better circumstances.

The opening of New Oxford Street has displaced many persons, who have had to find lodging elsewhere. To what extent this may have led to the over-crowding of Church Lane may be judged from facts detailed in the appended paper by Mr. Mann, which will also exhibit the sanitary state of this street. In reference to this subject it should be borne in mind that the Committee found several rooms untenanted in Church Lane.

*January 17th,* 1848.

Present—Colonel Sykes and the Agent.

The Committee took a general view of the street, and found it strewed from end to end with night soil, sweepings of houses, decayed vegetables, &c. Carrier Street, which is a *cul de sac,* runs at a right angle from near the centre of Church Lane; it terminates in a bulk-head against the backs of the new houses in Oxford Street: upon an open space in front of this bulk-head, and opposite the doors of the dwelling-houses, the inhabitants ease themselves night and day, and on this spot all kind of filth is thrown, the accumulations not being removed. Church Lane has not any sewer; the sewer of George Street sends off into Church Lane a ramification at right angles, which terminates within a few feet opposite the door of No. 1, Church Lane, and the landlady complains, that this trunk periodically chokes up, and inundates her cellar.

Your Committee have thus given a picture in detail of human wretchedness, filth, and brutal degradation, the chief features of which are a disgrace to a civilized country, and which your Committee have reason to fear, from letters that have appeared in the public journals, is but the type of the miserable condition of masses of the community, whether located in the small, ill-ventilated rooms of manufacturing towns, or in many of the cottages of the agricultural peasantry. In these wretched dwellings all ages and both sexes, fathers and daughters, mothers and sons, grown up brothers and sisters, stranger-adult males and females, and swarms of children, the sick, the dying, and the dead, are herded together with a proximity and mutual pressure which brutes would resist; where it is physically impossible to preserve the ordinary decencies of life; where all sense of propriety and self-respect must be lost, to be replaced only by a recklessness of demeanour which necessarily results from vitiated minds; and yet with many of the young, brought up in such hot-beds of mental pestilence, the hopeless, but benevolent, attempt is making to implant, by means of general education the seeds of religion, virtue, truth, order, industry, and cleanliness; but which seeds, to fructify advantageously, need, it is to be feared, a soil far less rank than can be found in these wretched abodes. Tender minds, once vitiated, present almost insuperable difficulties to reformation; bad habits and depraved feelings gather with the growth and strengthen with the strength. It is not properly within the province of your Committee to offer suggestions, but they cannot refrain from expressing their belief, that the surest way to improve the physical and moral condition of the labouring classes, and to give education a fair field, is for wealthy and benevolent individuals throughout the country, to form local associations, and by the aid of Parliament, to possess themselves of all such buildings as we have described, whether the house in the town, or the cottage in the country; to rebuild suitable roomy dwellings, properly drained, ventilated, and supplied with water, and to rent them so CHEAP to the poor, that they shall have no excuse for herding together like animals. In this way the great evils of over-crowding may be remedied for that large class of our labouring population which is prepared to adopt habits of cleanliness and decency: but nothing short of compulsory legislation can meet the case of the low lodging-houses and rooms sub-let after the manner of those described in this Report.

Nothing can be conceived more mischievous than the system of sub-letting in almost universal operation in the houses inspected by your Committee. The owner of the property letts his houses to a sub-landlord, this sub-landlord letts his rooms to individual tenants, and these tenants lett off the sides or corners of the rooms to individuals or families. Cheap houses will go far to give the death-blow to this fatal system; and to build cheap houses, deserving of the name, appears to your Committee a work of preventive charity worthy of all encouragement.

### Abstract of Report of Committee.

| No. of House. | No. of Room. | Cubic Contents. | Occupants. | | | | | No. of Families. | Number of Bedsteads. | Remarks. | Cubic Feet of Air to each Person. |
|---|---|---|---|---|---|---|---|---|---|---|---|
| | | | Males above 20. | Females above 20. | Males under 20. | Females under 20. | Total. | | | | |
| 2 | Ground, 1 and 2.... | { 1,092 / 815 } | 8 | 5 | 4 | 5 | 22 | 3 | 6 | | 86 |
| „ | Cellar ........... | .. | 1 | 3 | 4 | 3 | 11 | 1 | .. | | .. |
| „ | 1st floor ......... | 1,985 | 3 | 3 | 4 | 6 | 16 | 3 | 3 | | 124 |
| „ | 2nd floor ......... | 1,823 | 3 | 2 | 3 | 4 | 12 | 2 | 2 | | 152 |
| 3 | Ground, 1 and 2.... | { 1,925 / 140 } | 5 | 5 | 3 | 4 | 17 | 4 | 5 | | 121 |
| „ | 1st floor ......... | 1,989 | 3 | 5 | 5 | 4 | 17 | 4 | 1 | | 117 |
| „ | 2nd floor ......... | 1,989 | 1 | 1 | 3 | 3 | 8 | 1 | 2 | | 248 |
| „ | 1, back ........... | 625 | 1 | 2 | 2 | 2 | 7 | 1 | 1 | | 89 |
| 4 | Ground, 1 and 2.... | { 1,092 / 681 } | 4 | 9 | 2 | 4 | 19 | 5 | 6 | | 93 |
| „ | 1st floor ......... | 1,768 | 5 | 5 | 4 | 2 | 16 | 4 | 1 | | 111 |
| „ | 2nd floor ......... | 1,768 | 5 | 6 | 9 | 3 | 23 | 5 | None. | Chiefly Irish. | 77 |
| „ | 1, back ........... | 792 | 1 | 1 | .. | 1 | 3 | 1 | 2 | | 264 |
| 5 | Ground, 1 and 2.... | 1,092 | 1 | 2 | 1 | .. | 4 | 1 | 2 | | 273 |
| „ | 1st floor ......... | 1,768 | 2 | 2 | 4 | 6 | 14 | 2 | 3 | | 126 |
| „ | 1, back ........... | 792 | 3 | 2 | 1 | 1 | 7 | 2 | None. | | 113 |
| „ | 2nd floor ......... | 1,768 | 6 | 6 | 5 | 5 | 22 | 6 | 1 | | 80 |
| 6 | Ground, 1.......... | 1,768 | 1 | 2 | .. | .. | 3 | 1 | 2 | | 589 |
| „ | 1st floor ......... | 1,768 | 1 | 3 | 2 | 1 | 7 | 3 | 2 | | 252 |
| „ | 2nd floor ......... | 1,768 | 4 | 5 | 2 | 1 | 12 | 2 | None. | | 147 |
| „ | 1, back ........... | 672 | 1 | 1 | 1 | 1 | 4 | 1 | 1 | | 168 |
| „ | 2, back ........... | 1,054 | 1 | 2 | 2 | 1 | 6 | 1 | 2 | | 176 |
| 7 | Ground, 1.......... | 1,178 | 7 | 5 | 7 | 3 | 22 | 3 | 4 | | 54 |
| „ | 1st floor ......... | 1,200 | 1 | 2 | 3 | .. | 6 | 1 | 2 | | 202 |
| „ | 1, back yard....... | 792 | 1 | 1 | 4 | .. | 6 | 1 | 1 | | 132 |
| „ | 2nd floor ......... | 1,210 | 2 | 2 | 6 | 2 | 12 | 2 | 5 | | 101 |
| „ | 1, back ........... | 625 | 1 | 1 | 2 | .. | 4 | 1 | 1 | | 156 |
| „ | 2, back ........... | 625 | 2 | 2 | 4 | 4 | 12 | 2 | None. | One room empty. | 52 |
| 8 | Ground, 1.......... | 1,210 | 2 | 2 | .. | 2 | 6 | 2 | 1 | | 202 |
| „ | 1st floor ......... | 1,225 | 2 | 3 | 4 | 1 | 10 | 2 | 3 | | 123 |
| „ | 2nd floor ......... | 1,223 | 3 | 2 | 3 | 1 | 9 | 2 | 1 | | 136 |
| „ | 1, back yard....... | 268 | .. | 1 | .. | 1 | 2 | 1 | 1 | | 134 |
| „ | 2, back yard....... | 1,210 | .. | 2 | .. | .. | 2 | 1 | 1 | | 605 |
| „ | 3, back room, yard.. | .. | 1 | 1 | 1 | .. | 3 | 1 | 1 | | .. |
| „ | 4, back room, yard.. | .. | 1 | 1 | .. | .. | 2 | 1 | 1 | | .. |
| „ | 3rd floor ......... | 1.210 | 3 | 5 | 3 | 3 | 14 | 3 | None. | | 86 |
| 9 | Ground, 1.......... | 1,210 | 2 | 2 | 3 | 2 | 9 | 1 | 2 | | 134 |
| „ | 2nd floor ......... | 1,210 | 2 | 2 | 3 | 1 | 8 | 2 | 2 | | 151 |
| „ | 3rd floor ......... | 1,210 | 1 | 1 | 4 | 3 | 9 | 1 | 2 | | 134 |
| 10 | 2nd floor ......... | 324 | 1 | 1 | .. | .. | 2 | 1 | 1 | | 162 |
| „ | 2nd floor, 2nd room | 652 | 3 | 2 | 1 | 5 | 11 | 2 | None. | 4 rooms empty in this house. | 59 |
| 11,12 & 13 | { A lodging-house, 30 rooms...... } | .. | .. | .. | .. | .. | .. | .. | .. | Nightly Lodgers. | .. |
| 14 | Ground, 1 aud 2.... | .. | 3 | 2 | 1 | .. | 6 | 1 | 2 | E | .. |
| „ | 1st floor, front...... | 419 | 2 | 1 | 1 | 1 | 5 | 1 | 2 | E | 84 |
| „ | 1st floor, back...... | 404 | .. | 2 | .. | 2 | 4 | 1 | 1 | E | 101 |
| „ | 2nd floor, front .... | 404 | 1 | 1 | .. | 1 | 3 | 1 | 1 | E | 135 |
| „ | 2nd floor, back .... | 449 | 1 | .. | .. | .. | 1 | 1 | | E | 378 |
| „ | Back yard ........ | 449 | 1 | 1 | .. | 1 | 3 | 1 | None. | E. Grinder. | 150 |
| 17 | Ditto, 2, room...... | 385 | 1 | 1 | 1 | .. | 3 | 1 | { 1 broken } | E. Sweep. | 128 |
| „ | Ditto, 3, back ...... | 1,320 | 1 | 2 | 1 | 2 | 6 | 1 | 1 | | 220 |
| „ | Ditto, 4, back ...... | 480 | 1 | 4 | .. | 1 | 6 | 1 | 1 | | 80 |
| „ | Ditto, 5, back...... | 420 | 2 | 3 | .. | 1 | 7 | 2 | 2 | | 60 |
| „ | Ditto, 6, room...... | 420 | 1 | 1 | 1 | .. | 3 | 1 | 1 | | 140 |
| 18 | Ground, 1.......... | 1,268 | .. | 3 | .. | .. | 3 | 1 | 1 | | 423 |
| „ | 1st floor ......... | 1,274 | 1 | 1 | 1 | 1 | 4 | 1 | 2 | E | 318 |
| „ | 1st, back ......... | 1,176 | .. | 2 | .. | .. | 2 | 1 | 1 | E | 588 |
| „ | 2nd floor ......... | . | 1 | 2 | .. | .. | 3 | 1 | 1 | E | .. |
| „ | 2nd floor, 2nd room | .. | 1 | 1 | 1 | 2 | 5 | 1 | 2 | E | .. |
| | Total ........ | .. | 111 | 138 | 117 | 97 | 463 | 100 | 90 | | |

E. means English.

    1000 cubic feet of air being deemed necessary for a single prisoner in England, and 800 cubic feet for a soldier in a barrack in India, it will be seen how miserably deficient the supply of air is to the inhabitants of these houses. The average supply is as nearly as possible 175 cubic feet of air, the largest 605, and the smallest 52.

*Statement of the Mortality prevailing in Church Lane during the last Ten Years, with the Sickness during the last Seven Months. Contained in a Letter addressed to Dr. Guy.* By HORACE MANN, Esq., *Barrister-at-Law.*

February 1st, 1848.

SIR,—Understanding that the Council of the Statistical Society have directed an investigation into the sanitary condition of Church Lane, in the Northern District of St. Giles in the Fields; and having myself, some months since, for my private satisfaction, made various inquiries and collected a few facts relating to the health of that locality; I have much pleasure in laying before the Council some of the results to which I have arrived, in order that they may make such use of them as may seem proper. My own inquiry embraced the whole of the North District of St. Giles, and more particularly Church Lane, Church Street, Clark's Buildings, Carrier Street, Crown Street, Monmouth Street, New Compton Street, and High Street; but I propose to confine this communication to Church Lane, except where a reference to other localities may appear, for the sake of comparison, desirable; reserving for some future occasion any remarks I may have to make upon the condition of the remainder of the above-named streets.

Population.

Church Lane, according to the Census enumeration of 1841, contained, in that year, 655 inhabitants unequally distributed among 27 houses; the population of which, severally, was then as follows:—

| | | | | |
|---|---:|---|---:|---|---:|
| | | Brought forward.... 244 | | Brought forward 391 | |
| No. 1 | 39 | No. 10 | 17 | No. 20 | 38 |
| ,, 2 | 33 | ,, 11 | 9 | ,, 21 | 17 |
| ,, 3 | 14 | ,, 12 | 8 | ,, 22 | 32 |
| ,, 4 | 27 | ,, 13 | 20 | ,, 23 | 49 |
| ,, 5 | 35 | ,, 14 | 17 | ,, 24 | 42 |
| ,, 6 | 29 | ,, 15 | 17 | ,, 25 | 31 |
| ,, 7 | 29 | ,, 16 | 21 | ,, 26 | 20 |
| ,, 8 | 13 | ,, 17 | 12 | ,, 27 | 25 |
| ,, 9 | 25 | ,, 18 | 26 | ,, 28 | 10 |
| Carried forward.... 244 | | Carried forward.... 391 | | Total ......... 655 | |

giving an average of rather more than 24 persons to each house.

I find, however, on glancing at the enumeration recently made under the sanction of your Society, that, at some period or other since 1841, the population of this Lane has greatly increased. This will be shown by a comparative statement of the number of inhabitants, in 1841 and 1847 respectively, in each of 12 houses investigated by the Society.

Taking the increase in the following 12 houses together as indicating the probable ratio of increase in the whole 27, the population in 1841 (655), would, in 1847, have increased to 1095; the ratio being 67 per cent.; and giving an average of more than 40 persons to each house, instead of 24 as in 1841.

c 2

|  | 1841 | 1847 |
|---|---|---|
| No. 2 | 33 | 61 |
| ,, 3 | 14 | 49 |
| ,, 4 | 27 | 61 |
| ,, 5 | 35 | 47 |
| ,, 6 | 29 | 32 |
| ,, 7 | 29 | 62 |
| ,, 8 | 13 | 48 |
| ,, 9 | 25 | 26 |
| ,, 10 | 17 | 13 |
| ,, 14 | 17 | 19 |
| ,, 17 | 12 | 28 |
| ,, 18 | 26 | 17 |
|  | 277 | 463—increase 186 |

The causes of this vast increase appear to me attributable to two distinct facts, which would also determine the period of its commencement:—1st. The "improvements" which were begun in the neighbourhood in 1844; and, 2nd. The Irish famines of 1846 and 1847.

The former of these causes would act in a very obvious way, and one which seems to raise a suspicion of the sanitary value of that kind of improvement which consists in occupying, with first or second rate houses, ground previously covered by the tenements of the poorer classes. The expelled inhabitants cannot, of course, derive any advantage from the new erections, and are forced to invade the yet remaining hovels suited to their means: the circle of their habitations is contracted while their numbers are increased; and thus a larger population is crowded into a less space. This consequence may induce a doubt whether the improvement, in this manner, of the external appearance of districts, may not be a means of affecting prejudicially their general health.

The latter of the above causes, also, had, no doubt, considerable influence in producing the increase. Out of the 655 persons of all ages who formed the population of Church Lane in 1841, 281—or about two-fifths—were *natives* of Ireland, and, with their families, constituted nearly the whole population. Of the great number of immigrants who, during the late disastrous years in Ireland, flocked as well into the metropolis as into other large towns of England, there can be no doubt that the vast majority sought naturally the spots frequented by their countrymen; and Church Lane must have felt considerably the effect of this accession.

I shall not attempt to settle the comparative importance of these two causes in producing the increase, and only allude to them because they affect a subsequent calculation of mortality. From them, however, I think it may be assumed that any increase resulting from the improvements did not commence until 1845; and that any increase resulting from Irish immigration did not commence until the early part of 1847. During the 7 years, from January 1, 1838 to December 31, 1844, the population may be fairly supposed to have been nearly stationary at the numbers ascertained by the Census of 1841.

## Mortality.

I will first examine the mortality in Church Lane during the period when its population may be taken to have been stationary, viz., during the 7 years 1838 to 1844, both inclusive. In those years there occurred a total of 92 deaths in this Lane; the average annual mortality produced by which may be shown thus,—

| | |
|---|---|
| Population of Church Lane, 1838–44 ...................... | 655 |
| Deaths in Church Lane, same period ...................... | 92 |
| Annual Mortality per cent. of the living .................... | 2·007, or 1 in 50. |

This is a rate of mortality extremely low, but easily explained by the fact that the residents in these wretched neighbourhoods are generally removed, when overtaken by illness, to the workhouse in their vicinity, or to hospitals; and their deaths, if occurring while so removed, are not, in the register, included amongst those of their usual dwelling-place. The truth of this explanation is rendered obvious by reference to a table in the Eighth Annual Report of the Registrar-General, which shows the mortality in the entire district of St. Giles to have been, during the above period (1838-44), as high as 2·690 per cent. of the population, or 1 death to 37 living.

The real state of the case will be made evident if the mortality be calculated according to the only correct method, viz.: by ascertaining the number of deaths which took place at each *age* out of a certain number living at the same age. In no other way can a fair comparison be made between one district and another, in order to test the influence of locality; since, if one contained a less proportion than another of very young children to adults, the aggregate mortality in the former would, of course, be less than in the latter; not resulting, however, necessarily, from a healthier atmosphere or less crowded dwellings; but certainly, in great measure, from the maturity of its population, less liable to disease.

The adoption of this method with respect to the mortality of Church Lane, from 1838 to 1844, will bring out the following result:—

| Age. | Population 1841. | Deaths in the seven years 1838–44. | Annual Mortality per 100 of the living. |
|---|---|---|---|
| Under 1 ........ | 12 | 26 | 30·95 |
| 1— 2 ........ | 5 | 16 | 45·71 |
| 2— 3 ........ | 19 | 13 | 9·77 |
| 3— 4 ........ | 16 | 4 | 3·57 |
| 4— 5 ........ | 19 | 2 | 1·50 |
| Under 5 ........ | 71 | 61 | 12·27 |
| 5—10 ........ | 67 | 5 | 1·07 |
| 10—15 ........ | 60 | 2 | ·48 |
| 15—25 ........ | 131 | 6 | ·65 |
| 25—35 ........ | 128 | 5 | ·56 |
| 35—45 ........ | 106 | 3 | ·40 |
| 45—55 ........ | 56 | 3 | ·76 |
| 55—65 ........ | 27 | 4 | 2·11 |
| 65—75 ........ | 4 | 1 | 3·57 |
| 75 & upwards | 2 | 2 | 14·28 |
| Not stated ... | 3 | .... | .... |
| All ages .... | 655 | 92 | 2·007 |

The following comparison between this mortality and that of other districts of the metropolis* will still further develope the actual position of this Lane:—

| Age. | ANNUAL MORTALITY OUT OF 100 LIVING. | | | | |
|---|---|---|---|---|---|
| | Church Lane. | St. Giles, (whole district). | Lambeth. | City of London. | Islington. |
| Under 1 | 30·95 | 28·24 | 20·48 | 19·35 | 15·92 |
| 1— 2 | 45·71 | 14·59 | 9·79 | 11·64 | 7·29 |
| 2— 3 | 9·77 | 6·67 | 4·77 | 5·78 | 3·59 |
| 3— 4 | 3·57 | 5·09 | 3·46 | 3·88 | 2·66 |
| 4— 5 | 1·50 | 3·50 | 2·31 | 3·03 | 1·87 |
| Under 5 | 12·27 | 11·56 | 8·25 | 8·94 | 6·31 |
| 5—10 | 1·07 | 1·32 | 1·17 | 1·34 | ·94 |
| 10—15 | ·48 | ·48 | ·45 | ·55 | ·47 |
| 15—25 | ·65 | ·63 | ·72 | ·52 | ·70 |
| 25—35 | ·56 | 1·06 | ·98 | ·91 | ·90 |
| 35—45 | ·40 | 1·83 | 1·56 | 1·58 | 1·40 |
| 45—55 | ·76 | 2·84 | 2·25 | 2·58 | 2·04 |
| 55—65 | 2·11 | 4·97 | 4·03 | 4·24 | 3·84 |
| 65—75 | 3·57 | 10·57 | 8·08 | 8·34 | 7·44 |
| 75 & upwards | 14·28 | 19·72 | 18·98 | 18.59 | 18·54 |
| All ages | 2·007 | 2·69 | 2·33 | 2·14 | 1·99 |

Thus, out of 100 children born, there will die without attaining the age of 1 year,—

|  |  |
|---|---|
| In Church Lane | 31 |
| ,, the whole of St. Giles's | 28 |
| ,, Lambeth | 20 |
| ,, the City of London | 19 |
| ,, Islington | 16 |

So, out of 100 children living at the age of 1 year, there will die without die without attaining the age of 2 years,—

|  |  |
|---|---|
| In Church Lane | 46 |
| ,, St. Giles | 15 |
| ,, Lambeth | 10 |
| ,, City of London | 12 |
| ,, Islington | 7 |

The smallness of the number of persons living and dying in Church Lane at these particular ages may, perhaps, be thought hardly to afford data sufficient for a fair comparison; take then the period from birth to 5 years:—

Out of a population, constantly kept up, 100 children living at any age between birth and 5 years, there will die annually, without attaining 5 years,—

* Extracted, by permission of the Registrar-General, from his forthcoming Eighth Annual Report.

| In Church Lane | 12·3 |
|---|---|
| ,, St. Giles | 11·6 |
| ,, Lambeth | 8·2 |
| ,, City of London | 8·9 |
| ,, Islington | 6·3 |

I take the mortality among children, because they are more exposed than adults to the action of local circumstances, and so present a better test of local influence; but in reading these comparisons, and especially the foregoing table, it must be remembered that, in consequence of the deaths in the workhouse and hospitals not being included, the actual mortality of Church Lane is considerably understated; while that of the other districts is fully rendered.

It will be seen that the mortality of the whole district of St. Giles is little below that of Church Lane. This arises from the fact that the great mass of its population is very little better circumstanced. Church Street, Carrier Street, Clark's Buildings, Kennedy Court, Fletcher's Court, Hampshire Hog Yard, &c., are precisely the same, as respects filth and over-crowding, as Church Lane: while Crown Street, New Compton Street, Monmouth Street (now Dudley Street), Little Earl Street, Denmark Street, Great White Lion Street, Great and Little St. Andrew Street, Short's Gardens, &c., &c., with the courts and alleys branching from them, are, as respects overcrowding, scarcely better, and doubtless feel the added influence of their pestilential neighbours.

The following is a comparison between 6 streets in the Northern District of St. Giles; and will show the mortality when less disturbed by the workhouse, as is the case with Clark's Buildings, Crown Street, Monmouth Street, and New Compton Street. High Street is a tolerable street, given for the sake of contrast.

| Age. | Church Lane. 1838–44. | Clark's Buildings. 1838–44. | Crown Street. 1837–47. | Monmouth Street. 1837–47. | New Compton Street. 1837–47. | High Street. 1837–47. | Lambeth. 1838–44. |
|---|---|---|---|---|---|---|---|
| | Per Cent. | Per Cent. | Per Cent. | Per Cent. | Per Cent. | Per Cent. | Per Cent. |
| Under 5 | 12·27 | 18·35 | 12·34 | 13·00 | 10·12 | 8·08 | 8·25 |
| 5—10 | 1·07 | 2·70 | 1·93 | 1·07 | 1·28 | ·96 | 1·17 |
| 10—15 | ·48 | ·45 | ·68 | ·24 | ·63 | ·23 | ·45 |
| 15—25 | ·65 | ·30 | 1·22 | ·29 | ·47 | ·28 | ·72 |
| 25—35 | ·56 | ·77 | ·44 | ·78 | ·75 | ·43 | ·95 |
| 33—45 | ·40 | 1·40 | 1·01 | 1·24 | 1·37 | ·82 | 1·57 |
| 45—55 | ·76 | 1·73 | 1·89 | 1·73 | 1·02 | 1·80 | 2·25 |
| 55—65 | 2·11 | 1·02 | 8·21 | 2·65 | 3·59 | 2·73 | 4·03 |
| 65—75 | 3·57 | 9·52 | 8·00 | 8·72 | 7·66 | 8·19 | 8·08 |
| 75 & upwards | 14·28 | 28·57 | 8.00 | 18·88 | 12·22 | 10·00 | 12·06 |
| All ages | 2·007 | 3·45 | 3·09 | 2·72 | 2·41 | 1·65 | 2·33 |

The influence of overcrowding will be seen by a statement of the progressive mortality in Church Lane during the last 3 years. In 1845, when the population may be assumed as between 600 and 700, the deaths (excluding those occurring in the workhouse) were 8: in 1846, when the population must have slightly increased, the deaths were 13: and in 1847, when the Irish immigration may be taken to have set in, raising the population, according to the previous estimate, to 1095, the deaths (still exclusive of those in the workhouse) increased to 52; being a proportion of 4·75 per cent., or 1 death out of 21 living.

### Disease.

The amount of sickness prevalent, and its character, are important auxiliary facts by which to estimate the health of districts; especially in cases like the present, where the omission of deaths taking place in workhouses and hospitals, and perhaps the escape altogether of some from registration, give an appearance much too favourable to the actual statement of mortality.

From inquiries made with your assistance at the St. Giles's workhouse, it appears that, from July 1, 1847 to January 27 of the present year, the number of persons living in Church Lane who received medical treatment (both in and out-patients) was 139; giving a proportion to the population of 12·7 per cent. Of these, 88 (or nearly two-thirds) *were cases of fever;* 13 of influenza; 8 of diarrhœa; 7 of bronchitis; 3 of small-pox; 2 of hooping cough; and the remainder of various other diseases. Five of these cases proved fatal; viz., 1 from influenza; 1 from measles; 1 from consumption; and 2 from typhus*.

The sickness was thus distributed amongst the different houses:—

| | Fever Cases. | Total Sickness. | | Fever Cases. | Total Sickness. | | Fever Cases. | Total Sickness |
|---|---|---|---|---|---|---|---|---|
| | | | Brt. frwd. | 53 | 78 | Brt. frwd. | 67 | 97 |
| No. 1 | 4 | 4 | No. 10 | 1 | 1 | No. 19 | 3 | 9 |
| ,, 2 | 5 | 7· | ,, 11 | 4 | 5 | ,, 20 | 1 | 1 |
| ,, 3 | 5 | 6 | ,, 12 | 1 | 1 | ,, 21 | 8 | 11 |
| ,, 4 | 3 | 6 | ,, 13 | 0 | 0 | ,, 22 | 1 | 3 |
| ,, 5 | 14 | 22 | ,, 14 | 1 | 1 | ,, 23 | 0 | 0 |
| ,, 6 | 5 | 7 | ,, 15 | 0 | 0 | ,, 24 | 2 | 6 |
| ,, 7 | 9 | 16 | ,, 16 | 2 | 4 | ,, 25 | 3 | 5 |
| ,, 8 | 7 | 8 | ,, 17 | 2 | 3 | ,, 26 | 0 | 0 |
| ,, 9 | 1 | 2 | ,, 18 | 3 | 4 | ,, 27 | 1 | 4 |
| | | | | | | ,, 28 | 2 | 3 |
| Carried frwd. | 53 | 78 | Carried frwd. | 67 | 97 | Total | 88 | 139 |

All these were cases receiving medical relief from the workhouse, either as in or out-patients. Other cases probably occurred, with or without private medical treatment, the number of which there are no ready means of ascertaining.

I am compelled, by the press of time, to omit some particulars relative to the occupations and duration of life of the inhabitants of this Lane and the surrounding neighbourhood; but I hope the foregoing facts and calculations may be serviceable to the Council.

I am, Sir,
Your obedient servant,
HORACE MANN.

*W. A. Guy, Esq., M.D.,*
*Honorary Secretary of the*
*Statistical Society of London.*

* It is right to state that we are indebted to the courtesy of Mr. Bennett, the House-Surgeon of the workhouse, for this information.

# QUARTERLY JOURNAL

OF THE

# STATISTICAL SOCIETY OF LONDON.

*AUGUST*, 1848.

*Report to the Council of the Statistical Society of London from a Committee of its Fellows appointed to make an Investigation into the State of the Poorer Classes in St. George's in the East, with the sum of £25 given for this purpose by* HENRY HALLAM, *Esq., F.R.S., aided by a Donation of £10 from* R. A. SLANEY, *Esq., M.P., and further sums from the General Resources of the Society.*

[Read before the Statistical Society of London, 17th April and 15th May, 1848.]

ST. GEORGE'S in the East was selected for this inquiry as a district comprising a considerable population of the labouring classes, resembling in condition the people of many surrounding localities, and offering, in fact, an example of the *average condition* of the poorer classes of the metropolis.

The general mass of the labouring population in urban localities, where they are subject to influences over which they have but a partial control, being now avowedly an object of public policy as well as philanthropic solicitude, the Committee, with the advice of the gentleman whose liberality had given it being, determined to make a complete and detailed examination, and a careful analytical statement of the condition of such a body of the poorer labouring classes of the metropolis, as their means would permit them to embrace within the limits of their inquiry, rather than devote those means to exhibiting the condition of any one of those lowest sinks of barbarism and vice, which sanitary and other reports have recently placed with such painful truth before the public. Investigation must not stop until these are removed, for they are but the local accumulation of general evils, which can never be completely dissipated until great changes have been accomplished in the whole frame of society. But since their population is, to some extent, the drainage from the grades next above them, we should rather hope to find a cure by cutting off the supply of degradation than by attempting to reform and elevate it in the lowest depths to which it can sink.

The St. Mary's district of St. George's in the East was accordingly selected for the elaborate analysis which it was determined to make; and the portion concerning which it was ultimately found practicable to obtain every varied item of information, was the great block of habitations included between White Horse Lane, which is the commencement of the Commercial Road, on the north, and Cable Street and the New Road on the south; and between the New Road on the east and Church Lane on the west. This is, in fact, the whole of St. Mary's district north of Cable Street; and it is one of those composed of dingy streets, of houses of small dimensions and moderate elevation, very closely packed in ill-ventilated streets and courts, such as are commonly inhabited by the working classes of the east end; and, indeed, it may be said, of all parts of London, beyond the limits of that congested band round its centre, where overcrowding is carried to the greatest excess.

The period occupied in the inquiry was chiefly the summer half of the year 1845, and the abstract was made in the course of the following year. Annexed is the form of a table in which the particulars relating to the several families in each house were carefully registered, after they had been collected, in note-books with marginal indications corresponding with the headings of this table. A complete re-arrangement of the materials was then made under the head of each occupation. From these second abstracts, the following tables have been compiled.

| Name and Condition of Street or Place.<br><br>1. Height of Houses, in Stories.<br>2. Length and Width of Place.<br>3. Open or not at each end.<br>4. Paving and Lighting.<br>5. Cleansing.<br>6. Sewerage.<br>7. Supply of Water. | Number of House. | Number of Families in the House. | Number in Family. | Male Children, under 16. | | Female Children, under 16. | | Able-bodied Males, above 16. | | Able-bodied Females above 16. | | Aged and Infirm Males. | | Aged and Infirm Females | |
|---|---|---|---|---|---|---|---|---|---|---|---|---|---|---|---|
| | | | | Well. | Ill. | Well. | Ill. | Well. | Ill. | Well. | Ill. | Well. | Ill. | Well. | Ill. |
| | | | | | | | | | | | | | | | |

| Age of Father when first Child born. | Age of Mother when first Child born. | Present Age of Mother. | Number of Children she has had. | Number now living. | Occupation and Weekly Earnings of head of Family. | Occupation and Weekly Earnings of others than the head of the Family. | Weekly Earnings of the whole. | Number of Times that the Family has Animal Food in the Week. |
|---|---|---|---|---|---|---|---|---|
| | | | | | | | | |

| Clothing. | | | | Rooms. | | | | | | | | Books. | | | Pictures. | | |
|---|---|---|---|---|---|---|---|---|---|---|---|---|---|---|---|---|---|
| | | | | | | | Furnished. | | | Cleansed. | | | | | | | | |
| 1. Sufficient, and Clean. | 2. Insufficient, but Clean. | 3. Sufficient, but Dirty. | 4. Insufficient, and Dirty. | Number. | Rent per Week. | Number of Beds. | Well. | Scantily. | Ill. | Well. | Tolerably. | Ill. | Serious. | Theatrical. | Miscellaneous. | Serious. | Theatrical. | Miscellaneous. |

| Number of Children attending School. | | | | | | | Religion. | | | | | |
|---|---|---|---|---|---|---|---|---|---|---|---|---|
| Infant and Dame Schools. | | Day Schools. | | Sunday Schools only. | | Payments made for the Schooling of Children in Day Schools. | Church of England. | Roman Catholics. | Methodists. | Jews. | Other religious denominations. | No religious profession. |
| Males. | Females. | Males. | Females. | Males. | Females. | | | | | | | |

| Newspapers generally read. | Country of Birth. | | | | | Length of Time in present Residence. | | Receiving what Gratuitous Medical Aid, if any. | No. of Persons in Benefit Societies. |
|---|---|---|---|---|---|---|---|---|---|
| | London. | England and Wales. | Ireland. | Scotland. | Foreign Parts. | Years. | Months. | | |

The annexed preliminary table shows the condition of all the streets in this region, with the exception of Upper and Middle Grove Streets, which are almost wholly occupied by persons in a condition of life somewhat above that of the poor labourers who surround them.

TABLE I.—*Names of Streets, Courts, and Places of St. Mary's District of St. George's in the E[...]
condition as regards Lighting and Pav[...]*

| Names of Streets, Courts, and Places. | Height of houses in stories. | Length of street in yards. | Width of street in feet. | Open at both ends. | Open at one end. | Various entrances. | Paved and lighted. | Paved but nor lighted. | Nei[...] pav[...] ne[...] ligh[...] |
|---|---|---|---|---|---|---|---|---|---|
| | Stories*. | Yards. | Feet. | | | | | | |
| Upper Grove Street | 2 | 600 | 24 | 1 | .. | .. | Well | .. | |
| Batty's Garden | 2 | 90 | Av. 8 | 1 | .. | .. | Partially | .. | |
| Henry Street | 2 | 120 | 17 | 1 | .. | .. | Well | .. | |
| Everard Street | 2 | 130 | 18 | 1 | .. | .. | Well | .. | |
| Rix Court | 2 | 60 | 9 | 1 | .. | .. | Partially | .. | |
| Rhan's Court | 2 | 18 | 10 | .. | 1 | .. | Well | .. | |
| Philip Street | 2 | 100 | 11 | 1 | .. | .. | Well | .. | |
| Splidts Terrace | 2 | 130 | Av. 15 | 1 | .. | .. | Well | .. | |
| Ellen Street | 2 | 220 | 16 | 1 | .. | .. | Well | .. | |
| Ellen Place | 2 | 40 | 12 | .. | .. | Opening in centre | Well | .. | |
| Ellen Court | 2 | 15 | 11 | .. | 1 | .. | .. | | 1 |
| Blacksmith's Arms Place | 2 | 50 | 12 | .. | .. | .. | Partially | .. | |
| Thomas Street | 2 | 130 | 30 | 1 | .. | .. | Well | .. | |
| Sarah Place | 2 | 20 | 13 | .. | 1 | .. | Well | .. | |
| Prince of Orange Court | 2 | 32 | 9 | 1 | .. | .. | Well | .. | |
| Globe Place | 2 | 40 | 7 | .. | 1 | .. | Well | .. | |
| Elizabeth Street | 2 | 130 | 27 | 1 | .. | .. | Partially | .. | |
| Severn Street | 2 | 96 | 27 | 1 | .. | .. | Well | .. | |
| Mary Ann Street | 2 | 100 | 27 | 1 | .. | .. | Well | .. | |
| North Street | 2, a few 3 | 300 | 30 | 1 | .. | .. | Well | .. | |
| Blacksmith's Arms Court | 2 | 40 | 9 | .. | .. | .. | Partially | .. | |
| Campbell's Place | 2 | 44 | Av. 12 | .. | 1 | .. | Well | .. | |
| Frederick Street | 2 | 120 | 16 | 1 | .. | .. | Well | .. | |
| Charles Street | 2 | 70 | 15 | 1 | .. | .. | Well | .. | |
| Providence Street | 2 | 118 | 21 | 1 | .. | .. | Well | .. | |
| Church Lane | 2 and 3 | 560 | 33 | 1 | .. | .. | Well | .. | |
| Hampshire Court | 2 | 30 | 12 | 1 | .. | .. | Well | .. | |
| Queen's Court | 2 | 20 | 12 | .. | 1 | .. | Well | .. | |
| Batty's Place | 2 | 16 | 11 | .. | 1 | .. | .. | 1 | |
| Abel Buildings | 2 | 18 | 11 | .. | 1 | .. | .. | | 1 |
| Christian Street. / Lower King Street | 2 and 3 | 550 | 33 | 1 | .. | .. | Well | .. | |
| Matilda Place | 2 | 16 | 8 | .. | 1 | .. | Well | .. | |
| Matilda Street | 2 | 32 | 12 | 1 | .. | .. | Well | .. | |
| Batty's Street | 2 and 3 | 150 | 27 | 1 | .. | .. | Well | .. | |
| Gloucester Buildings | 2 | 78 | 12 | .. | 1 | .. | Well | .. | |
| Batty's Court | 2 | 21 | 4 | .. | 1 | .. | Partially | .. | |
| Grove Court | 2 | 40 | 10 | .. | .. | { Narrow entrance in centre } | .. | .. | |
| Lower Berner's Street / Upper Berner's Street | 3 | 300 | 36 | .. | 1 | .. | Well | .. | |
| Lloyd's Court | 2 | 8 | 6 | .. | 1 | A narrow entrance | .. | .. | |
| London Terrace | 2 | 316 | 10½ | 1 | .. | .. | Well | .. | |
| Patriot Street | 2 | 55½ | 19½ | 1 | .. | .. | Well | .. | |
| Langdale Street | 2 | 81 | 24 | 1 | .. | .. | Bad | .. | |
| Norman's Buildings | 2 | 7 | 18 | .. | 1 | .. | Badly | .. | |
| James Place | 2 | 21 | 9 | .. | 1 | .. | .. | | |
| West Folly | 2 | 4 | 3 | .. | .. | .. | .. | | |
| Cross Street | 2 | 34 | 21 | 1 | .. | .. | Badly | .. | |
| Langdale Court | 2 | 3 | 3 | .. | .. | .. | Badly | .. | |
| Marmaduke Place | 2 | 32 | 12 | .. | 1 | .. | Well | .. | |
| Marmaduke Street | 2 | Not stated. | | 1 | .. | .. | Well | .. | |
| St. George's Court | 2 | 78 | 15 | 1 | .. | .. | Well | .. | |
| Amber Court | 2 | 11 | 4½ | .. | 1 | .. | .. | | 1 |
| Wellington Buildings, (Saml. St.) | 2 | 39 | 12 | .. | 1 | .. | Well | .. | |
| Waterloo Place, (Samuel Street) | 2 | 64 | 7½ | .. | 1 | .. | Badly | .. | |
| Samuel Street | 2 | 175 | 15 | 1 | .. | .. | { Paving bad; lighting good } | .. | |
| John Street | 2 and 3 | Not stated. | | 1 | .. | .. | Well | .. | |
| James Street | 2 | Not stated. | | .. | .. | .. | Well | .. | |
| St. George's Terrace | 2 | 170 | 4½ | .. | 1 | .. | Well | .. | |
| Marman Street | 2 | 112 | 27 | .. | .. | .. | Tolerably | .. | |
| Western Passage | 2 | 12 | 6 | 1 | .. | .. | Well | .. | |
| Marmaduke Court | 2 | 50 | 6 | .. | .. | Opening in centre | Well | .. | |
| Turner's Buildings, (Grove St.) | 2 | 29 | 18 | 1 | .. | .. | Well | .. | |
| Lower Grove Street | 2 | 140 | 27 | .. | .. | .. | Well | .. | |
| Middle Grove Street / Upper Grove Street | 2 | No detailed account given of these streets | | | | | — See Remarks | | |
| 63 Streets, Courts, and Places | .. | 6,085½ | 895½ | 32 | 20 | 4 | { Well... 42 / Partially or badly 12 } | 4 | |
| Average | .. | 103 | 15 | .. | .. | 7 | .. | .. | |

* Reckoning the ground floor as one story.    † If there were good and clean surface drains the drainage w[...]

-th of Cable Street, with the Height of Buildings, Length and Width of Streets, &c., and their
nsing, Drainage, and Supply of Water.

| Well cleaned | Tolerably cleaned | Badly cleaned | Good drainage | Tolerable drainage | Bad drainage | Plentiful supply three times a week | REMARKS. |
|---|---|---|---|---|---|---|---|
| .. | .. | .. | 1 | .. | .. | 1 | **Batty's Garden.**—At one end only open by an arch 3 ft. 10 in. wide and 9 ft. high. Many of the houses in this street have no back premises, neither light nor ventilation from behind, and consequently are close, damp, and unhealthy. The street is angular, and at one corner of the narrow part is a dust-heap, on which is thrown night-soil and refuse of every description, which saturates and penetrates through the walls to the premises behind, creating a most disgusting nuisance to the tenants. This dust-heap is directly opposite the door of one of the houses. Some of the privies are entirely choaked and cannot be used. |
| .. | 1 | .. | 1 | .. | 1 | 1 | |
| { 1 except east end } | | .. | 1 | .. | .. | 1 | |
| .. | .. | .. | 1 | .. | .. | 1 | |
| .. | .. | .. | 1 | .. | .. | 1 | |
| .. | .. | .. | 1 | .. | .. | 1 | |
| .. | .. | .. | 1 | .. | .. | 1 | |
| .. | .. | .. | 1 | .. | .. | 1 | |
| .. | .. | 1 | 1 | .. | .. | 1 | |
| .. | .. | .. | 1 | .. | .. | 1 | |
| .. | .. | 1 | 1 | .. | .. | 1 | |
| .. | .. | .. | 1 | .. | .. | 1 | |
| .. | .. | .. | 1 | .. | .. | 1 | |
| .. | 1 | .. | 1 | .. | .. | { 1 pipe to supply water to all ; say 10 houses. } | |
| .. | .. | .. | 1 | .. | .. | 1 | **Campbell's Place.**—These houses are very confined in the rear, having neither door nor window in the ground-floor. |
| .. | .. | .. | 1 | .. | .. | 1 | |
| .. | .. | .. | 1 | .. | .. | 1 | |
| .. | .. | .. | 1 | .. | .. | 1 | |
| .. | .. | .. | 1 | .. | .. | 1 | |
| .. | .. | .. | 1 | .. | .. | 1 | |
| .. | .. | .. | 1 | .. | .. | 1 | |
| .. | .. | .. | 1 | .. | .. | 1 | |
| .. | .. | .. | 1 | .. | .. | 1 | |
| .. | .. | .. | 1 | .. | .. | 1 | |
| .. | .. | 1 | 1 | .. | .. | 1 | **Batty's Court.**—No light or air behind. |
| .. | 1 | .. | 1 | .. | .. | { No water-butts, & only 1 cock for all the houses. } | |
| .. | .. | .. | 1 | .. | .. | 1 | |
| .. | .. | .. | 1 | .. | .. | 1 | |
| .. | 1 | .. | .. | .. | 1 | 1 | |
| 1 | .. | .. | .. | 1 | .. | 1 | **Patriot Street.**—Rooms small, 6 by 12. |
| .. | .. | 1 | .. | .. | 1 | 1 | **Norman's Buildings.**—Inhabitants complain greatly of damp, also of rats and beetles. |
| .. | .. | 1 | .. | .. | 1 | 1 | |
| .. | .. | 1 | .. | .. | 1 | 1 | |
| .. | .. | 1 | .. | .. | 1 | 1 | |
| .. | .. | 1 | .. | .. | 1 | 1 | |
| .. | .. | .. | .. | 1 | .. | 1 | **Marmaduke Place.**—Good houses. |
| .. | .. | 1 | .. | .. | 1 | 1 | **Marmaduke St.**—Houses generally in bad condition |
| .. | .. | 1 | .. | .. | 1 | 1 | **St. George's Court.**—Houses generally dilapidated. Rooms 12 by 10. |
| 1 | .. | .. | .. | 1 | .. | 1 | **Wellington Buildings.**—Houses have no back yards and are infested with beetles and bugs |
| .. | 1 | .. | .. | .. | 1 | 1 | **Waterloo Place.**—No. 14 to 20 rebuilding. |
| .. | 1 | .. | .. | .. | 1 | 1 | |
| .. | .. | .. | 1 | .. | .. | 1 | |
| .. | .. | 1 | 1 | .. | .. | 1 | **St. George's Terrace.**—Houses in **very bad** repair. |
| .. | 1 | .. | .. | .. | 1 | 1 | |
| .. | .. | 1 | .. | .. | .. | 1 | |
| 1 | .. | .. | .. | 1 | .. | 1 | **Marmaduke Court.**—Inhabitants very poor. |
| .. | .. | 1 | .. | .. | .. | 1 | |
| .. | .. | 1 | .. | .. | .. | 1 | **Lower Grove Street.**—Chiefly respectable. |
| .. | .. | .. | .. | .. | .. | .. | **Middle Grove Street.**—Same length as Upper Grove Street. Between Upper and Lower Grove Street open at each end, Nos. 4, 5, 6, and 7, as Upper Grove Street. |
| 6 | 17 | 44 | 4 | 14 | 61 | | |
| .. | 5 | .. | .. | 1 | .. | | |

:d good ; if they were less clean, tolerable ; if obstructed and filthy, bad. All the drainage is by the surface.

Illness, in the meaning of the following table, is such as produces confinement to the house, and incapacity for labour or exertion. The proportion of such illness is small; and the appearance of the children, even, is very healthy, wherever three is a sufficiency of food; for they are early sent, as much as possible, out of the confined rooms of their parents, though sometimes into little, filthy, smoky, dame schools, by no means preferable; except that they have to pass through the streets to arrive at them. Others of these schools, however, are clean and fairly ventilated, and kept by persons with habits of order and propriety.

TABLE II.

*Population and State of Health of the Families of the Working Classes in St. Mary's District of St. George's in the East, north of Cable Street.*

|  | | Well. | Ill. | Whole Population. |
|---|---|---|---|---|
| Number of families visited ........ | 1,802 | | | |
| Male children under 15 ............... | .... | 1,636 | 49 | |
| Female children under 15 ........... | .... | 1,632 | 28 | |
| | | 3,268 | 77 | = 3,345 |
| Adult males ............................. ...... | .... | 1,886 | 42 | |
| Adult females ............................. | .... | 2,005 | 88 | |
| | | 3,891 | 130 | = 4,021 |
| Aged and infirm males ............... | .... | 38 | 15 | |
| Aged and infirm females............... | .... | 60 | 18 | |
| | | 98 | 33 | = 131 |
| Population not classified............... | .... | .... | .... | = 11 |
| Total of families, exclusive of single men and women ........... | .... | 7,257 | 240 | = 7,508 |
| Single men in families.................... | 88 | .... | .... | |
| Single women in families............... | 64 | .... | .... | |
| Adult males ............................. | .... | 122 | .... | = 122 |
| Adult females ............................. | .... | 67 | 3 | = 70 |
| Aged and infirm males ............... | .... | 3 | .... | = 3 |
| Aged and infirm females............... | .... | 4 | 4 | = 8 |
| 1204 houses visited. Families... | 1,954 | 7,453 | • 247 | = 7,711 |

TABLE III.

*Country of the Heads of the Families.*

| | Families. | Single Men. | Single Women. | Total Families. |
|---|---|---|---|---|
| London | 857 | 27 | 29 | 913 |
| England and Wales | 622 | 31 | 21 | 674 |
| Ireland | 159 | 5 | 6 | 170 |
| Scotland | 42 | .... | 1 | 43 |
| Foreign parts | 100 | 10 | ..... | 110 |
| Not ascertained | 22 | 15 | 7 | 44 |
| Total | 1,802 | 88 | 64 | 1,954 |

The excess of foreigners, indicated by this table, is partly attributable to some foreign sailors having their homes here, but chiefly to the sugar-bakers, being nearly all Germans; and to their credit it ought to be added, that they are a cleanly, orderly, and well-conducted body of men, chiefly worshippers at the German chapel in the neighbourhood.

The total population—men, women, and children—included in the scope of the present inquiry is here seen to be 7,711, comprised in 1,204 houses, and 1,954 families; reckoning as a separate family every one whose earnings were not thrown into some common stock, for boarding and lodging.  125 single men included in the inquiry, are thus reckoned to form 88 families; because some of them lodge together; and 78 single women and widows without incumbrance, make, in like manner, 64 families; an excess of gregariousness on the part of the men which is worthy of observation.

The economical condition of single persons of both sexes being altogether different from that of the great mass of the population, they are kept under separate heads in the following abstract, as also are 151 widows, with incumbrance, the total number in whose families amounts to 577, or nearly 3½ in each family, while the general average of the district is 4.  The remaining 1,651 families, including 6,991 individuals, or 4¼ individuals to each, are classified, as far as possible, according to the *occupation* of the head of each; being that circumstance which brings in its train the most numerous and most potent of the influences which affect the relative condition of all.  Every occupation which had any considerable number of the heads of families engaged in it, is, in fact, separately specified in the following tables, and they are 27 in number; leaving a surplus of 396 families, including 1,663 individuals, still unclassed, under the head of miscellaneous.  These, however, are all brought together in a separate sheet, similar to those in which the whole of the particulars concerning each of the other groups is abstracted.  Annexed is a list of these groups, with the numbers in each, from which it will appear that the number of mere "labourers" (in great part about the docks) is alone nearly equal to all the "miscellaneous;" while of shoemakers there are 101, gunsmiths 87, carpenters 76, tailors 72, sailors 67, coopers 64, carmen 50, &c. This list is followed by a classification of the "miscellaneous," under the heads of their several occupations.

TABLE IV.—

| | Trades. | Number of Families. | Population. | Average number to each Family | Earnings of Heads of Families Classified. | | | | | | | | Total Earnings of Heads of Families. |
|---|---|---|---|---|---|---|---|---|---|---|---|---|---|
| | | | | | Not exceeding 10s. | 11s. to 15s. | 16s. to 20s. | 21s. to 25s. | 26s. to 30s. | 31s. to 40s. | 41s. and upwards | Unknown | £   s. |
| 27 | Labourers | 363 | 1,478 | 4·0 | 30 | 141 | 103 | 51 | 17 | 11 | 6 | 4 | 5,596  6 |
| 25 | Gunsmiths | 87 | 384 | 4·4 | .. | 2 | .. | 3 | 3 | 24 | 55 | .. | 3,635  0 |
| 14 | Gunmakers | 26 | 106 | 4·1 | .. | .. | 7 | 10 | 7 | 2 | .. | .. | 658  0 |
| 26 | Shoemakers | 101 | 393 | 3·9 | 16 | 26 | 34 | 16 | 8 | 1 | .. | .. | 1,766  0 |
| 17 | Bricklayers | 31 | 134 | 4·3 | 2 | 1 | 3 | 15 | 8 | .. | .. | 2 | 686  ( |
| 21 | Coopers | 64 | 264 | 4·1 | 1 | 6 | 15 | 15 | 22 | 2 | 2 | 1 | 1,603  ( |
| 10 | Engineers | 20 | 82 | 4·1 | .. | .. | 1 | 2 | 9 | 7 | 1 | .. | 629  ( |
| 6 | Umbrella-makers | 11 | 59 | 5·4 | .. | 2 | 2 | 2 | 2 | 2 | 1 | .. | 292  ( |
| 18 | Porters | 34 | 164 | 4·8 | 3 | 13 | 10 | 7 | .. | .. | .. | 1 | 561  ( |
| 20 | Carmen | 50 | 219 | 4·4 | 1 | 6 | 38 | 2 | 1 | .. | .. | 2 | 869  ( |
| 7 | Butchers | 13 | 60 | 4·6 | .. | 3 | 6 | 1 | 1 | .. | .. | 2 | 207  ( |
| 12 | Sugar-bakers | 24 | 114 | 4·7 | .. | .. | 9 | 15 | .. | .. | .. | .. | 509 |
| 13 | Bakers | 26 | 102 | 3·9 | 2 | 2 | 15 | 2 | 1 | 1 | .. | 3 | 425 |
| 15 | Painters | 28 | 128 | 4·6 | 1 | 4 | 3 | 7 | 8 | .. | .. | 5 | 541 |
| 9 | Watermen | 20 | 85 | 4·2 | 1 | 5 | 3 | 9 | 1 | 1 | .. | .. | 417 |
| 19 | Smiths | 34 | 135 | 4·0 | .. | .. | 4 | 25 | 3 | 1 | 1 | .. | 823 |
| 22 | Sailors | 67 | 243 | 3·6 | 19 | 36 | 1 | 1 | 1 | ... | .. | 9 | 689 |
| 23 | Tailors | 72 | 344 | 4·8 | 6 | 15 | 25 | 10 | 11 | 2 | 3 | .. | 1,545 |
| 16 | Cigar-makers | 29 | 115 | 4·0 | .. | 2 | 5 | 3 | 7 | 7 | 3 | 2 | 822 |
| 24 | Carpenters | 76 | 351 | 4·6 | 4 | 3 | 8 | 26 | 28 | 2 | 1 | 4 | 1,826 |
| 1 | Gun-stock-makers | 7 | 37 | 5·3 | .. | .. | .. | .. | 4 | 2 | 1 | .. | 256 |
| 4 | Tin-workers | 10 | 59 | 6·0 | 1 | .. | 2 | 5 | 2 | .. | .. | .. | 212 |
| 2 | Wheelwrights | 8 | 32 | 4·0 | .. | .. | 1 | 5 | 2 | .. | .. | .. | 200 |
| 5 | Shopmen | 11 | 41 | 3·7 | .. | .. | 2 | 6 | 3 | .. | .. | .. | 268 |
| 11 | Policemen | 21 | 86 | 4·1 | .. | .. | 18 | 3 | .. | .. | .. | .. | 394  1 |
| 3 | Printers | 9 | 44 | 5·0 | .. | .. | 3 | 5 | 1 | .. | .. | .. | 209 |
| 8 | Clerks | 13 | 69 | 5·3 | .. | .. | .. | 7 | 4 | 1 | .. | 1 | 321 |
| 28 | Miscellaneous | 396 | 1,663 | 4·2 | 48 | 52 | 96 | 78 | 52 | 18 | 7 | 45 | 7,466 |
| | Total Families | 1,651 | 6,991 | 4·2 | 135 | 319 | 414 | 331 | 206 | 84 | 81 | 81 | 33,427 |
| | Widows, with incumbrance and of Miscellaneous occupations | 151 | 517 | 3·4 | 114 | 19 | 4 | 1 | .. | 1 | .. | 12 | 1,078 |
| | Single Men of Miscellaneous Trades | 88 | 125 | 1·4 | 6 | 19 | 23 | 37 | 10 | 17 | 5 | 8 | 2,716 |
| | Single Women and Widows without incumbrance & of Miscellaneous occupations | 64 | 78 | 1·2 | 63 | 4 | .. | .. | .. | .. | .. | 11 | 458 |
| | Total Families | 1,954 | 7,711 | 4·0 | 318 | 361 | 441 | 369 | 216 | 102 | 86 | 112 | 37,680 |

Occupations and Earnings.

| Average Earnings of Heads of Families | Total Earnings of Subordinate members of Families. | Average Earnings of each Subordinate member of a Family. | Average Earnings of Subordinates upon the whole of the Families. | Total Earnings of Families Classified. | | | | | | | | Total Earnings of whole. | Average Earnings of whole. |
|---|---|---|---|---|---|---|---|---|---|---|---|---|---|
| | | | | Not exceeding 10s | 11s. to 15s. | 16s. to 20s. | 21s. to 25s. | 26s. to 30s. | 31s. to 40s. | 41s. and upwards | Unknown | | |
| s. d. | £ s. | s. d. | s. d. | | | | | | | | | £ s. | s. d. |
| 15 7 | [290] 1,283 9 | 4 5 | 3 7 | 19 | 95 | 149 | 62 | 18 | 11 | 6 | 3 | 6,880 3 | 19 1 |
| 41 9 | [29] 303 6 | 10 6 | 3 3 | .. | 2 | .. | 2 | 1 | 20 | 62 | .. | 3,938 6 | 45 3 |
| 25 4 | [6] 39 6 | 6 7 | 1 6 | .. | .. | 6 | 8 | 8 | 3 | 1 | .. | 697 6 | 26 10 |
| 17 5 | [69] 325 9 | 4 9 | 3 3 | 12 | 10 | 30 | 29 | 12 | 8 | .. | .. | 2,091 9 | 20 8 |
| 23 8 | [17] 84 3 | 9 11 | 2 8 | 2 | 2 | 4 | 9 | 7 | 7 | .. | .. | 770 3 | 24 10 |
| 25 5 | [34] 182 6 | 5 4 | 2 10 | 2 | 4 | 11 | 10 | 21 | 12 | 4 | .. | 1,785 6 | 27 11 |
| 31 5 | [6] 20 0 | 3 4 | 1 0 | .. | .. | 1 | 1 | 7 | 10 | 1 | .. | 649 0 | 32 5 |
| 26 6 | [4] 28 6 | 7 1 | 2 7 | .. | .. | .. | 5 | 3 | 2 | 1 | .. | 320 6 | 29 1 |
| 17 0 | [26] 120 0 | 4 7 | 3 8 | .. | 8 | 8 | 9 | 7 | 1 | .. | 1 | 681 6 | 20 8 |
| 18 1 | [45] 310 6 | 6 11 | 6 3 | 2 | 4 | 8 | 25 | 4 | 5 | 2 | .. | 1,179 6 | 23 7 |
| 18 10 | [8] 42 6 | 5 4 | 3 10 | .. | 1 | 3 | 3 | 3 | 1 | .. | 2 | 249 6 | 22 8 |
| 21 3 | [16] 58 0 | 3 0 | 2 5 | .. | .. | 3 | 18 | 2 | 1 | .. | .. | 567 0 | 23 7 |
| 18 6 | [16] 73 0 | 3 7 | 2 11 | 2 | 2 | 13 | 5 | 2 | 1 | .. | 1 | 498 0 | 19 11 |
| 23 6 | [16] 86 6 | 5 5 | 3 2 | 3 | .. | 7 | 7 | 7 | 2 | 1 | 1 | 627 6 | 23 3 |
| 20 10 | [14] 112 0 | 8 0 | 5 7 | .. | 2 | 5 | 6 | 2 | 1 | 4 | .. | 529 0 | 26 5 |
| 24 3 | [22] 101 6 | 4 7 | 3 0 | .. | .. | 1 | 16 | 11 | 4 | 2 | .. | 924 6 | 27 2 |
| 11 10 | [52] 276 6 | 5 4 | 4 5 | 11 | 14 | 32 | 2 | 3 | 1 | .. | 4 | 965 6 | 15 4 |
| 21 6 | [41] 221 6 | 5 5 | 3 1 | 3 | 10 | 19 | 17 | 9 | 10 | 4 | .. | 1,767 3 | 24 6 |
| 30 5 | [17] 128 0 | 7 6 | 4 7 | .. | 2 | 2 | 4 | 5 | 10 | 5 | 1 | 950 0 | 33 11 |
| 25 4 | [37] 226 9 | 6 1 | 3 0 | 5 | 2 | 5 | 23 | 25 | 13 | 3 | .. | 2,052 9 | 27 0 |
| 36 7 | [3] 13 0 | 4 4 | 1 10 | .. | .. | .. | .. | 2 | 4 | 1 | .. | 269 0 | 38 5 |
| 21 2 | [11] 85 6 | 7 9 | 8 7 | .. | .. | 1 | 3 | 3 | 2 | 1 | .. | 297 6 | 29 9 |
| 25 2 | [5] 25 6 | 5 1 | 3 2 | .. | .. | 1 | 1 | 5 | 1 | .. | .. | 225 6 | 28 2 |
| 24 4 | [7] 50 6 | 7 2 | 4 7 | .. | .. | 1 | 4 | 3 | 2 | 1 | .. | 318 6 | 28 11 |
| 18 10 | [17] 65 0 | 3 10 | 3 1 | .. | .. | 7 | 9 | 5 | .. | .. | .. | 459 10 | 21 10 |
| 23 3 | [6] 25 0 | 4 2 | 2 9 | .. | .. | 2 | 2 | 4 | 1 | .. | .. | 234 0 | 26 0 |
| 26 9 | [4] 44 0 | 11 0 | 3 8 | .. | .. | .. | 5 | 3 | 3 | 1 | 1 | 365 0 | 30 5 |
| 21 3 | [192] 1,142 3 | 5 11 | 3 2 | 37 | 43 | 76 | 80 | 73 | 37 | 16 | 34 | 8,608 3 | 23 9 |
| 20 3 | [1,010] 5,475 3 | 5 5 | 3 6 | 98 | 201 | 395 | 365 | 255 | 173 | 116 | 48 | 38,902 10 | 23 1 |
| 7 9 | [58] 345 9 | 5 11 | 2 5 | 98 | 26 | 14 | 4 | 1 | 1 | .. | 7 | 1,423 9 | 9 11 |
| 23 3 | .. | .. | .. | 5 | 8 | 17 | 21 | 10 | 8 | 15 | 4 | 2,716 6 | 32 4 |
| 6 10 | .. | .. | .. | 50 | 4 | 1 | .. | 1 | .. | .. | 8 | 458 0 | 8 2 |
| 19 11 | [1,068] 5,821 0 | 5 5 | 3 5 | 251 | 239 | 427 | 390 | 267 | 182 | 131 | 67 | 43,501 1 | 23 1 |

TABLE V.—*Classification of the Heads of Families included under the term "Miscellaneous" in the preceding Table, according to their Occupations.*

| Families. | | Families. | |
|---|---|---|---|
| Agents | 3 | Brought forward | 158 |
| Actor | 1 | Draper | 1 |
| Accountant | 1 | Dairyman | 1 |
| Artists | 2 | Engravers | 2 |
| Box-makers | 2 | Excisemen | 2 |
| Basket and Brush-makers | 6 | Excise-officer | 1 |
| Boiler-makers | 4 | Fishmongers | 6 |
| Bedstead-makers | 3 | Foremen | 4 |
| Block and Last-makers | 3 | Firemen | 3 |
| Brass-workers | 2 | Furriers | 2 |
| Brass-polisher | 1 | French-polishers | 2 |
| Brass-founder | 1 | Founder | 1 |
| Brewers | 4 | Gas-workers | 2 |
| Bell-founder | 1 | Grocers | 6 |
| Boat-builder | 1 | General-dealers | 5 |
| Bookbinders | 3 | Gas-stoker | 1 |
| Builder | 1 | Glass-cutters | 2 |
| Broker | 1 | Gate-keeper | 1 |
| Brass-finisher | 1 | Ginger-beer-seller | 1 |
| Bell-hanger | 1 | Hatters | 7 |
| Boot-blocker | 1 | Hair-dressers | 2 |
| Bookseller | 1 | Hawkers | 5 |
| Chimney-sweepers | 2 | House of ill-fame | 1 |
| Coal-whippers or porters | 9 | In East India-house | 1 |
| Coachmen | 2 | In Docks | 2 |
| Cabmen | 2 | In Post-office | 4 |
| Coppersmiths | 2 | In Tower | 1 |
| Coachmakers | 3 | Jewellers | 4 |
| Costermongers | 13 | Japanners | 2 |
| Cabinet-makers | 10 | Ironmonger | 1 |
| Cellarmen | 6 | Interpreter | 1 |
| Corn-porters | 2 | Lamplighter | 1 |
| Cork-cutters | 12 | Lucifer-maker | 1 |
| Custom-house-officers | 7 | Milkmen | 6 |
| Coach-trimmer | 1 | Mathematical-instrument-makers | 4 |
| Confectioners | 5 | Masons | 3 |
| Comb-makers | 2 | Maltster | 1 |
| Cap-maker | 1 | Millwright | 1 |
| Coach-plater | 1 | Millman | 1 |
| Carvers and gilders | 7 | Messengers | 4 |
| Case-maker | 1 | Marine-store | 1 |
| Chair-maker | 1 | Oilman | 1 |
| Corn-dealers | 3 | Ostlers | 5 |
| Chemists | 2 | Old-clothesman | 1 |
| Coffee-roasters | 2 | Omnibus-driver | 1 |
| Chair-bottomer | 1 | Opticians | 2 |
| Chandler's-shop | 1 | Pot-maker | 1 |
| Colour-maker | 1 | Plumbers | 4 |
| Cane-worker | 1 | Public-singer | 1 |
| Captains | 3 | Pencil-maker | 1 |
| Draymen | 4 | Plasterers | 6 |
| Dyers | 3 | Pewterer | 1 |
| Drover | 1 | Poulterers | 2 |
| Dock-constable | 1 | Paper-maker | 1 |
| Dealers | 2 | Polisher | 1 |
| Carried forward | 158 | Carried forward | 283 |

TABLE V.—*Continued.*

| Families. | | Families. | |
|---|---|---|---|
| Brought forward ..............283 | | Brought forward ..............331 | |
| Postman | 1 | Seller of trimming | 1 |
| Pensioners | 8 | Ship storesman | 1 |
| Picture-frame-makers | 2 | Servant | 1 |
| Paper-hanger | 1 | Surveyor | 1 |
| Paviour | 1 | Turners | 4 |
| Publican | 1 | Toy-makers | 2 |
| Pew-opener | 1 | Travellers | 2 |
| Packers | 2 | Tanner | 1 |
| Riggers | 6 | Trimmer | 1 |
| Rope-maker | 1 | Timber-seller | 1 |
| Rule-maker | 1 | Tide-waiter | 1 |
| Satin-dresser | 1 | Vat-makers | 2 |
| Ship-carpenter | 1 | Weavers | 2 |
| Sawyers | 10 | Watchmen | 6 |
| Soldiers | 2 | Watchmakers | 5 |
| Soap-makers | 2 | Warehousemen | 5 |
| Scale-maker | 1 | Wire-workers | 2 |
| Sail-makers | 4 | Waiter | 1 |
| Spiceman | 1 | Trades not given | 26 |
| Salesman | 1 | | |
| | | Total of Families ........ 396 | |
| Carried forward .............. 331 | | | |

From the following (Table VI.), which shows the occupations, earnings, and ages of the single men, widows with incumbrance, and single women, it will be seen that the former are chiefly very young men, especially those in the trades, earning good wages; while in the two latter classes we find much greater diversity of age, with very limited means, derived from the narrow range of employments available for female hands, especially if unaccompanied by a vigorous frame and habits of bodily exertion. The extent of such employments, as compared with the number of struggling competitors for them, being always limited, their remuneration is always very low. The relative superiority of men's earnings over those of the women, and even over those of the women and children combined, in the metro-polis, as compared with most of the manufacturing districts, is thus very conspicuously shown. The "distressed needlewomen," are un-doubtedly a numerous class, in most parts, and especially in this part of the metropolis; unprotected women, in this district alone, being no fewer than 229, while the number of unmarried men is only 125. A glance at the tables which show their scanty earnings, and the numerous families which are dependent upon two-thirds of them, will convey a sufficient idea of the position of moral as well as pecuniary difficulty in which they are placed. Some of the women included in this class are, indeed, widowed only by the abandonment of their husbands. All, however, are living unprotected, with families dependent upon them.

All those specified as unfortunate females appear, with only a few exceptions, to be persons of respectable outward manners and conduct, for the houses of prostitution were expressly excepted from inquiry, beyond a rough enumeration of them and of their inmates, since they form a distinct feature in society, which it was not our present purpose to investigate. Unhappily there are many houses of this description within the topographical limits of the present inquiry, frequented chiefly by sailors, low mechanics, and labourers, at least fifty coming within the observation of your Committee's agents.

TABLE VI.

*Occupations of Single Men, Single Women, and Widows with Incumbrance, showing the Number of Families and Persons to each Trade, with their Ages and Earnings.*

SINGLE MEN.

| | Families. | No. | Total Ages. | Average Age. | Total Earnings. | | | Average Earnings. | |
|---|---|---|---|---|---|---|---|---|---|
| | | | | | £ | *s.* | | *s.* | *d.* |
| | | | [16] | | [18] | | | | |
| Labourers | 17 | 22 | 662 | 41·4 | 263 | 0 | | 14 | 7 |
| | | | [1] | | [2] | | | | |
| Basket-makers | 2 | 3 | 22 | 22·0 | 39 | 0 | | 19 | 6 |
| | | | [2] | | [2] | | | | |
| Seaman | 1 | 1 | 55 | 27·5 | 25 | 0 | | 12 | 6 |
| | | | | | [1] | | | | |
| Porter | 1 | 1 | .... | .... | 18 | 0 | | 18 | 0 |
| | | | [4] | | [11] | | | | |
| Coopers | 6 | 12 | 109 | 27·2 | 269 | 0 | | 24 | 6 |
| | | | [5] | | [7] | | | | |
| Tailors | 3 | 6 | 174 | 34·8 | 156 | 0 | | 22 | 3 |
| | | | [9] | | [20] | | | | |
| Gunsmiths | 9 | 21 | 215 | 23·9 | 756 | 0 | | 37 | 10 |
| | | | [4] | | [4] | | | | |
| Cigar-makers | 3 | 3 | 111 | 27·7 | 125 | 0 | | 31 | 3 |
| | | | | | [2] | | | | |
| French-polishers | 2 | 2 | .... | .... | 55 | 0 | | 27 | 6 |
| | | | [12] | | [12] | | | | |
| Shoemakers | 10 | 13 | 336 | 28·0 | 242 | 0 | | 20 | 2 |
| | | | [3] | | [3] | | | | |
| Carmen | 2 | 2 | 69 | 23·0 | 54 | 0 | | 18 | 0 |
| | | | [1] | | [1] | | | | |
| Ditto (Jobbing) | 1 | 1 | 40 | 40·0 | 5 | 0 | | 5 | 0 |
| | | | [1] | | [1] | | | | |
| Painter | 1 | 1 | 30 | 30·0 | 30 | 0 | | 30 | 0 |
| | | | [1] | | [1] | | | | |
| Cobler | 1 | 1 | 65 | 65·0 | 9 | 0 | | 9 | 0 |
| | | | | | [2] | | | | |
| Printers | 2 | 3 | .... | .... | 48 | 0 | | 24 | 0 |
| | | | [1] | | [2] | | | | |
| Boiler-makers | 2 | 2 | 19 | 19·0 | 49 | 0 | | 24 | 6 |
| | | | | | [1] | | | | |
| Butcher | 1 | 1 | .... | ·· | 15 | 0 | | 15 | 0 |
| | | | [3] | | [4] | | | | |
| Carpenters | 3 | 3 | 130 | 43·3 | 95 | 0 | | 23 | 9 |
| | | | [63] | | [94] | | | | |
| Carried forward | 67 | 98 | 2,037 | .... | 2,253 | 0 | | .... | |

TABLE VI.—*Continued.*

SINGLE MEN.

| | Families. | No. | Total Ages. | Average Age. | Total Earnings. | Average Earnings. |
|---|---|---|---|---|---|---|
| | | | | | £   s. | s.   d. |
| Brought forward ........ | 67 | 98 | [63] 2,037 | .... | [94] 2,253   0 | .... |
| Pensioners (one works as a Labourer) ...................... | 3 | 4 | [2] 135 | 67·5 | [1] 6   0 | 6   0 |
| Dyer ............................... | 1 | 1 | [1] 30 | 30·0 | [1] 25   0 | 25   0 |
| Chair-makers ...................... | 2 | 2 | [2] 53 | 26·5 | [2] 42   0 | 21   0 |
| Bookbinder ......................... | .... | 1 | [1] 19 | 19·0 | [1] 12   0 | 12   0 |
| Ironmonger.......................... | .... | 1 | [1] 19 | 19·0 | [1] 12   0 | 12   0 |
| Sugar-bakers ...................... | 2 | 3 | [3] 67 | 22·3 | [3] 68   0 | 22   8 |
| Mathematical-instrument-maker ...................... | 1 | 1 | [1] 22 | 22·0 | [1] 30   0 | 30   0 |
| Smith ............................... | 1 | 1 | [1] 28 | 28·0 | [1] 24   0 | 24   0 |
| Costermonger ...................... | 1 | 3 | [3] 68 | 22·7 | [3] 30   0 | 10   0 |
| Hair-dresser ...................... | 1 | 1 | [1] 25 | 25·0 | [1] 25   0 | 25   0 |
| Map-mounter ...................... | 1 | 1 | [1] 40 | 40·0 | [1] 25   0 | 25   0 |
| Hatter ............................. | 1 | 1 | [1] 22 | 22·0 | [1] 25   0 | 25   0 |
| Cap-maker ...................... | 1 | 1 | [1] 23 | 23·0 | [1] 21   0 | 21   0 |
| Glass-cutter....................... | 1 | 1 | [1] 21 | 21·0 | [1] 18   0 | 18   0 |
| Clerk ............................... | 1 | 1 | [1] 36 | 36·0 | [1] 31   6 | 31   6 |
| Engineer ........................... | 1 | 1 | [1] 20 | 20·0 | [1] 30   0 | 30   0 |
| Ragman ........................... | 1 | 1 | .... | .... | [1] 6   0 | 6   0 |
| Broker.............................. | 1 | 1 | .... | .... | [1] 33   0 | 33   0 |
| Trade unknown ................... | 1 | 1 | .... | .... | .... | .... |
| Total........ | 88 | 125 | [85] 2,665 | 31·3 | [117] 2,716   6 | 23   3 |

TABLE VI.—*Continued.*

SINGLE WOMEN AND WIDOWS.

| | Families. | No. | Total Ages. | Average Age. | Total Earnings. | Average Earnings. |
|---|---|---|---|---|---|---|
| | | | | | *s. d.* | *s. d.* |
| | | | | | [1] | |
| Unfortunate females | 3 | 5 | .... | .... | 10  0 | 10  0 |
| | | | [1] | | [1] | |
| Straw-bonnet-maker | 1 | 1 | 45 | 45·0 | 15  0 | 15  0 |
| | | | [1] | | [2] | |
| Schoolmistresses | 2 | 3 | 68 | 68·0 | 11  0 | 5  6 |
| | | | [3] | | [3] | |
| Do., working also with the needle | 1 | 3 | 105 | 35·0 | 20  0 | 6  8 |
| | | | [33] | | [41] | |
| Needlewomen | 33 | 41 | 1,282 | 38·8 | 238  0 | 5  9 |
| | | | [1] | | [1] | |
| Tailoress | 1 | 1 | 30 | 30·0 | 6  0 | 6  0 |
| | | | [5] | | [5] | |
| Charwomen | 4 | 4 | 287 | 57·4 | 29  0 | 5  9 |
| | | | [1] | | [1] | |
| Laundress | 1 | 1 | 65 | 65·0 | 8  0 | 8  0 |
| | | | [1] | | [1] | |
| Gun-polisher | 1 | 1 | 18 | 18·0 | 10  0 | 10  0 |
| | | | [2] | | [2] | |
| Dress-makers | 2 | 2 | 62 | 31·0 | 25  0 | 12  6 |
| | | | [1] | | [1] | |
| Nurse | 1 | 1 | 52 | 52·0 | 10  0 | 10  0 |
| | | | [1] | | [1] | |
| Stay-maker | 1 | 1 | 36 | 36·0 | 9  0 | 9  0 |
| | | | [2] | | [2] | |
| Mangle-keepers | 2 | 2 | 85 | 42·5 | 17  0 | 8  6 |
| | | | [1] | | [1] | |
| General shop | 1 | 1 | 39 | 19·5 | 10  0 | 10  0 |
| | | | [1] | | [1] | |
| Shoebinder | 1 | 1 | 42 | 21·0 | 5  0 | 5  0 |
| | | | | | [1] | |
| Shirt-maker | 1 | 1 | .... | .... | 15  0 | 15  0 |
| Slop workers | 1 | 2 | .... | .... | .... | .... |
| | | | [1] | | [1] | |
| Yeast-maker | 1 | 1 | 65 | 65·0 | 10  0 | 10  0 |
| Coal-wharf-keeper | 1 | 1 | .... | .... | .... | .... |
| | | | [1] | | [1] | |
| Waistcoat-maker | 1 | 1 | 25 | 25·0 | 10  0 | 10  0 |
| | | | [2] | | | |
| Supported by friends | 3 | 3 | 143 | 71·5 | .... | .... |
| | | | [1] | | | |
| Uncertain | 1 | 1 | 74 | 74·0 | .... | .... |
| | | | [59] | | [67] | |
| Total | 64 | 78 | 2,523 | 42·8 | 458  0 | 6  10 |

TABLE VI.—*Continued.*

WIDOWS WITH INCUMBRANCE.

| | Families. | No. | Total Ages. | Average Age. | Total Earnings. | | Average Earnings. | |
|---|---|---|---|---|---|---|---|---|
| | | | | | *s.* | *d.* | *s.* | *d.* |
| Greengrocer.................... | 1 | 2 | [1] 37 | 37·0 | .... | | .... | |
| Fishmonger.................... | 1 | 5 | [1] 57 | 57·0 | .... | | .... | |
| Schoolmistresses.................. | 3 | 7 | [2] 72 | 36·0 | [2] 13 | 0 | 6 | 6 |
| Washerwomen..................... | 11 | 41 | [11] 551 | 50·1 | [11] 110 | 6 | 10 | 6 |
| Needlewomen ........................ | 54 | 179 | [54] 2,418 | 44·8 | [54] 524 | 0 | 9 | 8 |
| Tailoresses ...................... | 3 | 9 | [2] 100 | 50·0 | [3] 23 | 0 | 7 | 8 |
| Charwomen ...................... | 20 | 77 | [20] 926 | 46·3 | [20] 157 | 3 | 7 | 10 |
| Laundresses........................... | 13 | 50 | [13] 665 | 51·1 | [12] 172 | 0 | 14 | 4 |
| Silk-winder .................... | 1 | 6 | [1] 49 | 49·0 | [1] 11 | 0 | 11 | 0 |
| Dress-makers ...................... | 2 | 8 | [1] 43 | 43·0 | [2] 34 | 0 | 17 | 0 |
| Nurses............................ | 2 | 5 | [2] 96 | 48·0 | [2] 21 | 0 | 10 | 6 |
| Mattress-maker .................. | 1 | 5 | [1] 36 | 36·0 | [1] 10 | 0 | 10 | 0 |
| Mangle-keepers .................. | 6 | 19 | [5] 245 | 49·0 | [6] 49 | 0 | 8 | 2 |
| Shopkeepers ...................... | 6 | 16 | [6] 251 | 41·8 | [5] 47 | 0 | 9 | 5 |
| Chandler's shop .................. | 1 | 2 | [1] 61 | 61·0 | .... | | .... | |
| Shirt-makers ...................... | 3 | 8 | [3] 108 | 36·0 | [3] 14 | 0 | 4 | 8 |
| Slop-workers ...................... | 4 | 15 | [4] 135 | 33·7 | [4] 12 | 6 | 3 | 2 |
| Coffee shop .......................... | 1 | 4 | [1] 30 | 30·0 | [1] 20 | 0 | 20 | 0 |
| Market servants .................. | 1 | 2 | [1] 50 | 50·0 | [1] 5 | 0 | 5 | 0 |
| Waistcoat-makers .............. | 3 | 8 | [3] 103 | 34·3 | [3] 32 | 0 | 16 | 0 |
| Supported by friends or children ................} | 13 | 47 | [12] 602 | 50·1 | [12] 168 | 6 | 14 | 0 |
| Pew-opener ...................... | 1 | 2 | [1] 60 | 60·0 | .... | | .... | |
| **Total** .................... | 151 | 517 | [146] 6,695 | 45·9 | [143] 1,423 | 9 | 9 | 11 |

**TABLE VII.—*Rents of Dwellings.***

*Columns 5–22 below (the rent bands, "Paying no Rent…" and "Not ascertained") fall under the heading* **Weekly Rents paid by Families.**

| No. | Trades | Number of Families | Average Earnings of each Family (s. d.) | 1s. to 1s. 6d. | 1s. 6d. to 2s. | 2s. to 2s. 6d. | 2s. 6d. to 3s. | 3s. to 3s. 6d. | 3s. 6d. to 4s. | 4s. to 4s. 6d. | 4s. 6d. to 5s. | 5s. to 5s. 6d. | 5s. 6d. to 6s. | 6s. to 6s. 6d. | 6s. 6d. to 7s. | 7s. to 7s. 6d. | 7s. 6d. to 8s. | 8s. to 10s. | 10s. to 20s. | Paying no Rent, whether as Proprietors or otherwise | Not ascertained | Total Rents Weekly | Average Rents per Week (s. d.) |
|---|---|---|---|---|---|---|---|---|---|---|---|---|---|---|---|---|---|---|---|---|---|---|---|
| 27 | Labourers | 363 | 19 1 | 34 | 73 | 60 | 42 | 29 | 88 | 22 | 29 | 8 | 0 | 4 | 8 | | 3 | 2 | | 4 | 1 | 1160 11 [388] | 3 3 |
| 25 | Gun-smiths* | 87 | 45 3 | | 4 | 9 | 8 | 14 | 19 | 6 | 10 | 6 | 2 | 2 | 1 | 4 | | | | | 2 | 349 5 [85] | 4 1 |
| 14 | Gun-makers* | 26 | 26 10 | | 1 | 7 | 1 | 3 | 1 | 2 | 2 | 4 | 1 | 1 | 1 | 1 | 1 | | | | | 111 8 [96] | 4 3 |
| 26 | Shoemakers | 101 | 20 8 | 6 | 11 | 19 | 12 | 14 | 10 | 10 | 8 | 2 | 1 | 3 | 2 | 1 | 1 | | | | 1 | 360 5 [100] | 3 6 |
| 17 | Bricklayers | 31 | 24 10 | 3 | 3 | 4 | 3 | 4 | 4 | 1 | 5 | | | | 3 | | 1 | | | | | 117 9 [31] | 3 9 |
| 21 | Coopers | 64 | 27 11 | 2 | 4 | 13 | 10 | 5 | 8 | 8 | 9 | 4 | 2 | 1 | 1 | | | | | 2 | | 228 0 [69] | 3 8 |
| 10 | Engineers | 20 | 32 5 | 1 | 1 | 8 | 4 | 1 | 5 | 1 | 1 | | | | | | | 1 | | 2 | | 64 0 [18] | 3 7 |
| 0 | Umbrella-makers | 11 | 29 1 | | 1 | | 1 | 2 | 1 | 2 | 2 | | | | | | 2 | | | | | 61 0 [11] | 4 8 |
| 18 | Porters | 34 | 20 8 | 3 | 3 | 6 | 4 | 6 | 6 | 1 | 4 | | 3 | | | | | 1 | | | | 118 6 [34] | 3 6 |
| 20 | Carmen | 50 | 23 7 | 2 | 5 | 9 | 6 | 9 | 4 | 5 | 4 | | 1 | 2 | | | 2 | | | | | 186 1 [50] | 3 2 |
| 7 | Butchers | 13 | 22 8 | | 2 | 1 | | 8 | 2 | 2 | 2 | 1 | | | | | | 1 | | | | 49 0 [13] | 3 9 |
| 12 | Sugar bakers | 24 | 23 7 | | 1 | 4 | 3 | 2 | 5 | 3 | 3 | | | 1 | 1 | 1 | | | | | | 96 6 [24] | 4 0 |
| 13 | Bakers | 26 | 19 11 | 1 | 6 | 3 | 2 | 2 | 5 | | 1 | | | 2 | 1 | | 1 | 1 | | | 1 | 95 2 [28] | 3 10 |
| 16 | Painters | 28 | 23 3 | 3 | 3 | 7 | 1 | 4 | 3 | | 1 | | | 2 | 2 | 1 | | | | 1 | | 94 6 [201] | 3 6 |

| | | | | | | | | | | | | | | | | | | | | | |
|---|---|---|---|---|---|---|---|---|---|---|---|---|---|---|---|---|---|---|---|---|---|
| 10 | Smiths | 31 | 27 | 2 | 4 | 15 | 1 | 10 | 6 | 5 | 7 | 4 | 2 | 1 | 2 | 2 | 1 | 2 | : | : | [67] 225 |
| 22 | Sailors | 67 | 15 | 4 | 9 | 11 | 11 | 6 | 6 | 7 | 7 | 9 | 10 | 1 | 1 | 1 | : | 3 | : | 1 | [71] 263 |
| 23 | Tailors | 72 | 24 | 6 | 2 | : | 4 | 5 | 5 | 3 | 3 | 4 | 2 | 4 | : | : | : | : | : | : | [39] 109 |
| 16 | Cigar-makers | 29 | 33 | 11 | 1 | 4 | 3 | 7 | 7 | 11 | 11 | 7 | 12 | 3 | 5 | : | : | 3 | : | 1 | [75] 310 |
| 24 | Carpenters | 76 | 27 | 0 | : | 1 | 1 | 8 | 1 | 1 | 1 | : | : | 3 | : | : | : | : | : | : | [7] 25 |
| 1 | Gun-stock-makers* | 7 | 38 | 5 | : | : | 2 | 3 | : | 3 | 1 | 1 | : | : | 1 | : | : | : | : | : | [10] 43 |
| 4 | Tin-workers | 10 | 29 | 9 | : | : | 1 | 2 | 3 | 3 | 1 | : | : | 1 | : | 2 | : | : | : | : | [8] 27 |
| 2 | Wheelwrights | 8 | 28 | 2 | : | : | 2 | 1 | 2 | 2 | 1 | : | 1 | 1 | : | : | : | : | : | : | [11] 44 |
| 5 | Shopmen | 11 | 29 | 11 | : | 1 | 4 | 5 | 5 | 1 | : | 1 | 2 | : | 1 | 2 | 1 | 1 | : | : | [21] 84 |
| 11 | Policemen | 21 | 21 | 10 | : | 1 | 2 | 4 | : | : | 1 | : | : | : | : | : | 1 | : | : | : | [9] 34 |
| 3 | Printers | 9 | 26 | 0 | : | : | 4 | 4 | : | : | : | : | : | 2 | 1 | 1 | : | : | : | : | [13] 71 |
| 8 | Clerks | 13 | 30 | 5 | : | 1 | 1 | 1 | : | 1 | 1 | 2 | : | : | 5 | 1 | 1 | : | 5 | : | [380] 71 |
| 28 | Miscellaneous | 396 | 23 | 9 | 23 | 35 | 55 | 37 | 36 | 35 | 38 | 31 | 37 | 26 | 9 | 14 | 19 | 12 | 3 | 1 | 1,632 |
| | Total Families | 1,051 | 24 | 5 | 94 | 191 | 252 | 178 | 191 | 191 | 117 | 149 | 69 | 37 | 44 | 47 | 16 | 33 | 9 | 1 | [1,619] 6,030 |
| | Widows with Incumbrance | 151 | 9 | 11 | 37 | 30 | 15 | 13 | 9 | 11 | 2 | 9 | 6 | : | 4 | 7 | 1 | 3 | 1 | : | [148] 461 |
| | Single Men of Miscellaneous Trades | 88 | 32 | 4 | 7 | 17 | 24 | 8 | : | 6 | : | 3 | : | : | 1 | : | : | 1 | : | : | [66] 188 |
| | Single Women, and Widows without Incumbrance, and of Miscellaneous Occupations | 64 | 8 | 2 | 25 | 15 | 4 | 5 | 3 | 1 | : | : | : | 1 | : | : | : | 2 | : | : | [56] 125 |
| | Total Families | 1,054 | 23 | 1 | 163 | 253 | 295 | 204 | 203 | 209 | 119 | 161 | 75 | 38 | 49 | 54 | 18 | 39 | 10 | 1 | [1,891] 6,805 |

\* The Gunsmith is the maker of the barrel and other metal work; the Gun-stock-maker is the finisher of the wood work out of the rough stocks; and the Gun-maker is the man who fits the different parts, and finishes the article.

The wages are seen to vary (Table VI.), as usual, with the degree of skill required in the several trades; the lowest being those of the sailors, 11s. 10d. per week besides rations, and of the mere labourers, 15s. 7d. per week, on the average; the highest, those of the gunsmiths, 41s. 9d. per week; the general average being 20s. 2d. per week. Including the earnings of all the family, the incomes of the sailors average 15s. 4d. per week, of the labourers 19s. 1d., and of all the rest, various sums between 20s. and 40s., with the exception of the gunsmiths, whose total emoluments, per family, average 45s. 3d. per week. Necessity, on the one hand, in the poorer trades, and opportunity, on the other, in some of the better paid, cause the amount of subordinate earnings to equalize each other in the families of some of the men who earn, themselves, a very unequal amount of wages; while those unmoved by either peculiar necessity or peculiar opportunity, show least of pecuniary advantages derived from the labour of women and children. In a few cases, the earnings of a grown-up son give an excess which disturbs the average from its usual value as an index to the earnings of women and children, and it must carefully be borne in mind that there may be the most industry, and that of the most appropriate kind, in those families whose subordinate members add little or nothing to their pecuniary resources; for the labours and cares of the little household, in homes which can afford the employment of only casual if any domestic service, are quite sufficient to occupy all available time and ability in their proper discharge. In the case of the tailors, the proportion of the wife's earnings is greater than would appear from the table, because the females assist the men in the work, for which payment is entered under the head of the husband's wages; but, in all other cases, the additional sums are drawn from the sources indicated in the case of the unprotected women.

The preceding table (VII.) shows, in comparison with the average earnings of the families in each trade, their weekly payments for rent, carefully classified; the next following shows the number of rooms occupied by the families, and the number of persons to a room; while a third states the number of beds possessed by each, and the number of cases where there are one, two, three, or any greater number of persons to a bed. The only remarkable result is the moderate degree of crowding which prevails throughout the population. It is greatest, of course, in the families having only one room, with several little children, but it steadily decreases as each class increases in the number of its rooms and its beds, showing that this is a population entirely above the wretched system of sub-letting corners of the same room, which occasions such an accumulation of wretchedness, barbarism, and disease, in the few localities to which the rudest and most unsettled of the population resort. Want of space and ventilation in the rooms is, however, observed generally, and everyone can conceive how unfavourable it is to domestic quiet to have only one room for every purpose of repose and the *ménage*. Indeed, the possession of only one room, indicates a depression of habits and of health, which, if every grosser feature of misery were removed, would well deserve the solicitude of the philanthropist; the provision of a second room in town-life being as marked a step as the advancement from a hovel to a proper cottage in the country.

TABLE VIII.—*Number of Rooms occupied by each Family.*

| Trades | Number of Families | Average Earnings of Families (s. d.) | One Room — No. of Families | One Room — Population | One Room — No. of Persons to a Room | Two Rooms — No. of Families | Two Rooms — Population | Two Rooms — No. of Persons to a Room | Three Rooms — No. of Families | Three Rooms — Population | Three Rooms — No. of Persons to a Room | Four Rooms — No. of Families | Four Rooms — Population | Four Rooms — No. of Persons to a Room | Five Rooms — No. of Families | Five Rooms — Population | Five Rooms — No. of Persons to a Room | Six Rooms — No. of Families | Six Rooms — Population | Six Rooms — No. of Persons to a Room | Not Ascertained — No. of Families | Not Ascertained — Population | Total Given — No. of Families | Total Given — Population | Persons to a Room |
|---|---|---|---|---|---|---|---|---|---|---|---|---|---|---|---|---|---|---|---|---|---|---|---|---|---|
| Labourers | 363 | 19 1 | 169 | 542 | 3·2 | 103 | 479 | 2·3 | 72 | 371 | 1·7 | 17 | 82 | 1·3 | | | | 2 | 4 | 3 | | | 363 | 1,478 | 2·2 |
| Gunsmiths | 87 | 45 3 | 16 | 50 | 3·1 | 31 | 139 | 2·2 | 27 | 126 | 1·5 | 12 | 62 | 1·2 | | | | | | | | | 87 | 384 | 1·8 |
| Gunmakers | 26 | 26 10 | 16 | 38 | 3·1 | 4 | 18 | 2·2 | 8 | 37 | 1·5 | 1 | 6 | 1·5 | | | | | 8 | 8 | | | 26 | 106 | 2·0 |
| Shoemakers | 101 | 20 8 | 37 | 123 | 3·3 | 35 | 153 | 2·0 | 20 | 88 | 1·4 | 5 | 24 | 1·2 | 1 | 5 | 1·0 | | | | | | 101 | 393 | 2·0 |
| Bricklayers | 64 | 24 11 | 15 | 34 | 2·9 | 10 | 34 | 1·7 | 22 | 51 | 1·6 | 4 | 10 | 1·0 | | | | | | | | | 64 | 134 | 2·1 |
| Coopers | 20 | 27 1 | 15 | 44 | 2·9 | 23 | 92 | 2·0 | 8 | 38 | 1·5 | 4 | 17 | 1·3 | 1 | 6 | 1·2 | | 8 | | | | 64 | 264 | 1·8 |
| Engineers | 11 | 32 5 | 8 | 29 | 3·6 | 4 | 15 | 1·9 | 5 | 29 | 1·0 | 1 | 4 | | | | | | | | | | 20 | 82 | 1·9 |
| Umbrella-makers | 6 | 29 8 | | | | 3 | 14 | 2·0 | 11 | 52 | 1·8 | 6 | 36 | 1·0 | | 2 | | 1 | 4 | | | | 11 | 59 | 1·7 |
| Porters | 18 | 20 7 | 1 | 2 | 2·0 | 9 | 54 | 3·0 | 11 | 62 | 1·8 | 1 | 9 | 1·5 | | | | | | | | | 34 | 164 | 2·4 |
| Carmen | 50 | 23 8 | 13 | 54 | 4·1 | 14 | 64 | 2·3 | 23 | 113 | 1·8 | 6 | 36 | 2·2 | | 8 | | | | | | | 50 | 219 | 2·1 |
| Butchers | 7 | 22 7 | 19 | 57 | 3·0 | 7 | 28 | 2·0 | 13 | 73 | 1·8 | 1 | 6 | 1·5 | 1 | 13 | | 1 | 6 | | | | 13 | 60 | 1·7 |
| Sugar-bakers | 13 | 23 8 | | 10 | 3·3 | 7 | 29 | 2·3 | 2 | 13 | 1·3 | | 8 | | | | | | | | | | 21 | 114 | 1·9 |
| Bakers | 24 | 19 11 | 2 | 5 | 3·3 | 12 | 57 | 2·7 | 9 | 72 | 2·2 | | | | | | | | 2 | | | | 24 | 102 | 2·6 |
| Painters | 26 | 23 11 | 3 | 25 | 2·7 | 14 | 77 | 2·7 | 5 | 20 | 2·0 | 7 | 33 | 1·1 | | 8 | 1·6 | | | | | | 26 | 128 | 2·1 |
| Watermen | 9 | 26 5 | 2 | 24 | 2·8 | 14 | 74 | 1·7 | 8 | 47 | 1·4 | 3 | 19 | 1·3 | | 13 | | | | | | | 28 | 85 | 2·0 |
| Smiths | 34 | 34 10 | 9 | 36 | 3·0 | 14 | 53 | 1·8 | 5 | 34 | 1·3 | | 70 | 1·5 | 1 | 10 | | | | | | | 20 | 135 | 1·9 |
| Tailors | 67 | 15 5 | 18 | 93 | 3·1 | 27 | 97 | 1·8 | 9 | 40 | 1·5 | 7 | 16 | | 1 | | | | | | | | 34 | 243 | 1·9 |
| Cigar-makers | 73 | 24 9 | 28 | 66 | 2·5 | 11 | 128 | 2·9 | 9 | 111 | | 13 | 16 | | | | | | | | | | 67 | 344 | 1·6 |
| Carpenters | 29 | 27 9 | 21 | 65 | 3·1 | 30 | 36 | 2·3 | 20 | 46 | 1·6 | 3 | 8 | 1·3 | | | | | | | | | 72 | 115 | 1·8 |
| Gun-stock-maker | 76 | 33 9 | 6 | 15 | 2·5 | 4 | 19 | 3·1 | 9 | 104 | 1·3 | 2 | 11 | 2·0 | | | | | | | | | 76 | 351 | 2·4 |
| Tin-workers | 7 | 29 2 | 13 | 39 | 4·0 | 3 | 19 | 1·8 | 9 | 16 | 1·5 | 1 | 10 | 2·0 | | | | | | | | | 7 | 37 | 1·9 |
| Wheelwrights | 10 | 28 4 | 2 | 8 | 4·0 | 8 | 16 | 1·8 | 19 | 8 | 1·8 | 2 | 5 | 1·3 | | | | | 2 | | | | 10 | 59 | 1·7 |
| Shopmen | 8 | 28 6 | 2 | 9 | 4·0 | 9 | 19 | 2·3 | 2 | 14 | 1·3 | 1 | 11 | | | | | | | 1·0 | | | 8 | 82 | 2·1 |
| Policemen | 11 | 26 11 | 4 | 11 | 2·7 | 6 | 16 | 3·1 | 4 | 9 | 1·5 | 2 | | | | | | | | | | | 11 | 41 | 2·3 |
| Printers | 21 | 26 5 | 5 | 6 | 3·0 | 6 | 11 | 1·8 | 8 | 11 | 1·6 | 1 | | | | | | | 3 | | | | 21 | 86 | 1·5 |
| Clerks | 9 | 26 9 | 1 | 30 | 6·0 | 2 | 57 | 2·2 | 3 | 45 | 1·5 | 2 | 40 | 1·7 | | | 1·0 | | 3 | | | | 9 | 44 | 1·8 |
| Miscellaneous | 13 | 23 9 | 1 | 6 | 3·2 | 4 | 31 | 2·1 | 5 | 104 | 1·5 | | 246 | 1·4 | | 28 | | | 44 | | | 25 | 13 | 69 | |
| | 396 | | 119 | 887 | | 104 | 437 | | 107 | 495 | | 44 | | | 6 | | | 9 | | | 7 | | 349 | 1,637 | 2·0 |
| **Total Families** | 1,651 | 24 5 | 551 | 1,765 | 3·2 | 526 | 2,316 | 2·2 | 404 | 2,014 | 1·7 | 130 | 708 | 1·4 | 16 | 86 | 1·1 | 17 | 76 | | | 25 | 1,644 | 6,965 | 2·0 |
| Widows with incumbrance | 151 | 9 11 | 85 | 260 | 3·1 | 36 | 138 | 1·9 | 19 | 76 | 1·3 | 7 | 32 | 1·1 | 4 | 11 | ·5 | | | | 7 | | 151 | 517 | 1·9 |
| Total Families, exclusive of single Men and Women lodgers | 1,802 | 23 1 | 636 | 2,025 | 3·2 | 562 | 2,454 | 2·2 | 423 | 2,090 | 1·7 | 137 | 740 | 1·4 | 20 | 97 | | 17 | 76 | | 7 | 25 | 1,795 | 7,482 | 2·0 |

## TABLE IX.—Number of Beds to a Family.

| | Trades | Number of Families | Average Earnings of Families (s. d.) | One Bed — No. of Families | One Bed — Population | One Bed — No. of Persons to a Bed | Two Beds — No. of Families | Two Beds — Population | Two Beds — No. of Persons to a Bed | Three Beds — No. of Families | Three Beds — Population | Three Beds — No. of Persons to a Bed | Four Beds — No. of Families | Four Beds — Population | Four Beds — No. of Persons to a Bed | Five Beds — No. of Families | Five Beds — Population | Five Beds — No. of Persons to a Bed | Not ascertained — No. of Families | Not ascertained — Population | Total given — No. of Families | Total given — Population | Persons to a Bed |
|---|---|---|---|---|---|---|---|---|---|---|---|---|---|---|---|---|---|---|---|---|---|---|---|
| 97 | Labourers | 363 | 19 1 | 143 | 387 | 2·7 | 160 | 779 | 2·4 | 14 | 90 | 2·1 | | | | | | | 46 | 222 | 317 | 1,256 | 2·5 |
| 25 | Gunsmiths | 87 | 46 3 | 14 | 34 | 2·4 | 38 | 168 | 2·1 | 8 | 50 | 2·1 | | | | | | | 27 | 137 | 60 | 247 | 2·1 |
| 14 | Gunmakers | 26 | 26 10 | 15 | 47 | 3·1 | 10 | 52 | 2·6 | 1 | 7 | 1·8 | | | | | | | | | 26 | 106 | 2·8 |
| 26 | Shoemakers | 101 | 20 8 | 45 | 119 | 2·6 | 39 | 185 | 2·3 | 7 | 39 | 2·5 | | | | | | | 10 | 50 | 91 | 343 | 2·5 |
| 17 | Bricklayers | 31 | 24 10 | 12 | 30 | 2·5 | 12 | 58 | 2·4 | 1 | 23 | 2·0 | | | | | | | 4 | 23 | 27 | 111 | 2·3 |
| 21 | Coopers | 64 | 27 11 | 21 | 63 | 2·5 | 34 | 153 | 2·2 | 8 | 6 | 2·3 | | | | | | | 8 | 52 | 56 | 213 | 2·4 |
| 10 | Engineers | 29 | 32 5 | 8 | 19 | 2·3 | 10 | 50 | 2·5 | 1 | 7 | 2·6 | | | | | | | 1 | 6 | 19 | 76 | 2·5 |
| | Umbrella-makers | 11 | 29 11 | 2 | 6 | 3·0 | 6 | 29 | 2·4 | 2 | 16 | | | | | | | | 1 | 8 | 10 | 51 | 2·8 |
| 18 | Porters | 34 | 20 8 | 11 | 34 | 3·1 | 18 | 99 | 2·7 | | | | | | | | | | 5 | 31 | 29 | 133 | 2·3 |
| 20 | Carmen | 50 | 23 7 | 6 | 38 | 2·2 | 15 | 75 | 2·5 | 5 | 33 | 2·2 | | | | | | | 13 | 66 | 37 | 153 | 2·6 |
| 7 | Butchers | 13 | 22 8 | 3 | 10 | 3·3 | 4 | 19 | 2·3 | 1 | 8 | 2·6 | | | | | | | 5 | 23 | 8 | 37 | 2·6 |
| 12 | Sugar-bakers | 26 | 23 11 | 7 | 17 | 2·4 | 11 | 59 | 2·6 | 2 | 15 | 2·5 | | | | | | | 4 | 23 | 20 | 91 | 2·8 |
| 13 | Bakers | 26 | 19 3 | 15 | 44 | 2·9 | 7 | 38 | 2·7 | | | | | | | | | | 4 | 20 | 22 | 82 | 2·9 |
| 15 | Painters | 33 | 23 5 | 13 | 34 | 2·6 | 16 | 94 | 3·1 | 4 | 14 | 2·3 | | 9 | | | | | | | 28 | 128 | 2·3 |
| 9 | Watermen | 20 | 26 2 | 8 | 24 | 2·6 | 5 | 23 | 1·9 | 2 | 26 | 2·1 | | | | | | | 4 | 27 | 16 | 58 | 2·3 |
| 19 | Smiths | 34 | 27 4 | 6 | 100 | 2·4 | 20 | 83 | 2·3 | 6 | 13 | 2·1 | 1 | | 2·2 | | | | 9 | 42 | 25 | 93 | 2·4 |
| 22 | Sailors | 67 | 15 6 | 1 | 63 | 2·9 | 34 | 118 | 2·1 | 2 | 47 | 2·6 | | | | | | | 5 | 17 | 62 | 226 | 2·6 |
| 23 | Tailors | 72 | 24 1 | 34 | 19 | 2·8 | 15 | 177 | 2·6 | 8 | 13 | 2·1 | | | | | | | 10 | 58 | 62 | 286 | 2·0 |
| 16 | Cigar-makers | 29 | 33 0 | 22 | 69 | 3·0 | 32 | 64 | 1·8 | | 56 | 2·1 | | | | | | | 6 | 29 | 24 | 86 | 2·4 |
| 24 | Carpenters | 76 | 27 5 | 7 | | | 8 | 150 | 2·0 | 2 | | | | | | | | | 13 | 77 | 63 | 274 | 2·0 |
| 1 | Gun-stock-makers | 7 | 38 9 | | | | 2 | 8 | 2·0 | | 13 | 2·1 | | | | | | | 5 | 29 | 2 | 8 | 2·9 |
| 4 | Tin-workers | 10 | 29 9 | 3 | 7 | 2·3 | 6 | 28 | 2·3 | | | | | | | | | | 3 | 18 | 7 | 41 | 2·5 |
| 2 | Wheelwrights | 8 | 28 2 | | 10 | 2·5 | 4 | 19 | 2·3 | 1 | 7 | 2·3 | | | | | | | 1 | 6 | 9 | 26 | 2·3 |
| 5 | Shopmen | 11 | 28 11 | 4 | 29 | 3·2 | 5 | 19 | 1·9 | | | | | | | | | | 2 | 12 | 7 | 29 | 2·5 |
| 11 | Policemen | 21 | 21 10 | 9 | 4 | 4·0 | 11 | 50 | 2·3 | 1 | 7 | 2·3 | | | | | | | | | 6 | 86 | 2·4 |
| 3 | Printers | 9 | 26 0 | 1 | 6 | 2·5 | 5 | 23 | 2·3 | | | | | | | | | | 3 | 17 | 21 | 27 | 2·4 |
| 8 | Clerks | 13 | 30 5 | 2 | | | 5 | 25 | 2·5 | 1 | 17 | 2·1 | | | | | | | 5 | 32 | 8 | 37 | 2·4 |
| 28 | Miscellaneous | 396 | 23 9 | 167 | 479 | 2·8 | 138 | 652 | 2·3 | 28 | 177 | 2·1 | 5 | 33 | 1·6 | 1 | 11 | 2·2 | 57 | 310 | 339 | 1,852 | 2·4 |
| | **Total Families** | **1,651** | 24 5 | 619 | 1,709 | 2·8 | 674 | 3,227 | 2·4 | 101 | 666 | 2·2 | 6 | 42 | 1·7 | 1 | 11 | 2·2 | 250 | 1,835 | 1,401 | 5,655 | 2·46 |
| | Widows with incumbrance | 151 | 9 11 | 86 | 241 | 2·8 | 64 | 228 | 2·1 | 3 | 20 | 2·2 | | | | | | | 8 | 28 | 143 | 489 | 2·4 |
| | **Total Families, exclusive of Single Men and Women** }<br>Lodgers | **1,802** | 23 1 | 705 | 1,950 | 2·8 | 728 | 3,455 | 2·4 | 104 | 686 | 2·2 | 6 | 42 | 1·7 | 1 | 11 | 2·2 | 258 | 1,363 | 1,544 | 6,144 | 2·45 |

TABLE X.—*Food, Clothing, Furniture, and Cleanliness.*

| Trades | Number of Families | Average Earnings of Families (s. d.) | Once | Twice | Three Times | Four | Five | Six | Seven | Not Ascer-tained | Sufficient and Clean | Insufficient but Clean | Sufficient but Dirty | Insufficient and Dirty | Not Ascer-tained | Well | Scantily | Badly | Not Ascer-tained | Well | Tolerably | Badly | Not Ascer-tained |
|---|---|---|---|---|---|---|---|---|---|---|---|---|---|---|---|---|---|---|---|---|---|---|---|
| | | | | | | Number of Times the Families have Animal Food in the Week. | | | | | Clothing. | | | | | Rooms—How Furnished. | | | | Whether Cleansed. | | | |
| Labourers | 363 | 19 | 80 | 62 | 80 | 42 | 3 | 19 | 13 | 64 | 134 | 177 | 10 | 36 | 6 | 62 | 205 | 76 | 20 | 123 | 146 | 75 | 19 |
| Gunsmiths | 87 | 45 | 2 | . | 1 | . | . | 8 | 72 | 4 | 81 | 1 | . | 1 | 1 | 52 | 24 | 1 | 10 | 68 | 8 | 1 | 10 |
| Gunmakers | 26 | 26 | 15 | 2 | 23 | 10 | 1 | 3 | 8 | 20 | 12 | 13 | . | 19 | . | 7 | 15 | 4 | 4 | 7 | 15 | 4 | . |
| Shoemakers | 101 | 20 | 2 | 4 | 3 | 9 | 1 | 8 | 7 | 6 | 40 | 42 | 1 | 10 | . | 22 | 50 | 25 | 6 | 32 | 38 | 27 | 4 |
| Bricklayers | 31 | 24 | 3 | 3 | 7 | 10 | 1 | 3 | 13 | 18 | 15 | 13 | . | 2 | . | 9 | 16 | 5 | 1 | 12 | 15 | 3 | 1 |
| Coopers | 64 | 27 | . | . | 1 | . | . | 9 | 10 | 5 | 35 | 17 | 1 | 10 | 1 | 23 | 30 | 11 | . | 31 | 22 | 11 | . |
| Engineers | 20 | 32 | 1 | 4 | 1 | 1 | . | 7 | 2 | . | 16 | 4 | . | . | . | 8 | 11 | . | 5 | 8 | 6 | . | 1 |
| Umbrella-makers | 11 | 29 | . | 5 | 1 | 2 | . | 1 | 3 | . | 9 | 2 | . | 3 | 1 | 10 | 3 | 1 | . | 3 | 3 | . | . |
| Porters | 34 | 20 | 1 | 2 | 9 | 8 | 1 | 2 | 2 | 7 | 16 | 13 | . | 4 | 1 | 15 | 19 | 2 | 6 | 13 | 14 | 6 | 5 |
| Carmen | 50 | 23 | 4 | . | 9 | 2 | 1 | 2 | 3 | 8 | 33 | 15 | 1 | 2 | . | 10 | 29 | 3 | 8 | 28 | 16 | 1 | 1 |
| Butchers | 13 | 23 | 6 | 4 | 6 | 2 | . | 3 | 4 | 6 | 7 | 6 | 1 | . | 1 | 7 | 6 | 5 | 2 | 9 | 2 | 2 | . |
| Sugar-bakers | 24 | 19 | . | 5 | 5 | 2 | 1 | 4 | 4 | 2 | 15 | 5 | . | 1 | . | 8 | 12 | 3 | . | 14 | 9 | 4 | . |
| Bakers | 26 | 23 | . | 2 | 6 | 2 | . | 4 | 5 | 6 | 12 | 10 | . | 5 | 1 | 6 | 14 | 8 | 2 | 9 | 11 | 3 | 1 |
| Painters | 28 | 26 | 4 | 3 | 5 | 3 | 1 | 4 | 4 | 9 | 11 | 12 | . | 10 | 2 | 8 | 9 | 20 | 4 | 10 | 14 | 7 | 1 |
| Watermen | 20 | 27 | 5 | . | 4 | 3 | . | 3 | 5 | 10 | 22 | 7 | . | 1 | 1 | 6 | 21 | . | 6 | 13 | 7 | 20 | . |
| Smiths | 34 | 15 | 2 | 1 | 3 | 3 | 4 | 4 | 13 | 9 | 30 | 30 | . | 5 | . | 18 | 39 | 2 | 1 | 27 | 13 | 6 | 2 |
| Sailors | 67 | 24 | 17 | 16 | 12 | 3 | . | 2 | 2 | 10 | 32 | 28 | 3 | 10 | . | 12 | 33 | 6 | . | 26 | 25 | 7 | 1 |
| Tailors | 72 | 33 | 2 | 7 | 14 | 6 | 4 | 14 | 10 | 13 | 30 | 18 | 1 | 4 | 2 | 37 | 11 | 6 | 2 | 17 | 31 | 20 | 2 |
| Cigar-makers | 29 | 27 | 1 | 1 | 3 | 2 | . | 7 | 17 | 2 | 32 | . | . | 1 | . | 3 | 31 | . | 3 | 44 | 23 | 6 | 1 |
| Carpenters | 76 | 38 | 7 | 6 | 8 | 7 | 4 | 4 | 2 | 4 | 51 | 6 | . | 5 | . | 9 | 37 | . | 2 | 4 | 4 | 7 | . |
| Gun-stock-makers | 10 | 28 | . | . | 2 | . | . | . | . | 1 | 7 | 1 | . | . | 1 | 5 | 3 | . | . | 4 | . | . | . |
| Tin workers | 8 | 29 | . | . | . | . | . | 1 | 6 | 2 | 8 | 6 | . | 1 | . | 5 | 2 | . | 2 | 6 | . | 1 | . |
| Wheelwrights | 11 | 28 | 1 | . | 4 | 7 | . | . | . | 2 | 6 | 2 | . | . | . | 3 | 3 | 2 | 2 | 8 | 1 | 2 | 1 |
| Shopmen | 21 | 21 | . | 1 | 1 | . | . | 1 | 5 | 6 | 11 | 8 | . | 1 | . | 9 | 13 | . | 6 | 6 | 3 | . | . |
| Policemen | 9 | 26 | . | . | 1 | . | . | . | . | 1 | 7 | 2 | . | . | . | 5 | 4 | . | 6 | 12 | 1 | . | . |
| Printers | 13 | 30 | . | . | 4 | 7 | . | 1 | 6 | 2 | 13 | 6 | 2 | 5 | 1 | 5 | 23 | . | 2 | 8 | 3 | . | . |
| Clerks | 7 | 28 | . | . | 1 | 3 | . | . | . | 6 | 13 | 2 | . | . | . | 3 | 13 | 3 | 6 | 6 | 1 | 1 | . |
| Miscellaneous | 396 | 28 | 33 | 46 | 57 | 38 | 15 | 39 | 102 | 66 | 213 | 131 | 6 | 37 | 9 | 142 | 184 | 55 | 15 | 181 | 145 | 56 | 14 |
| **Total Families** | **1,651** | **24** | 198 | 177 | 264 | 187 | 33 | 182 | 329 | 281 | 870 | 578 | 29 | 147 | 27 | 527 | 806 | 243 | 75 | 747 | 586 | 245 | 73 |
| Widows with incumbrance | 151 | 9 | 68 | 24 | 27 | 13 | 1 | 3 | 2 | 13 | 48 | 81 | 5 | 15 | 2 | 23 | 83 | 41 | 4 | 44 | 66 | 36 | 5 |
| Single Men | 88 | 32 | 1 | . | 3 | 1 | . | 14 | 31 | 38 | 49 | 2 | 1 | 5 | 31 | 6 | 8 | 6 | 68 | 9 | 4 | 6 | 69 |
| Single Women & Widows without incumbrance | 64 | 8 | 25 | 8 | 2 | 4 | 1 | . | 6 | 18 | 28 | 21 | 1 | 3 | 11 | 9 | 28 | 10 | 17 | 21 | 18 | 8 | 17 |
| **Total Families** | **1,954** | **23** | 292 | 209 | 296 | 205 | 35 | 199 | 368 | 350 | 995 | 682 | 36 | 170 | 71 | 565 | 925 | 300 | 164 | 821 | 674 | 295 | 164 |

The average rent is seen to be no less than 3*s.* 7*d.* per week, or 9*l.* 6*s.* 4*d.* per year, which, on the total number of families (1,954), gives the enormous sum of 18,204*l.* 16*s.* 8*d.* The present Committee, in relation to this subject, would earnestly recal the attention of the Members of the Society to the practical suggestion contained in the Report of their Committee on the state of the working classes in the parishes of St. Margaret and St. John, Westminster, read at the Ordinary Meeting of the Society on the 16th of March, 1840, and which has already been the source of much good in the origination of societies for the improvement of the dwellings and the lodging-houses of the labouring classes, and offers a test from which yet more enlarged practical deductions might be drawn, at a time when express provisions for the physical and moral health of our vast urban populations are at length recognised as a part of the public policy of the empire.

"High rents are an evil of a practical nature from which the labouring classes are severely suffering; and a sufficient proof of this circumstance is afforded in the fact that large numbers of the families of the working population continue to reside, for months and years together, crowded within miserable dwellings, consisting of a single room, of very moderate size, for each family.

"As a remedy for such an obvious grievance, the Committee are desirous to show the advantage which may be derived from the outlay of a moderate amount of capital, in the erection of buildings containing sets of rooms suited to the accommodation of labouring families, in properly selected situations. For these dwellings, weekly rents should be required from the tenants, and a profit may, in this manner, be reasonably expected from capital judiciously invested, while advantages of still greater importance, both physical and moral, would be gained to society, from the removal of a serious cause of discontent among the working classes, and from the provision of a more correct and convenient arrangement of their household comforts, which may materially assist in the foundation of a superior moral character for the working population."

The state of these poor families, with regard to food, clothing, furniture, and cleanliness, is described in Table X. There seems to be indicated by the column showing the consumption of animal food, a classification into poor and sufficient feeding; the former being very clearly indicated by the two columns which represent those who obtain animal food only once or twice a week; being about one-fourth of the whole. None appeared to be over-fed. The state of the clothing is, in one sense more satisfactory; for while it is described as *sufficient* in 1,031 cases, and *insufficient* in 852, it is described as *dirty* in only 36 of the former cases, and 170 of the latter. The distribution of these latter numbers chiefly among the poorer occupations will be seen at a glance. Only 300 are returned as having rooms *ill furnished*, while 565 have rooms *well furnished*, but a number greater than both of these combined (925) are described as having only *scanty* furniture; terms which are tolerably expressive to those accustomed to visit the habitations of the poor. Ill furnished dwellings are those in which there are only a wretched bedstead, or a bed on the floor, a few broken chairs, and a table worth only a shilling or two, besides, perhaps, a box or chest, with a few paper pictures about the walls. Scantily furnished dwellings are those which contain a few chairs, a deal table, a flock bed, and a few cooking utensils, altogether indicating a struggle towards neatness, though scarcely towards comfort. While the dwellings described as well furnished, had, perhaps, a chest of drawers, a clock, really good tables, a carpet, mahogany chairs, and every article essential to comfort, and some even of luxury, such as a piano, violins, and other musical instruments, with foreign productions of curiosity, &c.

The rooms are badly cleaned in a greater number of cases than the clothing, viz., in 295, and in 674 they are but tolerably clean. Still, in one-half of the cases ascertained (821), they are described as well cleaned. The excess of inferior habits in the lower occupations will be traced generally. The casual dock labourers appear to be in the lowest condition, in proportion even to their poor means; while those whose homes are most comfortable, in proportion to their earnings, are, undoubtedly, the German sugar-bakers, and the mates of vessels, with only a part of the gunsmiths; others throwing away all the advantages of their superior earnings by thriftless habits.

Some evidence as to the religious and moral character of the people will be conveyed by the table which describes their profession of religion, the newspapers and periodical publications which they read, and the character of the books and pictures found in their apartments.

TABLE XI.
*Religious Profession of Heads of Families.*

| Religious Profession. | Heads of Families. |
| --- | --- |
| Church of England | 1,328 |
| Wesleyan Methodists | 64 |
| Other Denominations of Dissenters | 177 |
| Roman Catholics | 168 |
| Jews | 35 |
| No religion | 152* |
| Not ascertained | 30 |
| Total | 1,954 |

* Under this head are included one or two Mahommedans.

This extensive profession of attachment to the Gospel is a hopeful sign, though the limited extent to which the Wesleyans and other denominations of Dissenters, appear to have penetrated into this mass of population, is rather remarkable, and will justify a feeling of doubt with regard to the profession made by some of belonging to the Established Church.

There is reason to believe, however, that the above statement gives a very fair representation of the results which would be arrived at amidst large bodies of the working classes, whether in town or country; though a different result would probably be shown in the manufacturing districts.

The following are the periodical publications in use among the
population:—

TABLE XII.

*Newspapers Read by the Families visited.*

|  | Families. | Single Men. | Single Women. | Total Families. |
|---|---|---|---|---|
| Times | 22 | .... | .... | 22 |
| Advertiser | 284 | 23 | .... | 307 |
| Dispatch | 327 | 27 | .... | 354 |
| Lloyd's Gazette | 476 | 38 | .... | 514 |
| Sunday Times | 9 | .... | .... | 9 |
| Watchman | 1 | .... | .... | 1 |
| Railway Bell | 1 | .... | .... | 1 |
| Nonconformist | 2 | .... | .... | 2 |
| Bell's Life | 4 | .... | .... | 4 |
| Cleave's Gazette | 1 | .... | .... | 1 |
| National | 2 | .... | .... | 2 |
| Builder | 1 | .... | .... | 1 |
| News of the World | 1 | :... | .... | 1 |
| Family Herald | 1 | .... | .... | 1 |
| Birmingham Herald | 1 | .... | .... | 1 |
| Various | 10 | .... | .... | 10 |
| Not reading Papers | 29 | .... | .... | 29 |
| Not ascertained | 630 | .... | 64 | 694 |
| Total | 1,802 | 88 | 64 | 1,954 |

This is not a cheering picture; the great use made of the capacity
to read being, so far as this statement indicates, in ministering to mere
excitement.  Out of 1,260 cases in which the circumstances with
regard to reading were ascertained, it was wholly in " Lloyd's Gazette,"
the " Weekly Dispatch," and the " Advertiser," in every case, except
22 in which the " Times " is read, 34 in which other miscellaneous
prints are taken in, and only 29 in which no newspaper whatever is
read.

**TABLE XIII.—Books and Pictures.**

| Trades | Number of Families | Average Earnings of Families | Number of Books: Serious | Theatrical | Miscellaneous | Averages of each kind where any: Serious | Theatrical | Miscellaneous | Number of Families possessing each Class of Books: Serious | Theatrical | Miscellaneous | Serious and Theatrical | Theatrical and Miscellaneous | Serious and Miscellaneous | All Classes of Books | No Books | Number of Pictures: Serious | Theatrical | Miscellaneous | Average of each kind where any: Serious | Theatrical | Miscellaneous | Number of Families possessing each Class of Pictures: Serious | Theatrical | Miscellaneous | Theatrical and Serious | Serious and Miscellaneous | Theatrical and Miscellaneous | All Classes of Pictures | No Pictures |
|---|---|---|---|---|---|---|---|---|---|---|---|---|---|---|---|---|---|---|---|---|---|---|---|---|---|---|---|---|---|---|
| 27 Labourers | 363 | 19 3 | 1,033 | 3 | 960 | 4 | 3 | 7 | 117 | 1 | 16 | | | | | 105 | 301 | 96 | 1,610 | 3 | 3 | 6 | 8 | 4 | 130 | | | | 21 | 97 |
| 25 Gunsmiths | 87 | 45 1 | 293 | 5 | 527 | 6 | 5 | 10 | 15 | | | | | | | 18 | 82 | 48 | 416 | 3 | 3 | 7 | 2 | | 24 | 2 | | | 11 | 26 |
| 14 Gunmakers | 26 | 26 3 | 72 | | 110 | 5 | | 11 | 12 | | 3 | | | | | 8 | 5 | | 58 | 2 | | 4 | | 2 | 14 | | | | | 10 |
| 26 Shoemakers | 101 | 20 8 | 333 | | 364 | 6 | | 9 | 32 | | 8 | | | | | 27 | 70 | 26 | 393 | 2 | | 6 | 2 | | 38 | | | | 3 | 31 |
| 17 Bricklayers | 31 | 24 0 | 87 | | 60 | 4 | | 9 | 13 | | 2 | | | | | 14 | 20 | 4 | 114 | 3 | | 5 | 1 | 1 | 10 | | | | | 11 |
| 21 Coopers | 64 | 27 1 | 160 | | 240 | 4 | | 7 | 23 | | 2 | | | | | 5 | 69 | 51 | 349 | 3 | 1 | 7 | | | 23 | | | | | 6 |
| 10 Engineers | 20 | 38 5 | 41 | | 90 | 5 | | 7 | 9 | | | | | | | 3 | 8 | 3 | 85 | 4 | 5 | 7 | 3 | | 9 | | | | 1 | 12 |
| 6 Umbrella-makers | 11 | 29 7 | 79 | | 299 | 4 | | 37 | 14 | | 2 | | | | | 11 | 23 | 2 | 52 | 2 | 3 | 6 | | | 6 | | | | | 9 |
| 18 Porters | 34 | 24 8 | 133 | 3 | 87 | 4 | | 7 | 6 | 1 | | | | | 1 | 2 | 28 | 10 | 133 | 3 | 3 | 6 | | | 16 | | | 4 | 2 | 7 |
| 20 Carmen | 50 | 23 7 | 44 | | 171 | 3 | | 7 | 15 | | 1 | | | | | 9 | 12 | 8 | 260 | 2 | 3 | 7 | | 1 | 22 | | | 4 | 1 | 6 |
| 7 Butchers | 13 | 22 11 | 45 | | 37 | 4 | | 7 | 5 | | | | | | | 6 | 7 | 2 | 40 | 2 | | 6 | | | 10 | | | 4 | 2 | 9 |
| 12 Sugar-bakers | 24 | 23 3 | 64 | | 75 | 4 | | 7 | 6 | | 2 | | | | | 8 | 15 | 4 | 63 | 2 | | 6 | | | 11 | 1 | | 6 | 4 | 11 |
| 13 Bakers | 26 | 19 5 | 76 | | 91 | 3 | | 11 | 7 | | | | | | | 4 | 19 | 5 | 95 | 2 | | 6 | | | 12 | 2 | | 4 | 1 | 3 |
| 15 Painters | 21 | 23 4 | 75 | 3 | 151 | 3 | | 13 | 8 | 1 | 1 | | | | | 11 | 32 | 10 | 118 | 2 | 2 | 7 | | | 10 | 1 | | 6 | 1 | 10 |
| 9 Watermen | 20 | 26 6 | 182 | 7 | 106 | 6 | 2 | 8 | 8 | | 2 | | | | | 15 | 30 | 31 | 104 | 2 | 2 | 6 | | | 31 | | | 4 | | 17 |
| 22 Smiths | 34 | 27 1 | 189 | 1 | 210 | 6 | 1 | 6 | 23 | 1 | 1 | | | | | 11 | 11 | 6 | 163 | 2 | 2 | 6 | 1 | | 35 | | | | 4 | 24 |
| 23 Sailors | 67 | 15 0 | 72 | | 144 | 7 | | 7 | 7 | | 2 | | | | | 15 | 63 | 8 | 272 | 3 | 2 | 8 | | | 15 | | | 3 | | 23 |
| 16 Tailors | 72 | 24 5 | 346 | | 91 | 4 | 3 | 11 | 23 | | 2 | | | | | 8 | 6 | 8 | 242 | 3 | 2 | 8 | 1 | | 28 | 1 | | 3 | | 4 |
| 24 Cigar-maker | 29 | 28 9 | 35 | | 319 | 5 | | 11 | 10 | | | | | | | 11 | 6 | 8 | 174 | 3 | | 9 | 1 | | 5 | | | | | 2 |
| 1 Carpenters | 76 | 27 2 | 57 | | 15 | 6 | | 8 | 2 | | 1 | | | | | 3 | 6 | | 12 | 3 | | 10 | 1 | | 28 | | 1 | | 1 | 1 |
| 4 Gun-stock-makers | 7 | 38 11 | 29 | | 75 | 3 | | 6 | 2 | | | | | | | 2 | 6 | | 59 | 5 | | 5 | 1 | | | | | | | 2 |
| 2 Tin-workers | 10 | 29 0 | 45 | | 40 | 4 | | 7 | 10 | | 2 | | | | | 1 | 6 | | 64 | 5 | 4 | 7 | | | 4 | | | 1 | | 7 |
| 5 Wheelwrights | 8 | 28 2 | 49 | 3 | 66 | 9 | | 12 | 3 | | | | | | | 3 | 9 | | 88 | 5 | 1 | 8 | | | 5 | | 1 | | | 2 |
| 11 Shopmen | 11 | 28 1 | 49 | | 48 | 5 | | 16 | 2 | | 1 | | | | | 2 | 14 | | 65 | 2 | | 8 | | | 6 | 1 | | | | 1 |
| 3 Policemen | 21 | 26 0 | 57 | 4 | 157 | 6 | 3 | 17 | 10 | | 2 | | | | | 3 | 17 | | 66 | 2 | | 9 | | | 4 | | | | | 2 |
| 8 Printers | 13 | 30 5 | 7 | 17 | 106 | 5 | 4 | 12 | 2 | 1 | | | | | | 2 | 7 | 8 | 87 | 3 | 2 | 5 | 1 | | 4 | | | | | 7 |
| 28 Miscellaneous | 396 | 23 9 | 1,426 | | 2,750 | 5 | 2 | 16 | 118 | 1 | 9 | | 5 | 1 | 5 | 108 | 193 | 91 | 1,465 | 2 | 3 | 6 | 13 | 2 | 153 | 2 | 1 | 2 | 13 | 148 |
| **Total Families** | **1,651** | 24 5 | (1,172) 5,200 | (7) 47 | (724) 7,585 | 4 | 3 | 10 | 497 | 3 | 53 | | 5 | | 8 | 422 | (429) 1,097 | (155) 439 | (1,096) 6,959 | 2 | 3 | 6 | 36 | 12 | 639 | 3 | | | 73 | 504 |
| Widows with incumbrance | 151 | 9 11 | (108) 443 | (1) 1 | (51) 375 | 1 | | 7 | 62 | | 8 | | | | 1 | 35 | (36) 100 | (9) 18 | (90) 506 | 3 | 2 | 6 | 4 | 1 | 51 | 1 | | | 1 | 56 |
| Single Men | 88 | 32 4 | (10) 38 | | (9) 75 | | | 8 | 3 | | 2 | | | | | 76 | (3) 7 | (2) 4 | (10) 63 | 2 | 2 | 6 | | 1 | 7 | 1 | | | 1 | 77 |
| Single Women & Widows without incumbrance | 64 | 8 0 | (32) 115 | | (22) 118 | 3 | | 5 | 11 | | | | | | | 31 | (16) 49 | | (88) 162 | 3 | | 6 | 2 | | 14 | | | | | 34 |
| **Total Families** | **1,954** | 23 1 | (1,323) 5,791 | (18) 48 | (889) 8,153 | 4 | 2 | 10 | 573 | 3 | 63 | | 5 | 1 | 9 | 564 | (484) 1,253 | (166) 460 | (1,221) 7,730 | 2 | 3 | 6 | 42 | 14 | 711 | 3 | | | 75 | 671 |

TABLE XIII.—Books and Pictures.

The classification of the books and pictures found in the houses, which has been adopted in the accompanying table, has been made in deference to a former classification in like inquiries. The head "Miscellaneous" is designed to include the miscellaneous books, chiefly of narrative, and seldom of "useful knowledge," which are found in the houses of the poorer classes, distinct from the books of religion and morality comprised under the name of "serious," and the melodramatic works which, chiefly, are designated by the term "theatrical." The total number of books found in the district was no less than 13,992, giving an average of upwards of 11 for each of the families in which they were found; 564 appearing to be without books of any kind; a proportion upwards of one-fourth of the total number. Only 58 books were found to be theatrical, while 5,791 are classed as serious, and 8,153 as miscellaneous. The former were found in only 18 families of the whole number visited, while all three classes were found in 9 of these; serious as well as theatrical in 5 more of them; and miscellaneous as well as theatrical in another; leaving but 3 in which theatrical books only were found. Both serious and miscellaneous books were found in 736 families; serious books only in 573; and miscellaneous books only in 63. The possession of books is, in fact, almost universal; and in the families in which each kind of books was found at all, therefore, there were, on an average, 4 serious, 10 miscellaneous, and 3 theatrical. The extent to which the habit of reading prevails, challenges, therefore, still more minute investigation into the direction given to it, an investigation which should extend to some simple observation upon the apparent *use*, as well as the actual possession, of the books, and a yet further classification of them. It is more than one-fourth of the houses which are without "serious" books, under which name are generally included the Holy Scriptures and books of prayer; and to what extent these are really used it must be impossible to ascertain statistically, but it would be very important to determine whether or not they appeared to be most used in the houses where they were accompanied by an equal or perhaps greater proportion of miscellaneous books. The impression of the agents is, that, in far the greater number of families which they visited, of all the books which they found in them, the "Bible" and "Testament" were those least read.

The decoration of the walls with pictures prevails to nearly the same degree as the possession of books of some kind. The total number of pictures observed was no fewer than 9,443, of which 7,730 had miscellaneous, 1,253 serious, and 460 theatrical subjects; the proportions of the miscellaneous and theatrical being greater in the pictures than in the books; the numbers of each kind in the families where they were found at all, averaging, of the serious 2, of the theatrical 3, and of the miscellaneous 6. These numbers give upwards of 8 to a family, in the case of all the families indulging in this sort of decoration. In the abodes of 75 families were found pictures of all these denominations; in 364, serious and miscellaneous pictures; in 711, miscellaneous pictures only; in 74, miscellaneous and theatrical; in 42, pictures on religious subjects only; in 14, on theatrical subjects only; in 3, on both serious and theatrical subjects. In 671, or one-third of the abodes, there was no decoration whatever by pictures. Those usually found were little paper prints, tricked out in glaring colours, and enclosed in little black frames of wood; while a few, especially the marine prints, were really good.

One very gratifying fact is, that 622, or upwards of one-third of the heads of families are connected with Benefit Societies. On the other hand, however, 50 families were in the actual receipt of gratuitous medical relief.

TABLE XLV.

*Families Receiving Gratuitous Medical Aid; and Heads of Families Connected with Friendly Societies.*

|  | Families. | Single Men. | Single Women. | Total Families. |
|---|---|---|---|---|
| Receiving gratuitous Medical aid | 50 | .... | .... | 50 |
| Balance of Families ................... | 1,752 | .... | .... | 1,752 |
| Total ....................... | 1,802 | .... | .... | 1,802 |
| Connected with Friendly Societies | 622 | 54 | 1 | 677 |
| Balance of Families ................. | 1,180 | 34 | 63 | 1,277 |
| Total ................. ........ | 1,802 | 88 | 64 | 1,954 |

Again, the great length of time which a large proportion of them have occupied their present habitations, indicates, in the main, a steadiness of character which is worthy of observation, if we take into account the large proportion of forced migration which attaches to a number of the trades; if only from one part of the town to another.

TABLE XV.

*Length of Time which the Heads of Families have Resided in their Present Dwellings.*

|  | Families. | Single Men. | Single Women. | Total Families. |
|---|---|---|---|---|
| From 1 week to 4 weeks ............ | 60 | 3 | 2 | 65 |
| ,,  1 month to 6 months ........ | 369 | 10 | 12 | 391 |
| ,,  6    ,,    1 year............. | 270 | 17 | 13 | 300 |
| ,,  1 year    3   ,, ............... | 467 | 18 | 12 | 497 |
| ,,  3    ,,    6   ,, ............... | 269 | 8 | 6 | 283 |
| ,,  6    ,,    9   ,, ............... | 148 | 3 | .... | 151 |
| ,,  9    ,,   12   ,, ............... | 69 | .... | 4 | 73 |
| ,,  12   ,,   15   ,, ............... | 46 | .... | 2 | 48 |
| ,,  15   ,,   20   ,, ............... | 43 | .... | 1 | 44 |
| ,,  20   ,,   30   ,, ............... | 41 | 2 | 2 | 45 |
| ,,  30   ,,   40   ,, ............... | 4 | .... | 2 | 6 |
| ,,  40   ,,   50   ,, ............... | 1 | .... | .... | 1 |
| ,,  50    ,, and upwards ........ | 1 | .... | .... | 1 |
| Not ascertained .................. | 14 | 27 | 8 | 49 |
| Total ..................... | 1,802 | 88 | 64 | 1,954 |

The tables of the attendance of the children in schools, and the payments made by their parents for that attendance, are very interesting; indicating, as they do, an universal use of schools for some period of life, and obviously also for successive years. Of the quality of the schooling we have other and less flattering means of judging, by analogy.

*Attendance of the Children at Schools.*

| Attendance at | Males. | Females. | Total. |
|---|---|---|---|
| Infant and Dame Schools | 211 | 224 | 435 |
| Day Schools ................. | 455 | 376 | 831 |
| Total Day Schools........... | 666 | 600 | 1,266 |
| Sunday Schools ............... | 281 | 290 | 571 |
| Total School attendance.... | 947 | 890 | 1,837 |

Thus, upon the total population of 7,711, the attendance in day-schools is nearly 1 in 9; in infant and dame schools about 1 in 18; and in both combined 1 in 6, or approaching one-half of the number not exceeding 16 years of age. The number of young persons attending Sunday Schools is seen to be 571, or 1 in 13½ of the whole population, and 1 in 6 of the population not exceeding 16 years of age. Thus, the school attendance is respectable, even as shown by that in day-schools only, and when the "out-of-the-way schools" for the "little ones" are included, it is seen to wear an aspect which is unrivalled even by the most glowing statistics of voluntary education, in which they universally form so great a portion; probably, as here, about one-third. The Sunday School attendance is, without doubt, proportionably less here than in the manufacturing districts, because the absence of an extensive demand for juvenile labour relieves the pressure for secular instruction on the Sunday, which causes no small part of the excess in those districts.

The table of school payments affords a very interesting view of the payments which the several classes of families are willing to make for the schooling of their children, while, of all the families returned, the children of only 113 were receiving absolutely gratuitous education.

*Total Payments made for the Schooling by the Children of each Family.*

| Weekly Payments. | Families. |
|---|---|
| 1d. to 3d. | 250 |
| 3d. to 6d. | 449 |
| 6d. to 9d. | 186 |
| 9d. to 1s. | 127 |
| 1s. to 1s. 3d.... | 32 |
| 1s. 3d. to 1s. 6d..... | 37 |
| 1s. 6d. to 2s.... | 13 |
| 2s. to 3s. 6d.... | 15 |
| | 1,109 |
| Not paying anything though having children at school | 113 |
| Payments not ascertained though children at school.... | 44 |
| | 1,266 |
| No children at school, and therefore making no school payments, besides the single men and women........ | 536 |
| | 1,802 |

The total sum spent upon day schooling is thus 291s. = 14l. 11s. per week, or 1,056l. 12s. per annum, at a general average of 5¾d. per week, contributed by each family which pays for schooling at all, an amount which, if distributed over all the families, would be under 2d. per week each.

TABLE XVI.—*School Attendance and Payments.*

| Trades. | Number of Families. | Average Earnings of each Family. | | Children attending School. Infant, Dame, and Day. | | | | Total Infant, Dame, and Day | | Total Sunday Scholars | | Total Payments by each Family for Children attending Schools, where any. | | | | | | | | | | | Total Payments for Children. | | Average Payments. | |
|---|---|---|---|---|---|---|---|---|---|---|---|---|---|---|---|---|---|---|---|---|---|---|---|---|---|---|
| | | | | Male. | Female. | Male. | Female. | Male. | Female. | Male. | Female. | 1*d.* to 3*d.* | 3*d.* to 6*d.* | 6*d.* to 9*d.* | 9*d.* to 1*s.* | 1*s.* to 1*s.* 3*d.* | 1*s.* 3*d.* to 1*s.* 6*d.* | 1*s.* 6*d.* to 2*s.* | 2*s.* to 3*s.* 6*d.* | 3*s.* 6*d.* to 4*s.* 6*d.* | Gratis. | Not ascertained. | | | | |
| | | *s.* | *d.* | | | | | | | | | | | | | | | | | | | | *s.* | *d.* | *s.* | *d.* |
| Labourers | 363 | 19 | 1 | 36 | 42 | 78 | 73 | 114 | 115 | 50 | 50 | 62 | 84 | 26 | 20 | 3 | 4 | .. | .. | .. | 25 | 5 | (116) 46 | 8 | 0 | 2¾ |
| Gunsmiths | 87 | 45 | 3 | 32 | 21 | 26 | 18 | 58 | 39 | 20 | 25 | 8 | 24 | 15 | 24 | 6 | 16 | .. | .. | .. | 3 | 1 | (46) 30 | 9 | 0 | 8 |
| Gunmakers | 26 | 26 | 10 | .. | .. | 7 | 9 | 7 | 9 | 4 | 3 | 1 | 9 | 5 | .. | .. | .. | .. | .. | .. | 1 | .. | (8) 3 | 10 | 0 | 5¾ |
| Shoemakers | 101 | 20 | 8 | 10 | 8 | 16 | 12 | 26 | 20 | 11 | 7 | 8 | 25 | 5 | 2 | .. | .. | .. | .. | .. | 2 | 4 | (25) 10 | 5 | 0 | 5 |
| Bricklayers | 31 | 24 | 10 | 2 | 2 | 10 | 9 | 12 | 11 | 3 | 9 | 5 | 5 | 6 | 2 | .. | .. | 4 | .. | .. | 1 | .. | (11) 6 | 9 | 0 | 7¼ |
| Coopers | 64 | 27 | 11 | 6 | 6 | 13 | 13 | 19 | 19 | 5 | 5 | 10 | 14 | 4 | 3 | 5 | .. | .. | .. | .. | 1 | 1 | (22) 9 | 5 | 0 | 5 |
| Engineers | 20 | 32 | 5 | 3 | 2 | 7 | 6 | 10 | 8 | 2 | 3 | .. | 8 | 2 | 5 | .. | .. | .. | .. | .. | 3 | .. | (7) 4 | 3 | 0 | 7¼ |
| Umbrella-makers | 11 | 29 | 1 | 1 | 5 | 6 | 1 | 7 | 6 | .. | .. | .. | 4 | 2 | 2 | .. | 3 | .. | .. | .. | .. | 2 | (5) 4 | 0 | 0 | 9½ |
| Porters | 34 | 20 | 8 | 5 | 3 | 19 | 8 | 24 | 11 | 10 | 3 | 7 | 9 | 6 | .. | .. | .. | .. | .. | .. | 11 | 2 | (14) 5 | 1 | 0 | 4½ |
| Carmen | 50 | 23 | 7 | 9 | 11 | 11 | 15 | 20 | 26 | 10 | 13 | 10 | 16 | 14 | .. | .. | .. | .. | .. | .. | 6 | .. | (19) 8 | 9 | 0 | 5½ |
| Butchers | 13 | 22 | 8 | 1 | 4 | 6 | 3 | 7 | 7 | 1 | 5 | 1 | 5 | 5 | 2 | .. | .. | .. | .. | .. | 1 | .. | (6) 2 | 9 | 0 | 5½ |
| Sugar-bakers | 24 | 23 | 7 | 4 | 2 | 10 | 10 | 14 | 12 | 6 | 1 | .. | 17 | .. | 2 | .. | .. | .. | .. | .. | 4 | 3 | (8) 4 | 2 | 0 | 6¼ |
| Bakers | 26 | 19 | 11 | 3 | 3 | 9 | 10 | 12 | 13 | 4 | 10 | .. | 7 | 15 | .. | .. | .. | .. | .. | .. | 3 | .. | (7) 3 | 11 | 0 | 6¾ |
| Painters | 28 | 23 | 3 | 3 | 4 | 5 | 8 | 8 | 12 | 4 | 5 | 4 | 12 | 2 | .. | .. | .. | .. | .. | .. | 2 | .. | (11) 3 | 10 | 0 | 4¼ |
| Watermen | 20 | 26 | 5 | 2 | .. | 7 | 4 | 9 | 4 | 3 | 3 | 2 | 3 | 2 | .. | .. | .. | .. | .. | .. | 6 | .. | (5) 1 | 9 | 0 | 4¼ |
| Smiths | 34 | 27 | 2 | 1 | 9 | 8 | 6 | 4 | 15 | 5 | 7 | 4 | 11 | .. | 4 | .. | .. | .. | .. | .. | .. | .. | (12) 5 | 1 | 0 | 6 |
| Sailors | 67 | 15 | 4 | 7 | 8 | 12 | 12 | 19 | 20 | 13 | 3 | 12 | 20 | 6 | .. | .. | .. | .. | .. | .. | 1 | .. | (22) 8 | 11 | 0 | 4¾ |
| Tailors | 72 | 24 | 6 | 9 | 9 | 25 | 17 | 34 | 26 | 16 | 15 | 14 | 25 | 7 | 2 | 2 | .. | .. | .. | .. | 6 | 4 | (24) 9 | 10 | 0 | 5 |
| Cigar-makers | 29 | 33 | 11 | 6 | 6 | 6 | 5 | 12 | 11 | 7 | 7 | 5 | 9 | 6 | .. | .. | .. | .. | .. | .. | 2 | 1 | (11) 4 | 8 | 0 | 5 |
| Carpenters | 76 | 27 | 0 | 12 | 7 | 20 | 16 | 32 | 23 | 17 | 13 | 9 | 25 | 3 | 7 | 2 | 3 | .. | .. | .. | 2 | 3 | (30) 15 | 4 | 0 | 6 |
| Gun-stock-maker | 7 | 38 | 5 | 4 | 4 | .. | .. | 4 | 4 | 3 | 4 | .. | 2 | 4 | 2 | .. | .. | .. | .. | .. | .. | .. | (3) 2 | 1 | 0 | 8¼ |
| Tin-workers | 10 | 29 | 9 | 1 | 1 | 5 | 8 | 6 | 9 | 3 | 4 | .. | 5 | .. | .. | .. | .. | 4 | 4 | .. | 2 | .. | (5) 6 | 0 | 1 | 2½ |
| Wheelwrights | 8 | 28 | 2 | 1 | 2 | 1 | .. | 2 | 2 | .. | .. | .. | 4 | .. | .. | .. | .. | .. | .. | .. | .. | .. | (2) 1 | 0 | 0 | 6 |
| Shopmen | 11 | 28 | 11 | .. | 1 | 3 | 1 | 3 | 2 | 1 | 1 | 1 | 2 | .. | 2 | .. | .. | .. | .. | .. | .. | .. | (3) 1 | 9 | 0 | 7 |
| Policemen | 21 | 21 | 10 | 1 | 1 | 4 | 8 | 5 | 9 | 1 | 3 | .. | 5 | 4 | .. | 4 | .. | .. | .. | .. | 1 | .. | (6) 4 | 0 | 0 | 8 |
| Printers | 9 | 26 | 0 | 2 | 2 | 7 | 3 | 9 | 5 | 5 | 3 | .. | 2 | 2 | 2 | 4 | .. | .. | .. | .. | 4 | .. | (5) 3 | 10 | 0 | 9¼ |
| Clerks | 13 | 30 | 5 | 3 | 1 | 5 | 3 | 8 | 4 | 1 | 1 | .. | 5 | 2 | 3 | .. | 2 | .. | .. | .. | .. | .. | (7) 5 | 0 | 0 | 8½ |
| Miscellaneous | 396 | 23 | 9 | 37 | 45 | 110 | 78 | 147 | 123 | 60 | 59 | 62 | 70 | 35 | 43 | 5 | 8 | 5 | 11 | .. | 18 | 13 | (124) 65 | 11 | 0 | 6¼ |
| Total Families | 1651 | 24 | 5 | 201 | 209 | 431 | 356 | 632 | 565 | 265 | 262 | 225 | 427 | 178 | 127 | 32 | 36 | 13 | 15 | .. | 105 | 39 | (564) 280 | 0 | 0 | 6 |
| Widows with incumbrance | 151 | 9 | 11 | 10 | 15 | 24 | 20 | 34 | 35 | 16 | 28 | 25 | 22 | 8 | .. | .. | 1 | .. | .. | .. | 8 | 5 | (35) 11 | 3 | 0 | 4 |
| Total Families exclusive of Single Men and Single Women Lodgers | 1802 | 23 | 1 | 211 | 224 | 455 | 376 | 666 | 600 | 281 | 290 | 250 | 449 | 186 | 127 | 32 | 37 | 13 | 15 | .. | 113 | 44 | (599) 291 | 0 | 0 | 5¾ |

The following table will show the ages of the parents at the birth of their first child; and if it be assumed, that the birth of the first child, on the average, happened about one year after marriage, it will be seen that in both sexes the greatest number of marriages took place, between the ages of 21 and 25. However, it will be found that the marriages in the male sex have taken place generally at a much later period in life than among the female sex, for while out of 1,488 marriages 170 only of the males were under 20 years of age, as many as 461 females were under the same age. On the other hand, while 236 only of the females were between the ages of 26-30, there were as many as 391 males at those ages. Again, while there were only 68 females married above the ages of 30, it will be found that as many as 223 males were married above that age.

| Age of Fathers. | Age of Mothers. | | | | | | | Total. |
|---|---|---|---|---|---|---|---|---|
| | 14—15. | 16—20. | 21—25. | 26—30. | 31—35. | 36—40. | 41—45. | |
| 14—15 | .... | .... | .... | .... | .... | .... | .... | .... |
| 16—20 | 8 | 115 | 38 | 8 | 1 | .... | .... | 170 |
| 21—25 | 5 | 218 | 418 | 57 | 6 | .... | .... | 704 |
| 26—30 | .... | 87 | 184 | 108 | 9 | 3 | .... | 391 |
| 31—35 | 2 | 18 | 55 | 40 | 19 | 2 | .... | 136 |
| 36—40 | .... | 8 | 15 | 21 | 8 | 3 | 1 | 56 |
| 41—45 | .... | .... | 5 | 1 | 6 | 3 | 2 | 17 |
| 46—50 | .... | .... | 6 | 2 | 1 | 2 | .... | 11 |
| 51—55 | .... | .... | .... | 1 | 1 | .... | .... | 2 |
| 56 | .... | .... | .... | .... | .... | .... | 1 | 1 |
| Total | 15 | 446 | 721 | 238 | 51 | 13 | 4 | 1,488 |

Tables A, B, C, D, and E, exhibit facts of considerable interest and importance. They are arranged to show the influence of the age at marriage on the number of children born, and the mortality of those children. Table A represents the results of those marriages, in which the birth of the first child took place when the mother was between the ages 16-20. The first column represents the number of years which have elapsed since the birth of the first child. The

Second—The number of families over which the observations extend; the

Third—The number of children born; the

Fourth—The number of children then alive; the

Fifth—The number dead; the

Sixth—The rate of mortality per cent., and the

Seventh—The average number of children born to each family within the given periods of years set forth in the first column, as having elapsed since the birth of the first child.

Tables B, C, and D represent the same class of facts for families in which the birth of the first child took place between the quinquennial ages 21-25, 26-30, and 31-35; and Table E includes the results for all the marriages formed at whatever period of life they may have taken place.

Tables *a*, *b*, *c*, *d*, and *e* are abridgments of the preceding tables. The first point deserving of attention in those figures, is the circumstance that those marriages formed at an earlier period of life, are more prolific than those formed at a later period. The gross results for each group of *facts* is as follows :—

The average number of children } 16—20 } was 6·07 to each family.
to each family, in which the birth } 21—25 } ,, 5·15 ,,
of the first child took place between } 26—30 } ,, 4·87 ,,
the ages of ............................ } 31—35 } ,, 3·94 ,,

To the results presented in this form, however, it may be objected, that the number of years elapsed between the birth of the first child over the time to which the facts are collected, is, on the average, greater in the case of the earlier marriages than in the later, and hence the greater number of children. This objection, true in principle, will be found, under a closer analysis of the figures, to materially alter the relative bearing of the results. The following abstract will show the average number of children to each marriage, at the respective periods of 10, 20, 30, and 40 years after the birth of the first child, for each class of marriages formed at the four different quinquennial periods of life.

| Years elapsed since Birth of First Child. | Average Number of Children to each Marriage, formed at Ages | | | |
|---|---|---|---|---|
| | 16—20. | 21—25. | 26—30. | 31—35. |
| 10 | 5·05 | 4·51 | 4·42 | 3·44 |
| 20 | 7·68 | 7·01 | 6·43 | 3·00 |
| 30 | 8·41 | 7·89 | 6·80 | 7·00 |
| 40 | 10·85 | 8·24 | 5·00 | 4·00 |

It is thus obvious, that marriages formed under the age of 25, are more prolific than those formed after that age, and that those formed between 16 and 20 years of age are still more so than those at any of the superior ages.

In connexion with these results, it is important to view the rate of mortality of the children born in marriages contracted at the same period of life.

The gross mortality up to all ages of } 16—20 } was 46·11 per cent.
the whole children born in families in } 21—25 } ,, 41·07 ,,
which the first child was born, between } 26—30 } ,, 39·61 ,,
the ages of ............................ } 31—35 } ,, 37·56 ,,

These figures are of course subject to the objection just alluded to, but the following abstract will show the results in a corrected form.

| Years elapsed since Birth of First Child. | Mortality per cent. of the Children born to Marriages formed at Ages | | | |
|---|---|---|---|---|
| | 16—20. | 21—25. | 25—30. | 31—35. |
| 10 | 36·87 | 37·09 | 37·89 | 35·48 |
| 20 | 47·44 | 43·10 | 44·36 | 16·67 |
| 30 | 53·03 | 43·89 | 48·53 | 64·29 |
| 40 | 63·12 | 57·14 | 68·00 | 50·00 |

From this abstract it is obvious, that of the three first periods, the children born of marriages formed in the quinquennial term of life, 21-25, are subject to a less rate of mortality than those of the period immediately preceding or immediately following, the rate of mortality in the most advanced period, 31-35, is very irregular, and no doubt arises from the small number of families included in that group. The two preceding series of facts furnish materials for the solution of a very interesting and highly important question, namely, what is the effect of the marriages formed at those different terms of life on the ultimate increase of population? By the first of the two preceding abstracts it was found, that the earlier the period at which marriage was contracted, the greater the number of children born; but by the second abstract a difference is observable in the rate of mortality of the various periods, and this must disturb the results in the first class of facts.

Let $a$ represent the results given in the first abstract; $b$ represent those given in the second; then $a - \dfrac{a \times b}{100}$ = the actual increase resulting from each marriage to the population. The following is an abstract of the results thus arrived at:

| Years elapsed since Birth of First Child. | Children alive by each Marriage contracted at the following Ages. | | | |
|---|---|---|---|---|
| | 16—20. | 21—25. | 26—30. | 31—35. |
| 10 | 3·19 | 2·84 | 2·75 | 2·22 |
| 20 | 4·04 | 4·09 | 3·58 | 2·50 |
| 30 | 3·95 | 4·43 | 3·50 | 2·50 |
| 40 | 4·00 | 3·53 | 1·60 | 2·00 |

It hence follows, that marriages formed under 25 years of age increase the population more than those formed above that age; and on a close examination it will be found, that there is very little difference in this respect between marriages contracted at ages 16-20 and 21-25, the rate of increase, however, being somewhat higher in the former period. With regard to the last two quinquennial terms at which marriage is formed, it will be seen that the rate of increase is not so great for ages 26-30 as in that immediately preceding, and in the period 31-35 the rate of increase is still less; in fact, the earlier the period of marriage the greater the increase resulting to the population, the difference between the first and second periods being very little, between the second and third very considerable, about 23 per cent., and between the third and fourth about 20 per cent.

In the consideration of these facts and observations, although they relate to 1,506 families, from which have resulted 8,034 births, and of which 4,616 children, or 57·46 per cent., are still alive, it must be borne in mind that they include only one class of the community, and may be subject to disturbing influences, such as to destroy their character as a type of the general population; however, there is reason to suppose that these results may be a more faithful representative of the condition of the whole population, than if they were derived from a like number of facts from either the middling or higher classes of Society. On reflection it will also be found, that the unfruitful marriages are not included in any of those 1,506 families, all included being more or less productive. Likewise, the marriages are all those in which one or both the parents are still alive, and consequently the results of fruitful marriages, in which the parents have died before the lapse of the given period of years brought under review, are excluded. An influence, independent of the relative number of marriages at each age, will further affect the results arising from the varying rates of mortality at the different terms of life, even when equal numbers only at those periods are considered; and it will follow, that fewer marriages of limited fruitfulness will be excluded from the groups at the younger ages, the effect of which must be to show in the preceding figures a reduced ratio of children at each marriage formed at those periods of life, compared with that which would appear were all cases included. The relative bearing of all the results are therefore so far modified. Also, the children still alive, composing 57·46 per cent. of all born, may, subsequent to the period now under observation, and when classified according to the ages at marriage of their parents, show a very different rate of mortality from that indicated in the respective classes by those who have hitherto died, and still more extended observations would be required to show, whether any and what difference exist, in the fruitfulness of the marriages in the succeeding generation. Lastly, all these remarks have had reference to the age of the mother only at birth of her first child.

The next point to which attention is directed, is the rate of mortality experienced by the children of those families. This will be seen by an inspection of Tables A, B, C, D, and E, as well as the abridgments of those tables, but as these, from their peculiar construction, as well as from the small number of families in some of the years, cause various irregularities in the results, the following graduated abstract will exhibit the rate of mortality for all the groups included in the preceding tables. The mortality in the first year of life appears to be remarkably low, being only 11·86 per cent., while, according to the Fourth Report of the Registrar-General. The mortality during the first year of life was for—

| | | |
|---|---|---|
| England and Wales | 17·355 | per cent. |
| For the County of Surrey | 13·278 | ,, |
| For the Metropolis | 20·124 | ,, |
| For Liverpool | 28·157 | ,, |

It will further be seen, from the following abstract, column 6, that of 100 children born, 62·76 live to complete their tenth year:

| No. of Years since Birth of 1st Child. | No. of Children Born. (Corrected.) | No. of Children Alive. (Corrected.) | No. of Children Dead. | Decrements from Birth to each Age. | Living. |
|---|---|---|---|---|---|
| 1 | 59 | 52 | 7 | 11·86 | 88·14 |
| 2 | 88 | 69 | 19 | 21·59 | 78·41 |
| 3 | 99 | 76 | 23 | 28·23 | 71·77 |
| 4 | 150 | 107 | 43 | 28·66 | 71·34 |
| 5 | 187 | 132 | 55 | 29·41 | 70·59 |
| 6 | 210 | 148 | 62 | 29·52 | 70·48 |
| 7 | 210 | 147 | 63 | 30·00 | 70·00 |
| 8 | 236 | 159 | 77 | 32·63 | 67·37 |
| 9 | 233 | 151 | 82 | 35·19 | 64·81 |
| 10 | 239 | 150 | 89 | 37·24 | 62·76 |
| 11 | 264 | 161 | 103 | .... | .... |
| 12 | 282 | 169 | 113 | .... | .... |
| 15 | 1,324 | 813 | 511 | 38·60 | 61·41 |
| 20 | 1,386 | 779 | 607 | 43·80 | 56·21 |
| 25 | 1,027 | 561 | 466 | 45·37 | 54·63 |
| 30 | 893 | 465 | 428 | 47·93 | 52·07 |
| 35 | 453 | 204 | 249 | 54·97 | 45·03 |
| 40 | 361 | 138 | 223 | 61·77 | 38·23 |
| 45 | 163 | 70 | 93 | 57.06 | 42·95 |
| 50 | 68 | 22 | 46 | 67·65 | 32·35 |
| 55 | 28 | 8 | 20 | 71·43 | 28·57 |
| 60 | 27 | 8 | 19 | 70·37 | 29·63 |

but according to the same report of the Registrar-General, the number out of 100 born who live to complete their tenth year is,—

For England and Wales ..................................................... 70·61
For the County of Surrey ................................................. 75·42
For the Metropolis .......................................................... 64·92
For Liverpool ................................................................. 48·21

while, according to the following well-known life-tables, the number out of 100 born who live to complete their tenth year is by the—

Carlisle Table (Milne) ..................................................... 64·60
Sweden (Nicander) .......................................................... 63·03
Select Lives in France (Deparcieux) ................................. 60·04
Towns in France (Duvillard) ........................................... 55·11
Northampton (Price) ....................................................... 48·71
Montpellier (Monyue) ...................................................... 43·58

Again, the numbers living to complete their 20th and their 30th years, according to each of the above authorities, is as follows:—

| Description of Table. | Out of 100 Born there live to complete their | |
|---|---|---|
| | 20th Year. | 30th Year. |
| According to result in this Paper ........ | 56·21 | 52·07 |
| England and Wales .......... | 66·06 | 60·33 |
| County of Surrey .......... | 70·89 | 65·56 |
| Metropolis .......... | 61·68 | 56·67 |
| Liverpool .......... | 44·81 | 40·35 |
| Carlisle .......... | 60·90 | 56·42 |
| Sweden .......... | 59·03 | 53·91 |
| Select Lives in France .......... | 55·58 | 50·05 |
| Towns in France .......... | 50·22 | 43·82 |
| Northampton .......... | 44·05 | 37·64 |
| Montpellier .......... | 40·97 | 36·62 |

Beyond the age of 30, the facts in this paper are not sufficiently numerous to warrant a comparison being instituted between them and other life tables, but from the illustrations already brought forward, it will be seen that the rate of mortality in the first year of life, is less than in any other of those cases. Again, with respect to the decrement of life between birth and the tenth year, it is greater than that for England and Wales, the county of Surrey, the Metropolis, the Carlisle Table, and that for the kingdom of Sweden, but less than the decrement for the select lives in France, the towns in France, Northampton, Liverpool, and Montpellier.

With respect to the decrements of life up to the ages of 20 and 30, they will be found to hold the same relative situation as that for age 10, being intermediate between Sweden and the select lives of France.

These remarks being applicable to all the changes and fluctuations, taking place from birth up to the various ages at which the comparisons are instituted, any irregularity in the mortality of one period, the first year of life for example, will disturb the results for all the subsequent ages. In order, therefore, to avoid the effects of the force of this element, it may be important to test the relative value of the different classes of facts, by a comparison of the equation of life for the different mortality tables. The following gives the result thus arrived at, for one-fourth of the integral or original number.

| Age of Comparison, or that from which the equation is derived. | Results of this Paper. | England and Wales. | County of Surrey. | Metropolis. | Liverpool. | Carlisle. | Sweden | Select Lives in France. | Towns in France. | Northampton. | Montpellier. |
|---|---|---|---|---|---|---|---|---|---|---|---|
| 10 | 24·00 | 31·25 | 34·00 | 31·00 | 27·00 | 33·34 | 32·90 | 29·60 | 24·54 | 22·72 | 28·36 |
| 20 | 20·00 | 26·04 | 29·00 | 26·00 | 21·00 | 27·16 | 25·40 | 26·31 | 19·32 | 17·14 | 22·35 |
| 30 | 17·00 | 18·49 | 26·00 | 19·00 | 16·00 | 22·67 | 21·72 | 23·33 | 14·84 | 14·46 | 18·08 |

In viewing the decrements of life from birth only, it was found that the results of this paper were intermediate in the scale between the table for Sweden and that for the select lives in France, that comparison was of course affected by the rate of mortality in infant life; but in the above tables, where the results of advanced life only enter into the figures, it is seen that the mortality is higher than that of all the tables, except those for the towns of France and for Northampton.

It is hence obvious, that so far as the facts here brought forward can be relied on, the mortality of infant life is very low, and that of advanced life high.

Lest the results of this inquiry, however, should be deemed by some to fairly indicate the influence of locality on the duration of life, of the inhabitants of this district of Whitechapel, with equal truth for the early and advanced terms of life, it may be well to draw attention to the following abstract, showing the length of time which the principal members of families have resided in their dwellings.

| | Families. | Single Men. | Single Women. | Total. |
|---|---|---|---|---|
| From 1 week to 4 weeks | 60 | 3 | 2 | 65 |
| ,, 1 month to 6 months | 369 | 10 | 12 | 391 |
| ,, 6 months to 1 year | 270 | 17 | 13 | 300 |
| ,, 1 year to 3 years | 467 | 18 | 12 | 497 |
| ,, 3 ,, 6 ,, | 269 | 8 | 6 | 283 |
| ,, 6 ,, 9 ,, | 148 | 3 | .... | 151 |
| ,, 9 ,, 12 ,, | 69 | .... | 4 | 73 |
| ,, 12 ,, 15 ,, | 46 | .... | 2 | 48 |
| ,, 15 ,, 20 ,, | 43 | .... | 1 | 44 |
| ,, 20 ,, 30 ,, | 41 | 2 | 2 | 45 |
| ,, 30 ,, 40 ,, | 4 | .... | 2 | 6 |
| ,, 40 ,, 50 ,, | 1 | .... | .... | 1 |
| ,, 50 and upwards | 1 | .... | .... | 1 |
| Not ascertained | 14 | 27 | 8 | 49 |
| | 1,802 | 88 | 64 | 1,954 |

It will thus be seen, that nearly two-thirds of the families have been less than three years in their present residence, and more than one-fourth between one and three years only. The term in " their present residence" will admit of the explanation that they may have been much longer in the same neighbourhood. Still many amongst those who have changed their dwellings must also have been recent inhabitants of the locality, and it must, therefore, follow, that the younger lives indicate more strictly the sanatory condition of the place than those of more advanced age. The high rate of mortality of the older lives now under review can, consequently, not be attributable to residence in Whitechapel, as the majority of the deaths in advanced life may have taken place elsewhere—one-thirteenth only of the families having occupied their present residences upwards of twelve years; but with respect to the deaths at the younger ages, the greater number of those must have happened in the locality, and hence the comparative healthiness of the district.

In regard to the state of health of the families surveyed in the district now under consideration, it may be interesting to subjoin the following abstract returned " well" and " ill."

*Population and State of Health of the Families of the Working Classes in St. Mary's District of St. George's in the East.*

Number of Families visited, 1,802.

| | Well. | Ill. | Whole Population. | No. of Families. |
|---|---|---|---|---|
| Male Children under 15 | 1,636 | 49 | | |
| Female Ditto | 1,632 | 28 | | |
| | 3,268 | 77 | =3,345 | 1,802 |
| Adult Males | 1,886 | 42 | | |
| Adult Females | 2,005 | 88 | | |
| Carried forward | 3,891 | 130 | =4,021 | .... |

*Population and State of Health of the Families of the Working Classes in St. Mary's District of St. George's in the East.—Continued.*

Number of Families visited, 1,802.

|  | Well. | Ill. | Whole Population. | No. of Families. |
|---|---|---|---|---|
| Brought forward ............ |  |  | 7,366 | 1,802 |
| Aged and Infirm Males ................ | 38 | 15 |  |  |
| Aged and Infirm Females................ | 60 | 18 |  |  |
|  | 98 | 33 | = 131 | .... |
| Population not classified ................ | .... | .... | 11 | .... |
| Total ................ | 7,257 | 240 | =7,508 | .... |
| Single Men as Families ................ | .... | .... | .... | 88 |
| Single Women as Families ............ | .... | .... | .... | 64 |
| Adult Males ........ .................... | 122 | .... | 122 | .... |
| Adult Females ............................ | 67 | 3 | 70 | .... |
| Aged and Infirm Males ................ | 3 | ... | 3 | .... |
| Aged and Infirm Females................ | 4 | 4 | 8 | .... |
| Grand Total ........ | 7,453 | 247 | 7,711 |  |
| Grand Total of Families.... | .... | .... | .... | 1,954 |

It is thus seen, that of the 7,711 persons here enumerated, 247, or 3·923 per cent. are returned as being " ill." These numbers include the children and those under 15 years of age. There is no authentic record of the proportion constantly sick in this country at all ages, including the young, but the records of Friendly Societies will admit of a comparison for every term of life from the age of 10 upwards; and this comparison will, to some extent, be strictly applicable, from the fact that of the 1,954 families now referred to, 677, or 34·135, were connected with Friendly Societies. The following will show the proportion recorded ill in those families at various terms of life, as well as the ratio constantly sick for the average of England and Wales, among the members of Friendly Societies.

|  |  | According to the results of this Paper. | Average of England & Wales. |
|---|---|---|---|
| Proportion Sick or Ill | In the Adult Population, aged 15 years and upwards, but not including the aged and infirm above the age of 70................... | 3·257 per cent. | 3·319 per cent. |
| Ditto........ | In the aged and infirm, above the age of 70 ........................ | 25·191 per cent. | 46·775 per cent. |
| Ditto........ | At all terms of life from the age of 15 and upwards ............ | 3·923 per cent. | 4·613 per cent. |

So far as the preceding facts are available as a test of health, it is obvious that the district now under consideration, must be regarded in a very favourable light.

TABLE XVII.—*Ages of each Parent when first Child born, Present*

| | Trades. | Number of Families. | Average Earnings of Families. | Age of Father Classified when first child Born. | | | | | | | Total Ages of Father. | Average Age of Father and Mother when first child Born. | |
|---|---|---|---|---|---|---|---|---|---|---|---|---|---|
| | | | *s. d.* | Under 20. | 20 to 25. | 25 to 30. | 30 to 35. | 35 to 40. | 40 and upwards. | Age not ascertained. | | Fathers' Age. | Mothers' Age. |
| 27 | Labourers | 363 | 19 1 | 14 | 118 | 95 | 44 | 17 | 10 | 65 | 7,787 | 26 | 23 |
| 25 | Gunsmiths | 87 | 45 3 | 5 | 49 | 16 | 3 | 2 | 1 | 11 | 1,822 | 24 | 21 |
| 14 | Gunmakers | 26 | 26 10 | 3 | 16 | 2 | ... | ... | ... | 5 | 462 | 22 | 20 |
| 26 | Shoemakers | 101 | 20 8 | 7 | 38 | 20 | 10 | 4 | 1 | 21 | 2,033 | 25 | 23 |
| 17 | Bricklayers | 31 | 24 10 | 2 | 15 | 5 | 3 | 1 | ... | 5 | 625 | 24 | 21 |
| 21 | Coopers | 64 | 27 11 | 5 | 18 | 20 | 6 | 4 | 2 | 9 | 1,472 | 27 | 22 |
| 10 | Engineers | 20 | 32 5 | 1 | 6 | 5 | 2 | ... | ... | 6 | 358 | 26 | 23 |
| 6 | Umbrella-makers | 11 | 29 1 | 1 | 5 | 3 | ... | ... | 1 | 1 | 252 | 25 | 23 |
| 18 | Porters | 34 | 20 8 | 1 | 16 | 10 | 5 | ... | ... | 2 | 795 | 25 | 22 |
| 20 | Carmen | 50 | 23 7 | 4 | 17 | 13 | 3 | 2 | ... | 11 | 961 | 25 | 23 |
| 7 | Butchers | 13 | 22 8 | 1 | 4 | 3 | 2 | ... | ... | 3 | 248 | 25 | 22 |
| 12 | Sugar-bakers | 24 | 23 7 | 2 | 2 | 10 | 5 | 3 | ... | 2 | 612 | 28 | 22 |
| 13 | Bakers | 26 | 19 11 | 2 | 9 | 7 | ... | ... | 1 | 7 | 466 | 25 | 22 |
| 15 | Painters | 28 | 23 3 | 2 | 8 | 8 | 2 | 2 | 1 | 5 | 602 | 26 | 22 |
| 9 | Watermen | 20 | 26 5 | 2 | 8 | 5 | 1 | ... | ... | 4 | 369 | 23 | 19 |
| 19 | Smiths | 34 | 27 2 | 1 | 15 | 9 | 1 | 1 | ... | 7 | 660 | 25 | 21 |
| 22 | Sailors | 67 | 15 4 | 4 | 19 | 17 | 7 | 4 | 3 | 13 | 1,456 | 27 | 23 |
| 23 | Tailors | 72 | 24 6 | 4 | 24 | 18 | 11 | 2 | 3 | 10 | 1,638 | 26 | 23 |
| 16 | Cigar-makers | 29 | 33 11 | 1 | 17 | 5 | 1 | 1 | ... | 4 | 611 | 24 | 22 |
| 24 | Carpenters | 76 | 27 0 | 4 | 29 | 23 | 9 | 2 | 2 | 7 | 1,772 | 26 | 23 |
| 1 | Gun-stock-maker | 7 | 38 5 | 1 | 2 | 2 | ... | ... | ... | 2 | 112 | 22 | 22 |
| 4 | Tin-workers | 10 | 29 9 | ... | 5 | 3 | 1 | ... | 1 | ... | 275 | 27 | 22 |
| 2 | Wheelwrights | 8 | 28 2 | ... | 2 | 1 | 2 | 1 | ... | 2 | 164 | 27 | 25 |
| 5 | Shopmen | 11 | 28 11 | 2 | 3 | 1 | 2 | ... | ... | 3 | 196 | 24 | 22 |
| 11 | Policemen | 21 | 21 10 | ... | 9 | 9 | 2 | ... | ... | 1 | 506 | 25 | 23 |
| 3 | Printers | 9 | 26 0 | ... | 5 | 4 | ... | ... | ... | ... | 217 | 24 | 23 |
| 8 | Clerks | 13 | 30 5 | 1 | 4 | 6 | 2 | ... | ... | ... | 333 | 26 | 24 |
| 28 | Miscellaneous | 396 | 23 9 | 13 | 136 | 110 | 32 | 15 | 15 | 75 | 8,372 | 26 | 23 |
| | Total Families | 1,651 | 24 5 | 83 | 599 | 430 | 156 | 61 | 41 | 281 | 35,176 | 26 | 23 |
| | Widows with incumbrance | 151 | 9 11 | 5 | 43 | 45 | 15 | 7 | 2 | 34 | 3,061 | 26 | 23 |
| | Total Families, exclusive of Single Men and Single Women Lodgers | 1,802 | 23 1 | 88 | 642 | 475 | 171 | 68 | 43 | 315 | 38,237 | 26 | 23 |

Ages of Parents, Number of Children they have had, &c.

| Total Ages of Mother. | Age of Mother Classified when first child Born. | | | | | | | Total of Mothers' present Age. | Total Children they have had. | Total Number they have now living. | Average of Mothers' Present Age, of Children they have had, and now Living. | | |
|---|---|---|---|---|---|---|---|---|---|---|---|---|---|
| | Age not ascertained. | Under 20. | 20 to 25. | 25 to 30. | 30 to 35. | 35 to 40. | 40 and upwards. | | | | Average Mothers' present age. | Average of children she has had. | Average of children now living. |
| 6,926 | 63 | 64 | 148 | 63 | 16 | 5 | 4 | (299) 11,730 | (301) 1,642 | (301) 904 | 39 | 5·4 | 3·0 |
| 1,635 | 11 | 14 | 54 | 5 | 3 | ... | ... | (75) 2,452 | (76) 379 | 236 | 33 | 4·9 | 3·1 |
| 427 | 5 | 8 | 12 | 1 | ... | ... | ... | (21) 630 | (21) 93 | 55 | 30 | 4·4 | 2·6 |
| 1,803 | 21 | 13 | 52 | 10 | 4 | 1 | ... | (79) 2,898 | (81) 408 | 238 | 37 | 5·1 | 2·9 |
| 564 | 4 | 8 | 16 | 3 | ... | ... | ... | (26) 984 | (27) 165 | 91 | 38 | 6·1 | 3·3 |
| 1,226 | 9 | 11 | 33 | 8 | 2 | 1 | ... | (56) 2,110 | (56) 295 | 153 | 38 | 5·3 | 2·7 |
| 322 | 6 | 2 | 9 | 3 | ... | ... | ... | (14) 442 | (14) 55 | 39 | 32 | 3·9 | 2·8 |
| 235 | 1 | 3 | 4 | 1 | 1 | 1 | ... | (10) 401 | (10) 68 | 34 | 40 | 6·8 | 3·4 |
| 709 | 2 | 8 | 17 | 5 | 2 | ... | ... | (31) 1,120 | (32) 185 | 108 | 36 | 5·8 | 3·4 |
| 912 | 10 | 5 | 26 | 7 | 2 | ... | ... | (40) 1,460 | (40) 209 | 121 | 36 | 5·2 | 3·0 |
| 218 | 3 | 2 | 6 | 1 | 1 | ... | ... | (22) 359 | (22) 52 | 35 | 36 | 5·2 | 3·5 |
| 488 | 2 | 6 | 9 | 6 | 1 | ... | ... | (19) 778 | (19) 110 | 71 | 35 | 5·0 | 3·2 |
| 425 | 7 | 4 | 11 | 3 | ... | 1 | ... | (23) 667 | (23) 99 | 58 | 35 | 5·2 | 3·0 |
| 519 | 5 | 7 | 10 | 4 | 2 | ... | ... | (16) 843 | (16) 135 | 75 | 37 | 5·9 | 3·3 |
| 312 | 4 | 9 | 6 | 1 | ... | ... | ... | (27) 593 | (27) 92 | 46 | 37 | 5·7 | 2·9 |
| 568 | 7 | 6 | 19 | 2 | ... | ... | ... | (56) 930 | (56) 141 | 77 | 34 | 5·2 | 2·8 |
| 1,283 | 11 | 11 | 25 | 16 | 2 | 2 | ... | (61) 2,028 | (62) 249 | 126 | 36 | 4·4 | 2·2 |
| 1,408 | 10 | 17 | 26 | 14 | 4 | 1 | ... | (25) 2,396 | (25) 368 | 230 | 39 | 5·9 | 3 7 |
| 555 | 4 | 6 | 14 | 3 | 2 | ... | ... | (69) 874 | (69) 109 | 65 | 35 | 4·4 | 2·6 |
| 1,575 | 7 | 16 | 33 | 15 | 3 | 2 | ... | (6) 2,786 | (6) 425 | 243 | 40 | 6·1 | 3·5 |
| 133 | 1 | 2 | 2 | 2 | ... | ... | ... | (10) 214 | (10) 36 | 24 | 36 | 6·0 | 4·0 |
| 227 | ... | 3 | 4 | 2 | 1 | ... | ... | (7) 410 | (7) 75 | 47 | 41 | 7·5 | 4·7 |
| 173 | 1 | 1 | 4 | 1 | ... | 1 | ... | (9) 254 | (9) 33 | 20 | 36 | 4·7 | 2·9 |
| 197 | 2 | 1 | 7 | 1 | ... | ... | ... | (20) 299 | (20) 40 | 19 | 33 | 4·4 | 2·1 |
| 455 | 1 | 2 | 13 | 5 | ... | ... | ... | (9) 707 | (9) 91 | 50 | 35 | 4·5 | 2·5 |
| 206 | ... | 2 | 4 | 3 | ... | ... | ... | (13) 308 | (13) 46 | 26 | 34 | 5·1 | 2·9 |
| 311 | ... | 1 | 6 | 5 | 1 | ... | ... | (315) 548 | (326) 72 | 48 | 42 | 5·5 | 3·7 |
| 7,473 | 73 | 57 | 168 | 76 | 17 | 4 | 1 | 12,429 | 1,693 | 1,026 | 39 | 5·2 | 3·1 |
| 4,285 | 270 | 289 | 738 | 266 | 64 | 19 | 5 | (1,368) 51,650 | (1,387) 7,365 | (1,387) 4,265 | 37·76 | 5·31 | 3·07 |
| 3,253 | 9 | 24 | 74 | 35 | 8 | 1 | ... | (145) 6,647 | (145) 841 | (145) 453 | 45·84 | 5·80 | 3·20 |
| 4,538 | 279 | 313 | 812 | 301 | 72 | 20 | 5 | (1,513) 58,297 | (1,532) 8,206 | (1,532) 4,718 | 38·53 | 5·36 | 3·08 |

TABLE XVIII.—*Total of Present Age of Married Women having no Children, classified according to Trades.*

| Trades. | Under 20. | 20 to 25. | 25 to 30. | 30 to 35. | 35 to 40. | 40 to 45. | 45 to 50. | 50 and upwards. |
|---|---|---|---|---|---|---|---|---|
| Labourers | .... | 282 | 130 | 188 | 222 | 86 | 93 | 131 |
| Gunsmiths | 19 | 62 | 77 | .... | .... | .... | .... | .... |
| Gunmakers | .... | .... | 25 | .... | .... | .... | .... | .... |
| Shoemakers | 19 | 22 | 27 | 94 | .... | .... | 142 | .... |
| Bricklayers | .... | .... | 28 | .... | .... | .... | .... | .... |
| Coopers | .... | 45 | 54 | .... | .... | .... | 88 | 50 |
| Engineers | 19 | 48 | .... | 30 | .... | .... | 47 | .... |
| Umbrella-makers | .... | .... | .... | .... | .... | .... | .... | .... |
| Porters | .... | .... | .... | .... | .... | .... | .... | .... |
| Carmen | .... | 21 | 110 | 30 | 35 | .... | 48 | .... |
| Butchers | 19 | .... | .... | 30 | .... | .... | .... | .... |
| Sugar-bakers | .... | 22 | 25 | .... | .... | .... | .... | .... |
| Bakers | .... | .... | 26 | 98 | .... | 40 | 47 | .... |
| Painters | .... | .... | 22 | 31 | .... | .... | 45 | .... |
| Watermen | .... | .... | .... | .... | ..л | 41 | 45 | ...: |
| Smiths | .... | 89 | .... | 62 | .... | 43 | .... | .... |
| Sailors | .... | 111 | 105 | .... | .... | 40 | .... | .... |
| Tailors | .... | 23 | 130 | .... | .... | 40 | .... | .... |
| Cigar-makers | .... | 20 | .... | .... | .... | .... | .... | .... |
| Carpenters | .... | 23 | 28 | .... | .... | 40 | .... | .... |
| Gun-stock-makers | .... | .... | .... | .... | .... | 43 | .... | .... |
| Tin-workers | .... | .... | .... | .... | .... | .... | .... | .... |
| Wheelwrights | .... | .... | .... | .... | 36 | .... | .... | .... |
| Shopmen | .... | 23 | 26 | .... | .... | .... | .... | .... |
| Widows with incumbrance | .... | .... | .... | .... | .... | .... | 48 | .... |
| Policemen | .... | .... | .... | .... | .... | .... | .... | .... |
| Printers | .... | .... | .... | .... | .... | .... | .... | .... |
| Clerks | .... | .... | ..↲ | .... | .... | .... | .... | .... |
| Miscellaneous | .... | 225 | 343 | 94 | 37 | 81 | 48 | 278 |
| Carried to Totals of present Age of Mothers having Children | 76 | 1,016 | 1,156 | 657 | 330 | 454 | 651 | 459 |

TABLE XIX.—*Number of Children Born and Living in Families, classified by the Mother's Age at the Birth of the First Child.*

A.—Age of Mother at Birth of first Child.—16 to 20.

| No. of Years since Birth of 1st Child. | No. of Families. | No. of Children Born. | Average No. of Children to each Family. | No. of Children Alive. | No. of Children Dead. | Mortality per Cent. |
|---|---|---|---|---|---|---|
| 1 | 13 | 13 | 1·00 | 13 | .... | .... |
| 2 | 11 | 16 | 1·45 | 13 | 3 | 18·75 |
| 3 | 9 | 15 | 1·66 | 13 | 2 | 13·33 |
| 4 | 21 | 56 | 2·66 | 35 | 21 | 37·50 |
| 5 | 14 | 43 | 3·07 | 30 | 13 | 30·23 |
| 6 | 16 | 60 | 3·75 | 40 | 20 | 33·33 |
| 7 | 23 | 78 | 3·39 | 55 | 23 | 29·49 |
| 10 | 86 | 434 | 5·05 | 274 | 160 | 36·87 |
| 15 | 80 | 520 | 6·50 | 301 | 219 | 42·12 |
| 20 | 56 | 430 | 7·68 | 226 | 204 | 47·44 |
| 25 | 44 | 353 | 8·48 | 178 | 175 | 49·57 |
| 30 | 39 | 328 | 8·41 | 154 | 174 | 53·03 |
| 35 | 15 | 118 | 7·87 | 45 | 73 | 61·86 |
| 40 | 13 | 141 | 10·85 | 52 | 89 | 63·12 |
| 45 | 4 | 33 | 8·25 | 23 | 10 | 30·30 |
| 50 | 5 | 64 | 12·80 | 16 | 48 | 75·00 |
| 55 | 2 | 18 | 9·00 | 5 | 13 | 72·22 |
| 60 | 2 | 28 | 14·90 | 8 | 20 | 71·43 |
| Total .... | 453 | 2,748 | 6·07 | 1,481 | 1,267 | 46·11 |

B.—Age of Mother at Birth of first Child.—21 to 25.

| No. of Years since Birth of 1st Child. | No. of Families. | No. of Children Born. | Average No. of Children to each Family. | No. of Children Alive. | No. of Children Dead. | Mortality per Cent. |
|---|---|---|---|---|---|---|
| 1 | 36 | 39 | 1·08 | 33 | 6 | 15·38 |
| 2 | 39 | 56 | 1·44 | 43 | 13 | 23·21 |
| 3 | 31 | 58 | 1·87 | 43 | 15 | 25·86 |
| 4 | 33 | 88 | 2·67 | 61 | 27 | 30·68 |
| 5 | 36 | 103 | 2·86 | 74 | 29 | 28·15 |
| 6 | 31 | 97 | 3·13 | 69 | 28 | 28·86 |
| 7 | 40 | 131 | 3·27 | 95 | 36 | 27·48 |
| 10 | 116 | 523 | 4·51 | 329 | 194 | 37·09 |
| 15 | 98 | 604 | 6·16 | 390 | 214 | 34·97 |
| 20 | 92 | 645 | 7·01 | 367 | 278 | 43·10 |
| 25 | 66 | 482 | 7·30 | 280 | 202 | 41·91 |
| 30 | 56 | 442 | 7·89 | 248 | 194 | 43·89 |
| 35 | 28 | 223 | 7·96 | 80 | 143 | 64·13 |
| 40 | 17 | 140 | 8·24 | 60 | 80 | 57·14 |
| 45 | 10 | 121 | 12·10 | 52 | 69 | 57·02 |
| 50 | 2 | 10 | 5·00 | 3 | 7 | 70·00 |
| 55 | .... | .... | .... | .... | .... | .... |
| 60 | .... | .... | .... | .... | .... | .... |
| Total .... | 731 | 3,762 | 5·15 | 2,217 | 1,545 | 41·07 |

TABLE XIX.—*Continued.*

C.—Age of Mother at Birth of first Child.—26 to 30.

| No. of Years since Birth of 1st Child. | No. of Families. | No. of Children Born. | Average No. of Children to each Family. | No. of Children Alive. | No. of Children Dead. | Mortality per Cent. |
|---|---|---|---|---|---|---|
| 1 | 6 | 6 | 1·00 | 6 | .... | .... |
| 2 | 9 | 15 | 1·66 | 12 | 3 | 20·00 |
| 3 | 12 | 22 | 1·83 | 17 | 5 | 22·73 |
| 4 | 10 | 36 | 3·60 | 20 | 16 | 44·44 |
| 5 | 7 | 17 | 2·43 | 14 | 3 | 17·41 |
| 6 | 7 | 19 | 2·71 | 18 | 1 | 5·26 |
| 7 | 9 | 39 | 4·33 | 30 | 9 | 23·07 |
| 10 | 43 | 190 | 4·42 | 118 | 72 | 37·89 |
| 15 | 37 | 195 | 5·27 | 128 | 67 | 34·36 |
| 20 | 40 | 257 | 6·43 | 143 | 114 | 44·36 |
| 25 | 17 | 103 | 6·06 | 55 | 48 | 46·60 |
| 30 | 20 | 136 | 6·80 | 70 | 66 | 48·53 |
| 35 | 9 | 69 | 7·67 | 50 | 19 | 27·54 |
| 40 | 10 | 50 | 5·00 | 16 | 34 | 68·00 |
| 45 | 2 | 8 | 4·00 | 4 | 4 | 50·00 |
| 50 | 2 | 7 | 3·50 | 5 | 2 | 28·57 |
| 55 | .... | .... | .... | .... | .... | .... |
| 60 | .... | .... | .... | .... | .... | .... |
| Total .... | 240 | 1,169 | 4·87 | 706 | 463 | 39·61 |

D.—Age of Mother at Birth of first Child.—31 to 35.

| No. of Years since Birth of 1st Child. | No. of Families. | No. of Children Born. | Average No. of Children to each Family. | No. of Children Alive. | No. of Children Dead. | Mortality per Cent. |
|---|---|---|---|---|---|---|
| 1 | 1 | 1 | 1·00 | .... | 1 | 100·00 |
| 2 | 1 | 1 | 1·00 | 1 | .... | .... |
| 3 | 2 | 4 | 2·00 | 3 | 1 | 25·00 |
| 4 | 2 | 4 | 2·00 | 3 | 1 | 25·00 |
| 5 | 0 | 0 | .... | 0 | 0 | .... |
| 6 | 6 | 20 | 3·33 | 16 | 4 | 20·00 |
| 7 | 4 | 21 | 5·25 | 11 | 10 | 47·62 |
| 10 | 9 | 31 | 3·44 | 20 | 11 | 35·48 |
| 15 | 1 | 4 | 4·00 | 2 | 2 | 50·00 |
| 20 | 8 | 24 | 3·00 | 20 | 4 | 16·67 |
| 25 | 8 | 49 | 6·13 | 26 | 23 | 46·94 |
| 30 | 2 | 14 | 7·00 | 5 | 9 | 64·29 |
| 35 | 4 | 16 | 4·00 | 11 | 5 | 31·25 |
| 40 | 1 | 4 | 4·00 | 2 | 2 | 50·00 |
| 45 | 1 | 4 | 4·00 | 3 | 1 | 25·00 |
| 50 | .... | .... | .... | .... | .... | .... |
| 55 | .... | .... | .... | .... | .... | .... |
| 60 | .... | .... | .... | .... | .... | .... |
| Total .... | 50 | 197 | 3·94 | 123 | 74 | 37·56 |

TABLE XIX.—*Continued.*

E.—Age of Mother at Birth of first Child.—Total Ages 14 to 43.

| No. of Years since Birth of 1st Child. | No of Families. | No. of Children Born. | Average No. of Children to each Family. | No. of Children Alive. | No. of Children Dead. | Mortality per Cent. |
|---|---|---|---|---|---|---|
| 1 | 56 | 59 | 1·05 | 52 | 7 | 11·86 |
| 2 | 60 | 88 | 1·46 | 69 | 19 | 21·59 |
| 3 | 54 | 99 | 1·83 | 76 | 23 | 23·23 |
| 4 | 68 | 190 | 2·80 | 122 | 68 | 35·79 |
| 5 | 57 | 163 | 2·86 | 118 | 45 | 27·61 |
| 6 | 63 | 208 | 3·30 | 151 | 57 | 27·40 |
| 7 | 78 | 273 | 3·50 | 195 | 78 | 28·57 |
| 10 | 259 | 1,197 | 4·62 | 752 | 445 | 37·18 |
| 15 | 223 | 1,361 | 6·10 | 841 | 520 | 38·21 |
| 20 | 203 | 1,395 | 6·87 | 779 | 616 | 44·16 |
| 25 | 137 | 1,001 | 7·31 | 545 | 456 | 45·55 |
| 30 | 118 | 927 | 7·86 | 481 | 446 | 48·11 |
| 35 | 59 | 445 | 7·54 | 196 | 249 | 55·96 |
| 40 | 41 | 335 | 8·17 | 130 | 205 | 61·19 |
| 45 | 17 | 166 | 9·76 | 72 | 94 | 56·63 |
| 50 | 9 | 81 | 9·00 | 24 | 57 | 70·37 |
| 55 | 2 | 18 | 9·00 | 5 | 13 | 72·02 |
| 60 | 2 | 28 | 14·00 | 8 | 20 | 71·43 |
| Total .... | 1,506 | 8,034 | 5·33 | 4,616 | 3,418 | 42·54 |

| A.—Age of Mother at Birth of 1st Child. 16 to 20. | | | | | | | B.—Age of Mother at Birth of 1st Child. 21 to 25. | | | | | | |
|---|---|---|---|---|---|---|---|---|---|---|---|---|---|
| No. of years since birth of 1st child. | No. of Families. | No. of Children born. | No. of Children alive. | No. of Children dead. | Mortality per cent. | Average No. of Children in each Family. | No. of years since birth of 1st child. | No. of Families. | No. of Children born. | No. of Children alive. | No. of Children dead. | Mortality per cent. | Average No. of Children to each Family. |
| 1 | 13 | 13 | 13 | .. | .. | 1·00 | 1 | 36 | 39 | 33 | 6 | 15·38 | 1·08 |
| 2 | 11 | 16 | 13 | 3 | 18·75 | 1·45 | 2 | 39 | 56 | 43 | 13 | 23·21 | 1·44 |
| 3 | 9 | 15 | 13 | 2 | 13·33 | 1·66 | 3 | 31 | 58 | 43 | 15 | 25·86 | 1·87 |
| 4 | 21 | 56 | 35 | 21 | 37·50 | 2·66 | 4 | 33 | 88 | 61 | 27 | 30·68 | 2·67 |
| 5 | 14 | 43 | 30 | 13 | 30·23 | 3·07 | 5 | 36 | 103 | 74 | 29 | 28·15 | 2·86 |
| 6 | 16 | 60 | 40 | 20 | 33·33 | 3·75 | 6 | 31 | 97 | 69 | 28 | 28·86 | 3·13 |
| 7 | 23 | 78 | 55 | 23 | 29·49 | 3·39 | 7 | 40 | 131 | 95 | 36 | 27·48 | 3·27 |
| 8 | 13 | 60 | 44 | 16 | 26·67 | 4·61 | 8 | 33 | 121 | 85 | 36 | 29·75 | 3·66 |
| 9 | 18 | 89 | 52 | 37 | 41·57 | 4·94 | 9 | 12 | 44 | 29 | 15 | 34·09 | 3·66 |
| 10 | 28 | 131 | 81 | 50 | 38·17 | 4·68 | 10 | 20 | 95 | 53 | 42 | 44·21 | 4·75 |
| 11 | 9 | 47 | 27 | 20 | 42·55 | 5·12 | 11 | 25 | 124 | 72 | 52 | 41·94 | 5·00 |
| 12 | 18 | 107 | 70 | 37 | 34·58 | 5·94 | 12 | 26 | 139 | 90 | 49 | 35·25 | 5·34 |
| 13 | 23 | 154 | 82 | 72 | 46·75 | 6·70 | 13 | 21 | 114 | 77 | 37 | 32·46 | 5·43 |
| 14 | 13 | 94 | 49 | 45 | 47·87 | 7·23 | 14 | 21 | 126 | 80 | 46 | 36·51 | 6·00 |
| 15 | 13 | 87 | 63 | 24 | 27·59 | 6·69 | 15 | 23 | 152 | 90 | 62 | 40·79 | 6·61 |
| 16 | 19 | 118 | 73 | 45 | 38·13 | 6·21 | 16 | 19 | 128 | 84 | 44 | 34·37 | 6·74 |
| 17 | 12 | 67 | 34 | 33 | 49·25 | 5·58 | 17 | 14 | 84 | 59 | 25 | 29·76 | 6·00 |
| 18 | 8 | 52 | 24 | 28 | 53·85 | 6·50 | 18 | 16 | 95 | 58 | 37 | 38·95 | 5·94 |
| 19 | 10 | 76 | 42 | 34 | 44·74 | 7·60 | 19 | 21 | 166 | 91 | 75 | 45·18 | 7·91 |
| 20 | 18 | 122 | 67 | 55 | 43·44 | 6·78 | 20 | 19 | 120 | 69 | 51 | 42·50 | 6·32 |
| 21 | 7 | 70 | 37 | 33 | 47·14 | 10·00 | 21 | 20 | 146 | 83 | 63 | 43·15 | 7·30 |
| 22 | 13 | 110 | 56 | 54 | 49·09 | 8·46 | 22 | 16 | 118 | 66 | 52 | 44·07 | 7·37 |
| 23 | 12 | 100 | 42 | 58 | 58·00 | 8·33 | 23 | 15 | 116 | 69 | 47 | 40·52 | 7·73 |
| 24 | 10 | 91 | 49 | 42 | 46·15 | 9·10 | 24 | 21 | 159 | 89 | 70 | 44·02 | 7·57 |
| 25 | 7 | 40 | 28 | 12 | 30·00 | 5·71 | 25 | 8 | 57 | 32 | 25 | 43·86 | 7·12 |
| 26 | 5 | 33 | 14 | 19 | 57·58 | 6·60 | 26 | 15 | 103 | 64 | 39 | 37·86 | 6·86 |
| 27 | 10 | 89 | 45 | 44 | 49·44 | 8·90 | 27 | 7 | 47 | 26 | 21 | 44·68 | 6·71 |
| 28 | 4 | 23 | 12 | 11 | 47·83 | 5·75 | 28 | 13 | 97 | 56 | 41 | 42·27 | 7·46 |
| 29 | 12 | 100 | 42 | 58 | 58·00 | 8·83 | 29 | 15 | 118 | 67 | 51 | 43·22 | 7·86 |
| 30 | 13 | 119 | 52 | 67 | 56·30 | 9·15 | 30 | 16 | 141 | 75 | 66 | 46·81 | 8·81 |
| 31 | 3 | 35 | 20 | 15 | 42·86 | 11·67 | 31 | 6 | 40 | 28 | 12 | 30·00 | 6·67 |
| 32 | 7 | 51 | 28 | 23 | 45·10 | 7·29 | 32 | 6 | 46 | 22 | 24 | 52 17 | 7·67 |
| 33 | 2 | 16 | 6 | 10 | 62·50 | 8·00 | 33 | 6 | 36 | 11 | 25 | 69·44 | 6·00 |
| 34 | 2 | 14 | 8 | 6 | 42·86 | 7·00 | 34 | 6 | 64 | 22 | 42 | 65·62 | 10·66 |
| 35 | 3 | 13 | 4 | 9 | 69·23 | 4·33 | 35 | 6 | 39 | 18 | 21 | 53·84 | 6·50 |
| 36 | 7 | 61 | 25 | 36 | 59·01 | 8·71 | 36 | 7 | 56 | 16 | 40 | 71·43 | 8·00 |
| 37 | 1 | 14 | 2 | 12 | 85·71 | 14·00 | 37 | 3 | 28 | 13 | 15 | 53·57 | 9·33 |
| 38 | 1 | 13 | 6 | 7 | 53·84 | 13·00 | 38 | 1 | 5 | 5 | .. | .. | 5·00 |
| 39 | 4 | 57 | 21 | 36 | 63·16 | 14·25 | 39 | 4 | 35 | 13 | 22 | 62·86 | 8·75 |
| 40 | 5 | 48 | 13 | 35 | 72·92 | 9·60 | 40 | 2 | 21 | 5 | 16 | 76·19 | 10·50 |
| 41 | 2 | 13 | 5 | 8 | 61·54 | 6·50 | 41 | 5 | 48 | 16 | 32 | 66·67 | 9·60 |
| 42 | 1 | 10 | 7 | 3 | 30·00 | 10·00 | 42 | 5 | 31 | 21 | 10 | 32·26 | 6·20 |
| 43 | 2 | 23 | 18 | 5 | 21·74 | 11·50 | 43 | 3 | 47 | 16 | 31 | 65·96 | 15·67 |
| 44 | 1 | 5 | 2 | 3 | 60·00 | 5·00 | 44 | 3 | 34 | 12 | 22 | 64·71 | 11·33 |
| 45 | .. | .. | .. | .. | .. | .. | 45 | 3 | 33 | 9 | 24 | 72·73 | 11·00 |
| 46 | .. | .. | .. | .. | .. | .. | 46 | 1 | 7 | 5 | 2 | 28·57 | 7·00 |
| 47 | 1 | 5 | 3 | 2 | 40·00 | 5·00 | 47 | .. | .. | .. | .. | .. | .. |
| 48 | .. | .. | .. | .. | .. | .. | 48 | 1 | 3 | .. | 3 | 100·00 | 3·00 |
| 49 | 3 | 33 | 8 | 25 | 75·76 | 11·00 | 49 | .. | .. | .. | .. | .. | .. |
| 50 | .. | .. | .. | .. | .. | .. | 50 | 1 | 7 | 3 | 4 | 57·14 | 7·00 |
| 51 | 1 | 14 | 5 | 9 | 64·28 | 14·00 | 51 | .. | .. | .. | .. | .. | .. |
| 52 | 1 | 17 | 3 | 14 | 82·35 | 17·00 | 52 | .. | .. | .. | .. | .. | .. |
| 53 | .. | .. | .. | .. | .. | .. | 53 | .. | .. | .. | .. | .. | .. |
| 54 | 2 | 18 | 5 | 13 | 72·22 | 9·00 | 54 | .. | .. | .. | .. | .. | .. |
| 55 | .. | .. | .. | .. | .. | .. | 55 | .. | .. | .. | .. | .. | .. |
| 56 | .. | .. | .. | .. | .. | .. | 56 | .. | .. | .. | .. | .. | .. |
| 57 | .. | .. | .. | .. | .. | .. | 57 | .. | .. | .. | .. | .. | .. |
| 58 | .. | .. | .. | .. | .. | .. | 58 | .. | .. | .. | .. | .. | .. |
| 59 | 1 | 15 | 7 | 8 | 53·33 | 15·00 | 59 | .. | .. | .. | .. | .. | .. |
| 60 | 1 | 13 | 1 | 12 | 92·31 | 13·00 | 60 | .. | .. | .. | .. | .. | .. |
|  | 453 | 2,748 | 1,481 | 1,267 | 46·11 | 6·07 |  | 731 | 3,762 | 2,217 | 1,545 | 41·07 | 5·15 |

| | C.—Age of Mother at Birth of 1st Child. 26 to 30. | | | | | | D.—Age of Mother at Birth of 1st Child. 31 to 35. | | | | | |
|---|---|---|---|---|---|---|---|---|---|---|---|---|
| No. of years since birth of 1st child. | No. of Families. | No. of Children born. | No. of Children alive. | No. of Children dead. | Mortality per cent. | Average No. of Children in each Family. | No. of years since birth of 1st child. | No. of Families. | No. of Children born. | No. of Children alive. | No. of Children dead. | Mortality per cent. | Average No. of Children in each Family. |
| 1 | 6 | 6 | 6 | .. | .. | 1·00 | 1 | 1 | 1 | .. | 1 | 100·00 | 1·00 |
| 2 | 9 | 15 | 12 | 3 | 20·00 | 1·66 | 2 | 1 | 1 | 1 | .. | .. | 1·00 |
| 3 | 12 | 22 | 17 | 5 | 22·73 | 1·83 | 3 | 2 | 4 | 3 | 1 | 25·00 | 2·00 |
| 4 | 10 | 36 | 20 | 16 | 44·44 | 3·60 | 4 | 2 | 4 | 3 | 1 | 25·00 | 2·00 |
| 5 | 7 | 17 | 14 | 3 | 17·41 | 2·43 | 5 | .. | .. | .. | .. | .. | .. |
| 6 | 7 | 19 | 18 | 1 | 5·26 | 2·71 | 6 | 6 | 20 | 16 | 4 | 20·00 | 3·33 |
| 7 | 9 | 39 | 30 | 9 | 23·07 | 4·33 | 7 | 4 | 21 | 11 | 10 | 47·62 | 5·25 |
| 8 | 5 | 14 | 12 | 2 | 14·28 | 2·80 | 8 | 4 | 11 | 7 | 4 | 36·36 | 2·75 |
| 9 | 10 | 52 | 33 | 19 | 36·54 | 5·20 | 9 | 1 | 3 | 2 | 1 | 33·33 | 3·00 |
| 10 | 12 | 54 | 33 | 21 | 38·89 | 4·50 | 10 | 3 | 15 | 10 | 5 | 33·33 | 5·00 |
| 11 | 6 | 18 | 12 | 6 | 33·33 | 3·00 | 11 | 1 | 2 | 1 | 1 | 50·00 | 2·00 |
| 12 | 14 | 52 | 28 | 24 | 46·15 | 5·20 | 12 | .. | .. | .. | .. | .. | .. |
| 13 | 14 | 64 | 42 | 22 | 34·37 | 4·71 | 13 | .. | .. | .. | .. | .. | .. |
| 14 | 8 | 48 | 23 | 25 | 52·08 | 6·00 | 14 | .. | .. | .. | .. | .. | .. |
| 15 | 1 | 9 | 5 | 4 | 44·44 | 9·00 | 15 | .. | .. | .. | .. | .. | .. |
| 16 | 8 | 37 | 29 | 8 | 21·62 | 4·62 | 16 | 1 | 4 | 2 | 2 | 50·00 | 4·00 |
| 17 | 6 | 37 | 29 | 8 | 21·62 | 6·17 | 17 | .. | .. | .. | .. | .. | .. |
| 18 | 8 | 34 | 21 | 13 | 38·23 | 4·25 | 18 | .. | .. | .. | .. | .. | .. |
| 19 | 8 | 41 | 25 | 16 | 39·02 | 5·12 | 19 | 3 | 9 | 9 | .. | .. | 3·00 |
| 20 | 11 | 91 | 44 | 47 | 51·65 | 8·27 | 20 | 2 | 5 | 3 | 2 | 40·00 | 2·50 |
| 21 | 6 | 51 | 30 | 21 | 41·18 | 8·50 | 21 | 1 | 3 | 2 | 1 | 33·33 | 3·00 |
| 22 | 7 | 40 | 23 | 17 | 42·50 | 5·71 | 22 | 2 | 7 | 6 | 1 | 14·28 | 3·50 |
| 23 | 2 | 6 | 3 | 3 | 50·00 | 3·00 | 23 | 2 | 16 | 6 | 10 | 62·50 | 8·00 |
| 24 | 6 | 35 | 22 | 13 | 37·14 | 5·83 | 24 | 1 | 3 | 3 | .. | .. | 3·00 |
| 25 | 2 | 12 | 4 | 8 | 66·66 | 6·00 | 25 | 3 | 16 | 6 | 10 | 62·50 | 5·33 |
| 26 | 3 | 26 | 7 | 19 | 73·08 | 8·67 | 26 | 1 | 11 | 8 | 3 | 27·27 | 1·10 |
| 27 | 4 | 24 | 19 | 5 | 20·83 | 6·00 | 27 | 1 | 3 | 3 | .. | .. | 3·00 |
| 28 | 5 | 38 | 16 | 22 | 57·89 | 7·60 | 28 | .. | .. | .. | .. | .. | .. |
| 29 | 5 | 30 | 20 | 10 | 33·33 | 6·00 | 29 | .. | .. | .. | .. | .. | .. |
| 30 | 5 | 23 | 13 | 10 | 43·48 | 4·60 | 30 | .. | .. | .. | .. | .. | .. |
| 31 | 1 | 2 | 2 | .. | .. | 2·00 | 31 | .. | .. | .. | .. | .. | .. |
| 32 | 4 | 43 | 19 | 24 | 55·81 | 10·75 | 32 | 2 | 14 | 5 | 9 | 64·28 | 7·00 |
| 33 | 3 | 20 | 19 | 1 | 5·00 | 6·67 | 33 | 2 | 4 | 3 | 1 | 25·00 | 2·00 |
| 34 | 3 | 18 | 13 | 5 | 27·77 | 6·00 | 34 | 1 | 7 | 3 | 4 | 57·14 | 7·00 |
| 35 | .. | .. | .. | .. | .. | .. | 35 | 1 | 5 | 5 | .. | .. | 5·00 |
| 36 | 1 | 14 | 6 | 8 | 57·14 | 14·00 | 36 | .. | .. | .. | .. | .. | .. |
| 37 | 2 | 17 | 12 | 5 | 29·41 | 8·50 | 37 | .. | .. | .. | .. | .. | .. |
| 38 | 2 | 11 | 2 | 9 | 81·81 | 5·50 | 38 | .. | .. | .. | .. | .. | .. |
| 39 | 3 | 20 | 9 | 11 | 55·00 | 6·67 | 39 | 1 | 4 | 2 | 2 | 50·00 | 4·00 |
| 40 | 3 | 17 | 3 | 14 | 82·35 | 5·67 | 40 | .. | .. | .. | .. | .. | .. |
| 41 | .. | .. | .. | .. | .. | .. | 41 | .. | .. | .. | .. | .. | .. |
| 42 | 2 | 2 | 2 | .. | .. | 1·00 | 42 | .. | .. | .. | .. | .. | .. |
| 43 | 1 | 6 | 3 | 3 | 50·00 | 6·00 | 43 | 1 | 4 | 3 | 1 | 25·00 | 4·00 |
| 44 | 1 | 2 | 1 | 1 | 50·00 | 2·00 | 44 | .. | .. | .. | .. | .. | .. |
| 45 | .. | .. | .. | .. | .. | .. | 45 | .. | .. | .. | .. | .. | .. |
| 46 | .. | .. | .. | .. | .. | .. | 46 | .. | .. | .. | .. | .. | .. |
| 47 | .. | .. | .. | .. | .. | .. | 47 | .. | .. | .. | .. | .. | .. |
| 48 | 1 | 4 | 3 | 1 | 25·00 | 4·00 | 48 | .. | .. | .. | .. | .. | .. |
| 49 | 1 | 3 | 2 | 1 | 33·33 | 3·00 | 49 | .. | .. | .. | .. | .. | .. |
| 50 | .. | .. | .. | .. | .. | .. | 50 | .. | .. | .. | .. | .. | .. |
| 51 | .. | .. | .. | .. | .. | .. | 51 | .. | .. | .. | .. | .. | .. |
| 52 | .. | .. | .. | .. | .. | .. | 52 | .. | .. | .. | .. | .. | .. |
| 53 | .. | .. | .. | .. | .. | .. | 53 | .. | .. | .. | .. | .. | .. |
| 54 | .. | .. | .. | .. | .. | .. | 54 | .. | .. | .. | .. | .. | .. |
| 55 | .. | .. | .. | .. | .. | .. | 55 | .. | .. | .. | .. | .. | .. |
| 56 | .. | .. | .. | .. | .. | .. | 56 | .. | .. | .. | .. | .. | .. |
| 57 | .. | .. | .. | .. | .. | .. | 57 | .. | .. | .. | .. | .. | .. |
| 58 | .. | .. | .. | .. | .. | .. | 58 | .. | .. | .. | .. | .. | .. |
| 59 | .. | .. | .. | .. | .. | .. | 59 | .. | .. | .. | .. | .. | .. |
| 60 | .. | .. | .. | .. | .. | .. | 60 | .. | .. | .. | .. | .. | .. |
| | 210 | 1,169 | 706 | 463 | 39·61 | 4·87 | | 50 | 197 | 123 | 74 | 37·56 | 3·94 |

E.—Age of Mother at Birth of 1st Child.  Total Ages.  14 to 43.

| No. of Years since Birth of 1st Child. | No. of Families. | No. of Children born. | No. of Children alive. | No. of Children dead. | Mortality per cent. | Average No. of Children to each Family. |
|---|---|---|---|---|---|---|
| 1 | 56 | 59 | 52 | 7 | 11·86 | 1·05 |
| 2 | 60 | 88 | 69 | 19 | 21·59 | 1·46 |
| 3 | 54 | 99 | 76 | 23 | 23·23 | 1·83 |
| 4 | 68 | 190 | 122 | 68 | 35·79 | 2·80 |
| 5 | 57 | 163 | 118 | 45 | 27·61 | 2·86 |
| 6 | 63 | 208 | 151 | 57 | 27·40 | 3·30 |
| 7 | 78 | 273 | 195 | 78 | 28·57 | 3·50 |
| 8 | 58 | 215 | 153 | 62 | 28·84 | 3·71 |
| 9 | 42 | 190 | 117 | 73 | 38·42 | 4·52 |
| 10 | 63 | 295 | 177 | 118 | 40·00 | 4·68 |
| 11 | 41 | 191 | 112 | 79 | 41·36 | 4·66 |
| 12 | 55 | 306 | 193 | 113 | 36·93 | 5·56 |
| 13 | 60 | 340 | 205 | 135 | 39·71 | 5·66 |
| 14 | 43 | 276 | 157 | 119 | 43·12 | 6·42 |
| 15 | 38 | 256 | 162 | 94 | 36·72 | 6·74 |
| 16 | 48 | 288 | 189 | 99 | 34·38 | 6·00 |
| 17 | 34 | 201 | 128 | 73 | 36·32 | 5·91 |
| 18 | 32 | 181 | 103 | 78 | 43·09 | 5·66 |
| 19 | 43 | 298 | 168 | 130 | 43·62 | 6·93 |
| 20 | 53 | 351 | 192 | 159 | 45·30 | 6·62 |
| 21 | 36 | 282 | 161 | 121 | 42·91 | 7·83 |
| 22 | 39 | 283 | 155 | 128 | 45·23 | 7·26 |
| 23 | 32 | 239 | 121 | 118 | 49·37 | 7·47 |
| 24 | 38 | 288 | 163 | 125 | 43·40 | 7·58 |
| 25 | 20 | 125 | 70 | 55 | 44·00 | 6·25 |
| 26 | 25 | 186 | 98 | 88 | 47·31 | 7·44 |
| 27 | 22 | 163 | 93 | 70 | 42·94 | 7·41 |
| 28 | 22 | 158 | 84 | 74 | 46·84 | 7·18 |
| 29 | 32 | 248 | 129 | 119 | 47·98 | 7·75 |
| 30 | 34 | 283 | 140 | 143 | 50·53 | 8·32 |
| 31 | 11 | 84 | 54 | 30 | 35·71 | 7·64 |
| 32 | 19 | 154 | 74 | 80 | 51·95 | 8·10 |
| 33 | 14 | 85 | 44 | 41 | 48·24 | 6·07 |
| 34 | 12 | 103 | 46 | 57 | 55·34 | 8·58 |
| 35 | 11 | 62 | 31 | 31 | 50·00 | 5·64 |
| 36 | 16 | 136 | 48 | 88 | 64·71 | 8·50 |
| 37 | 6 | 59 | 27 | 32 | 54·24 | 9·83 |
| 38 | 4 | 29 | 13 | 16 | 55·17 | 7·25 |
| 39 | 12 | 116 | 45 | 71 | 61·21 | 9·67 |
| 40 | 10 | 86 | 21 | 65 | 75·58 | 8·60 |
| 41 | 7 | 61 | 21 | 40 | 65·57 | 8·71 |
| 42 | 8 | 43 | 30 | 13 | 30·23 | 5·37 |
| 43 | 7 | 80 | 40 | 40 | 50·00 | 11·43 |
| 44 | 5 | 41 | 15 | 26 | 63·41 | 8·20 |
| 45 | 3 | 33 | 9 | 24 | 72·73 | 11·00 |
| 46 | 1 | 7 | 5 | 2 | 28·57 | 7·00 |
| 47 | 1 | 5 | 3 | 2 | 40·00 | 5·00 |
| 48 | 2 | 7 | 3 | 4 | 57·14 | 3·50 |
| 49 | 4 | 36 | 10 | 26 | 72·72 | 9·00 |
| 50 | 1 | 7 | 3 | 4 | 57·14 | 7·00 |
| 51 | 1 | 14 | 5 | 9 | 64·29 | 14·00 |
| 52 | 1 | 17 | 3 | 14 | 82·35 | 17·00 |
| 53 | .. | .. | .. | .. | .. | .. |
| 54 | 2 | 18 | 5 | 13 | 72·22 | 9·00 |
| 55 | .. | .. | .. | .. | .. | .. |
| 56 | .. | .. | .. | .. | .. | .. |
| 57 | .. | .. | .. | .. | .. | .. |
| 58 | .. | .. | .. | .. | .. | .. |
| 59 | 1 | 15 | 7 | 8 | 53·33 | 15·00 |
| 60 | 1 | 13 | 1 | 12 | 92·31 | 13·00 |
| | 1,506 | 8,034 | 4,616 | 3,418 | 42·54 | 5·33 |

TABLE XX.—*Average of Present Age of Mothers, of Respective Trades Classified, with Averages of Children Born, now Living, and Dead, to each ; also Average Age of Mother when First Child Born, with difference between that and Present Age.*

| Trades. | Under 20. | | | | | | 20 to 25. | | | | | |
|---|---|---|---|---|---|---|---|---|---|---|---|---|
| | Average Age of Mothers. | | | Average to each Mother of | | | Average Age of Mothers. | | | Average to each Mother of | | |
| | When First Child Born. | Present Age. | Difference. | Children Born. | Children now Living. | Dead. | When First Child Born. | Present Age. | Difference. | Children Born. | Children now Living. | Dead. |
| Labourers | 18·0 | 19·0 | 1·0 | 1·0 | 1·0 | .... | 19·8 | 23·1 | 3·3 | 2·4 | 1·5 | 0·9 |
| Gunsmiths | 17·0 | 19·0 | 2·0 | 2·0 | 2·0 | .... | 20·7 | 23 0 | 2·3 | 1·7 | 1·2 | 0·5 |
| Gunmakers | .... | .... | .... | .... | .... | .... | 19·0 | 22·4 | 3·4 | 2·4 | 1·6 | 0·8 |
| Shoemakers | .... | .... | .... | .... | .... | .... | 18·7 | 22·5 | 3·8 | 3·0 | 1·5 | 1·5 |
| Bricklayers | .... | .... | .... | .... | .... | .... | 20·0 | 23·0 | 3·0 | 2·0 | 2·0 | .... |
| Coopers | .... | .... | .... | .... | .... | .... | 18·6 | 23·0 | 4·4 | 2·6 | 1·8 | 0·8 |
| Engineers | .... | .... | .... | .... | .... | .... | .... | .... | .... | .... | .... | .... |
| Umbrella-makers | .... | .... | .... | .... | .... | .... | 18·0 | 22·0 | 4·0 | 3·0 | .... | 3·0 |
| Porters | 16·0 | 17·0 | 1·0 | 1·0 | 1·0 | .... | 19·0 | 22·0 | 3·0 | 2·0 | 1·5 | 0·5 |
| Carmen | .... | .... | .... | .... | .... | .... | 19·0 | 22·0 | 3·0 | 2·0 | 2·0 | .... |
| Butchers | .... | .... | .... | .... | .... | .... | 21·0 | 22·0 | 1·0 | 1·0 | 1·0 | .... |
| Sugar-bakers | .... | .... | .... | .... | .... | .... | 18·0 | 22·0 | 4:0 | 2·0 | 1·0 | 1·0 |
| Bakers | .... | .... | .... | .... | .... | .... | 21·0 | 23·0 | 2·0 | 1·0 | 1·0 | .... |
| Painters | .... | .... | .... | .... | .... | .... | | | | | | |
| Watermen | .... | .... | .... | .... | .... | .... | 17·3 | 22·6 | 5·3 | 2·0 | 1·7 | 0·3 |
| Smiths | .... | .... | .... | .... | .... | .... | 20·2 | 23·4 | 3·2 | 1·8 | 1·6 | 0·2 |
| Sailors | 16·0 | 19·0 | 3·0 | 1·0 | 1·0 | .... | 20·5 | 22·5 | 2·0 | 1·0 | 1·0 | .... |
| Tailors | .... | .... | .... | .... | .... | .... | 17·7 | 21·3 | 3·6 | 1·3 | 0·7 | 0·6 |
| Cigar-makers | .... | .... | .... | .... | .... | .... | 20·4 | 22·9 | 2·5 | 1·6 | 1·4 | 0·2 |
| Carpenters | .... | .... | .... | .... | .... | .... | 17·8 | 22·0 | 4·2 | 2·8 | 2·2 | 0·6 |
| Gun-stock-makers | .... | .... | .... | .... | .... | .... | 19·0 | 20·0 | 1·0 | 1·0 | 1·0 | .... |
| Tin-workers | .... | .... | .... | .... | .... | .... | 22·0 | 23·0 | 1·0 | 1·0 | 1·0 | .... |
| Wheelwrights | .... | .... | .... | .... | .... | .... | | | | | | |
| Shopmen | .... | .... | .... | .... | .... | .... | 21·0 | 23·5 | 2·5 | 2·0 | 2·0 | .... |
| Widows with incumbrance | .... | .... | .... | .... | .... | .... | 19·7 | 23·3 | 3·6 | 2·0 | 1·0 | 1·0 |
| Policemen | .... | .... | .... | .... | .... | .... | 21·2 | 22·7 | 1·5 | 1·0 | 0·7 | 0·3 |
| Printers | .... | .... | .... | .... | .... | .... | .... | .... | .... | .... | .... | .... |
| Clerks | .... | .... | .... | .... | .... | .... | | | | | | |
| Miscellaneous | 18·0 | 19·0 | 1·0 | 1·0 | 1·0 | .... | 20·1 | 22·7 | 2·6 | 1·9 | 1·3 | 0·6 |
| | 17·0 | 18·6 | 1·6 | 1·2 | 1·2 | .... | 19·7 | 22·7 | 3·0 | 2·0 | 1·4 | 0·6 |
| Averages of Total, including Married Women, having no children | 17·0 | 18·8 | .... | 0·7 | 0·7 | .... | 19·7 | 22·7 | .... | 1·4 | 1·0 | 0·4 |

TABLE XXI.—*Average of Present Age of Mothers, of Respective Trades Classif*
*Age of Mother when First Child Born, u*

| Trades. | 25 to 30. | | | | | | 30 to 35. | | | | |
| | Average Age of Mothers. | | | Average to each Mother of | | | Average Age of Mothers. | | | Average to Mother | |
| | When First Child Born. | Present Age. | Difference. | Children Born. | Children now living. | Dead. | When First Child Born. | Present Age. | Difference. | Children Born. | Children now Living. |
|---|---|---|---|---|---|---|---|---|---|---|---|
| Labourers | 21·5 | 27·2 | 5·7 | 3·0 | 2·0 | 1·0 | 21·6 | 31·4 | 9·8 | 4·9 | 2·7 |
| Gunsmiths | 20·9 | 27·3 | 6·4 | 3·6 | 2·4 | 1·2 | 21·4 | 32·0 | 10·6 | 5·3 | 3·9 |
| Gunmakers | 20·4 | 26·7 | 6·3 | 3·6 | 2·9 | 0·7 | 21·0 | 32·0 | 11·0 | 5·0 | 3·0 |
| Shoemakers | 21·8 | 26·6 | 4·8 | 2·7 | 1·5 | 1·2 | 22·8 | 31·8 | 9·0 | 4·7 | 3·6 |
| Bricklayers | 19·7 | 26·0 | 6·3 | 3·0 | 1·7 | 1·3 | 20·2 | 31·0 | 10·8 | 6·2 | 3·6 |
| Coopers | 21·3 | 27·1 | 5·8 | 3·4 | 2·2 | 1·2 | 23·3 | 31·7 | 8·4 | 4·8 | 2·1 |
| Engineers | 23·2 | 27·6 | 4·4 | 2·4 | 1 6 | 0·8 | 23·8 | 32·0 | 8·2 | 4·0 | 3·2 |
| Umbrella-makers | 20·0 | 27·0 | 7·0 | 3·5 | 2·5 | 1·0 | 22·0 | 32·0 | 10·0 | 6·0 | 5·0 |
| Porters | 21·2 | 26·6 | 5·4 | 3·4 | 2·8 | 0·6 | 21·1 | 31·5 | 10·4 | 6·6 | 3·7 |
| Carmen | 22·8 | 26·6 | 3·8 | 2·0 | 1·8 | 0·2 | 22·9 | 31·5 | 8·6 | 4·6 | 2·5 |
| Butchers | 21·5 | 28·0 | 6·5 | 3·5 | 2·0 | 1·5 | 21·0 | 32·0 | 11·0 | 3·0 | 3·0 |
| Sugar-bakers | 20·6 | 26·6 | 6·0 | 4·0 | 3·0 | 1·0 | 23·8 | 30·8 | 7·0 | 3·6 | 2·2 |
| Bakers | 20·2 | 26·0 | 5·8 | 3·2 | 2·2 | 1·0 | 22·2 | 31·4 | 9·2 | 4·8 | 3·6 |
| Painters | 20·2 | 26·6 | 6·4 | 3·6 | 2·4 | 1·2 | 21·5 | 31·2 | 9·7 | 4·4 | 2·5 |
| Watermen | 20·0 | 26·0 | 6·0 | 2·2 | 2·0 | 0·2 | .... | .... | .... | .... | .... |
| Smiths | 21·4 | 25·8 | 4·4 | 2·4 | 1·6 | 0·8 | 19·5 | 31·5 | 12·0 | 4·8 | 3·5 |
| Sailors | 22·1 | 27·6 | 5·5 | 3·3 | 2·0 | 1·0 | 21·5 | 32·6 | 11·1 | 5·2 | 1·9 |
| Tailors | 21·8 | 26.6 | 4·8 | 3·2 | 2·4 | 0·8 | 21·7 | 32·3 | 10·6 | 5·0 | 3·7 |
| Cigar-makers | 23·2 | 26·5 | 3·3 | 2·0 | 2·0 | .... | 19·0 | 32·0 | 13·0 | 5·7 | 3·3 |
| Carpenters | 21·8 | 26·5 | 4·7 | 2·0 | 1·7 | 0·3 | 22·6 | 31·8 | 9·2 | 4·2 | 3·3 |
| Gun-stock-makers | .... | .... | .... | .... | .... | .... | 21·0 | 31·5 | 10·5 | 7·0 | 3·0 |
| Tin-workers | 19·0 | 26·0 | 7·0 | 3·0 | 3·0 | .... | 19·0 | 32·0 | 13·0 | 7·0 | 5·0 |
| Wheelwrights | 21·3 | 26·0 | 4·7 | 2·0 | 1·7 | 0·3 | .... | .... | .... | .... | .... |
| Shopmen | 23·5 | 26·0 | 2·5 | 1·5 | 1·0 | 0·5 | 22·5 | 31·0 | 8·5 | 4·5 | 2·0 |
| Widows with incumbrance | 21·4 | 26·7 | 5·3 | 2·5 | 1·5 | 1·0 | 22·2 | 32·2 | 10·0 | 3·7 | 2·5 |
| Policemen | 22·5 | 25·5 | 3·0 | 1·5 | 1·5 | .... | 22·0 | 30·5 | 8·5 | 3·5 | 3·0 |
| Printers | 22·7 | 28·0 | 5·3 | 3·7 | 2·7 | 1·0 | 22·0 | 30·0 | 8·0 | 2·0 | 2·0 |
| Clerks | 23·5 | 27·5 | 4·0 | 3·0 | 2·5 | 0·5 | 24·0 | 31·5 | 7·5 | 5·0 | 4·0 |
| Miscellaneous | 21·1 | 27·0 | 5·9 | 3·2 | 2·3 | 0·9 | 22·2 | 31·7 | 9·5 | 4·2 | 2·7 |
| Averages of Total, | 21·4 | 26·9 | 5·5 | 3·0 | 2·1 | 0·9 | 22·0 | 31·7 | 9·7 | 4·7 | 2·9 |
| Averages of Total, including Married Women, having no children | 21·4 | 26·8 | .... | 2·6 | 1·8 | 0·8 | 22·0 | 31·7 | .... | 4·3 | 2·7 |

*with Averages of Children Born, now Living, and Dead to each; also Average Difference between that and Present Age.—Continued.*

| | 35 to 40. | | | | | | 40 to 45. | | | | | | 45 to 50. | | | | |
| --- | --- | --- | --- | --- | --- | --- | --- | --- | --- | --- | --- | --- | --- | --- | --- | --- | --- |
| Average Age of Mothers. | | | Average to each Mother of | | | Average Age of Mothers. | | | Average to each Mother of | | | Average Age of Mothers. | | | Average to each Mother of | | |
| When First Child Born. | Present Age. | Difference. | Children Born. | Children now Living. | Dead. | When First Child Born. | Present Age. | Difference. | Children Born. | Children now Living. | Dead. | When First Child Born. | Present Age. | Difference. | Children Born. | Children now Living. | Dead. |
| 3·3 | 37·0 | 13·7 | 5·1 | 3·1 | 2·0 | 23·4 | 41·5 | 18·1 | 6·3 | 3·6 | 2·7 | 23·9 | 46·8 | 22·9 | 7·7 | 4·0 | 3·7 |
| 3·0 | 35·9 | 8·9 | 5·1 | 3·5 | 1·6 | 20·2 | 41·0 | 20·8 | 8·5 | 6·2 | 2·3 | 20·3 | 46·3 | 26·0 | 10·3 | 4·0 | 6·3 |
| 3·2 | 35·5 | 12·3 | 7·0 | 2·7 | 4·3 | .... | .... | .... | .... | .... | .... | 16·5 | 46·5 | 30·0 | 6·5 | 3·5 | 3·0 |
| 1·8 | 36·4 | 14·6 | 6·3 | 3·2 | 3·1 | 23·1 | 42·4 | 18·3 | 8·2 | 4·2 | 4·0 | 20·2 | 46·2 | 26·0 | 6·2 | 3·5 | 2·7 |
| 2·4 | 37·2 | 14·8 | 4·2 | 3·2 | 1·0 | 21·3 | 40·5 | 19·2 | 8·0 | 4·8 | 3·2 | 21·5 | 47·5 | 26·0 | 12·5 | 3·5 | 9·0 |
| 2·0 | 37·5 | 15·5 | 3·5 | 2·1 | 1·4 | 23·2 | 42·0 | 18·8 | 7·6 | 3·5 | 4·1 | 22·8 | 45·8 | 23·0 | 6·6 | 3·8 | 2·8 |
| 1·7 | 36·0 | 14·3 | 5·7 | 3·7 | 2·0 | .... | .... | .... | .... | .... | .... | .... | .... | .... | .... | .... | .... |
| .... | .... | .... | .... | .... | .... | 21·0 | 41·0 | 20·0 | 3·0 | 2·0 | 1·0 | 27·7 | 47·3 | 19·6 | 10·7 | 5·0 | 5·7 |
| 4·0 | 37·5 | 13·5 | 7·5 | 4·2 | 3·3 | 23·6 | 41·8 | 18·2 | 5·6 | 3·8 | 1·8 | 21·7 | 45·3 | 23·6 | 7·0 | 2·3 | 4·7 |
| 3·0 | 37·0 | 14·0 | 5·4 | 3·2 | 2·2 | 21·4 | 41·1 | 19·7 | 8·0 | 3·6 | 4·4 | 23·0 | 47·0 | 24·0 | 7·0 | 5·5 | 1·5 |
| 9·0 | 37·0 | 18·0 | 3·5 | 3·5 | .... | 25·0 | 41·5 | 16·5 | 11·0 | 6·5 | 4·5 | 22·5 | 46·0 | 23·5 | 6·0 | 3·5 | 2·5 |
| 3·8 | 36·8 | 13·0 | 6·3 | 4·3 | 2·0 | 18·0 | 40·0 | 22·0 | 10·0 | 5·0 | 5·0 | 20·0 | 46·5 | 26·5 | 3·5 | 2·0 | 1·5 |
| 1·0 | 39·0 | 18·0 | 12·0 | 8·0 | 4·0 | 26·0 | 41·5 | 15·5 | 6·0 | 2·2 | 3·8 | 25·0 | 49·0 | 24·0 | 5·0 | 2·0 | 3·0 |
| 4·0 | 36·0 | 12·0 | 6·5 | 2·5 | 5·0 | 26·0 | 40·2 | 14·2 | 6·0 | 4·2 | 1·8 | 25·0 | 45·0 | 20·0 | 7·5 | 6·0 | 1·5 |
| 8·0 | 38·0 | 20·0 | 8·3 | 3·3 | 4·0 | 20·0 | 42·0 | 22·0 | 6·0 | 4·5 | 1·5 | 23·0 | 47·0 | 24·0 | 8·0 | 5·5 | 2·5 |
| 0·5 | 36·0 | 15·5 | 8·0 | 2·5 | 5·5 | 22·2 | 41·8 | 19·6 | 8·0 | 3·4 | 4·6 | 23·5 | 45·0 | 21·5 | 8·0 | 4·5 | 3·5 |
| 4·0 | 36·5 | 12·5 | 4·8 | 2·7 | 2·1 | 23·2 | 41·4 | 18·2 | 5·6 | 2·0 | 3·6 | 23·3 | 48·3 | 25·0 | 6·0 | 3·3 | 2·7 |
| 1·5 | 36·4 | 14·9 | 7·1 | 5·0 | 2·1 | 24·0 | 42·5 | 18·5 | 8·5 | 5·1 | 3·4 | 25·4 | 47·1 | 21·7 | 5·8 | 3·4 | 2·4 |
| 6·7 | 35·0 | 8·3 | 1·7 | 1·7 | .... | .... | .... | .... | .... | .... | .... | 24·0 | 48·0 | 24·0 | 11·0 | 10·0 | 1·0 |
| 3·8 | 37·0 | 13·2 | 5·9 | 3·5 | 2·4 | 22·7 | 41·6 | 18·9 | 7·4 | 4·1 | 3·3 | 21·0 | 46·6 | 25·6 | 8·4 | 3·8 | 4·6 |
| 0·0 | 38·0 | 19·0 | 10·0 | 10·0 | .... | 25·0 | 45·0 | 20·0 | 5·0 | 3·0 | 2·0 | 28·0 | 48·0 | 20·0 | 6·0 | 4·0 | 2·0 |
| .... | .... | .... | .... | .... | .... | 21·0 | 40·0 | 19·0 | 7·0 | 5·0 | 2·0 | 22·7 | 48·0 | 25·3 | 10·5 | 6·2 | 4·3 |
| 2·5 | 37·0 | 14·5 | 9·0 | 4·5 | 4·5 | .... | .... | .... | .... | .... | .... | 29·0 | 46·0 | 17·0 | 6·0 | 4·0 | 2·0 |
| .... | .... | .... | .... | .... | .... | .... | .... | .... | .... | .... | .... | 21·0 | 46·0 | 25·0 | 8·0 | 3·0 | 5·0 |
| 3·3 | 36·6 | 13·3 | 4·1 | 2·5 | 1·6 | 23·6 | 41·5 | 17·9 | 5·6 | 3·8 | 1·8 | 23·2 | 46·4 | 23·2 | 6·8 | 3·3 | 3·5 |
| 3·7 | 37·0 | 13·3 | 5·3 | 3·0 | 2·3 | 24·0 | 40·0 | 16·0 | 4·0 | 4·0 | .... | 24·0 | 46·7 | 22·7 | 8·7 | 4·7 | 4·0 |
| 3·7 | 38·0 | 17·5 | 6·3 | 3·3 | 3·0 | 22·5 | 40·0 | 17·5 | 7·0 | 3·0 | 4·0 | .... | .... | .... | .... | .... | .... |
| 1·0 | 38·0 | 7·0 | 4·0 | 3·0 | 1·0 | 20·0 | 42·0 | 22·0 | 10·0 | 8·0 | 2·0 | 22·0 | 45·7 | 23·7 | 6·0 | 3·7 | 2·3 |
| 4·1 | 36·9 | 12·8 | 5·3 | 3·7 | 1·6 | 23·3 | 41·9 | 18·6 | 6·9 | 4·3 | 2·6 | 23·8 | 46·9 | 23·1 | 7·2 | 3·8 | 3·4 |
| 3·1 | 36·8 | 13·7 | 5·4 | 3·3 | 2·1 | 23·2 | 41·6 | 18·4 | 6·8 | 3·9 | 2·9 | 23·3 | 46·7 | 23·4 | 7·4 | 3·9 | 3·5 |
| 3·1 | 36·8 | .... | 5·2 | 3·2 | 2·0 | 23·2 | 41·6 | ... | 6·5 | 3·8 | 2·7 | 23·3 | 46·7 | .... | 6·8 | 3·6 | 3·2 |

TABLE XXII.—*Average of Present Age of Mothers, of Respective Trades Classified, with Averages of Children Born, now Living, and Dead, to each ; also Average Age of Mother when First Child Born, with Difference between that and Present Age.—Continued.*

| Trades. | 50 and Upwards. | | | | | | Unknown. | | | | | |
|---|---|---|---|---|---|---|---|---|---|---|---|---|
| | Average Age of Mothers. | | | Average to each Mother of | | | Average Age of Mothers. | | | Average to each Mother of | | |
| | When First Child Born. | Present Age. | Difference. | Children Born. | Children now Living. | Dead. | When First Child Born. | Present Age. | Difference. | Children Born. | Children now Living. | Dead. |
| Labourers | 25·6 | 56·2 | 30·6 | 7·0 | 3·3 | 3·7 | 25·5 | Dead | .... | 6·0 | 3·5 | 2·5 |
| Gunsmiths | 24·6 | 54·6 | 30·0 | 9·7 | 4·9 | 4·8 | 22·0 | Dead | .... | 13·0 | 7·0 | 6·0 |
| Gunmakers | .... | .... | .... | .... | .... | .... | .... | .... | .... | .... | .... | .... |
| Shoemakers | 26·0 | 56·9 | 30·9 | 5·7 | 3·5 | 2·2 | 22·0 | Dead | .... | 5·5 | 4·5 | 1·0 |
| Bricklayers | 18·0 | 60·3 | 42·3 | 7·0 | 2·7 | 4·3 | 27·0 | Dead | .... | 6·0 | 4·0 | 2·0 |
| Coopers | 23·4 | 59·8 | 36·4 | 8·5 | 3·1 | 5·4 | .... | .... | .... | .... | .... | .... |
| Engineers | .... | .... | .... | .... | .... | .... | .... | .... | .... | .... | .... | .... |
| Umbrella-makers | 25·5 | 55·0 | 29·5 | 8·5 | 3·5 | 5·0 | .... | .... | .... | .... | .... | .... |
| Porters | 25·5 | 52·5 | 27·0 | 7·0 | 3·5 | 3·5 | 20·0 | Dead | .... | 10·0 | 7·0 | 3·0 |
| Carmen | 26·1 | 56·8 | 30·4 | 7·2 | 4·2 | 3·0 | · | .... | .... | .... | .... | .... |
| Butchers | .... | .... | .... | .... | ..·r | .... | .... | .... | .... | .... | .... | .... |
| Sugar-bakers | 23·5 | 57·5 | 34·0 | 7·5 | 4·5 | 3·0 | .... | .... | .... | .... | .... | .... |
| Bakers | 21·0 | 51·5 | 30·5 | 8·5 | 4·5 | 4·0 | .... | .... | .... | .... | .... | .... |
| Painters | 21·7 | 56·0 | 34·3 | 11·3 | 3·7 | 7·6 | .... | .... | .... | .... | .... | .... |
| Watermen | 20·5 | 64·5 | 44·0 | 12·0 | 1·5 | 10·5 | .... | .... | .... | .... | .... | .... |
| Smiths | 22·0 | 62·0 | 40·0 | 9·5 | 4·5 | 5·0 | .... | .... | .... | .... | .... | .... |
| Sailors | 25·0 | 54·7 | 29·7 | 4·9 | 2·4 | 2·5 | .... | .... | .... | .... | .... | .... |
| Tailors | 24·8 | 61·7 | 36·9 | 8·1 | 3·4 | 4·7 | 17·0 | Dead | .... | 8·0 | 7·0 | 1·0 |
| Cigar-makers | 23·0 | 56·0 | 33·0 | 9·1 | 3·5 | 5·6 | .... | .... | .... | .... | .... | .... |
| Carpenters | 25·0 | 55·7 | 30·7 | 8·4 | 4·3 | 4·1 | .... | .... | .... | .... | .... | .... |
| Gun-stock-makers | .... | .... | .... | .... | .... | .... | .... | .... | .... | .... | .... | .... |
| Tin-workers | 34·0 | 57·0 | 23·0 | 8·0 | 3·0 | 5·0 | .... | .... | .... | .... | .... | .... |
| Wheelwrights | 35·0 | 56·0 | 21·0 | 3·0 | 2·0 | 1·0 | .... | .... | .... | .... | .... | .... |
| Shopmen | .... | .... | .... | .... | .... | .... | .... | .... | .... | .... | .... | .... |
| Widows with incumbrance | 22·9 | 58·5 | 35·6 | 7·4 | 3·5 | 3·9 | .... | .... | .... | .... | .... | .... |
| Policemen | 23·3 | 50·6 | 27·3 | 8·0 | 1·7 | 6·3 | .... | .... | .... | .... | .... | .... |
| Printers | .... | .... | .... | .... | .... | .... | .... | .... | .... | .... | .... | .... |
| Clerks | 24·8 | 53·3 | 28·5 | 6·0 | 3·2 | 2·8 | .... | .... | .... | .... | .... | .... |
| Miscellaneous | 25·5 | 58·2 | 32·7 | 6·7 | 3·5 | 3·2 | 25·2 | Dead | .... | 5·5 | 3·7 | 1·8 |
| | | | | | | | | | | | | |
| Averages of Total including Married Women, having no children | 24·7 | 57·3 | 32·6 | 7·3 | 3·5 | 3·8 | 24·2 | Dead | .... | 6·4 | 4·3 | 2·1 |
| | 24·7 | 57·3 | .... | 7·1 | 3·4 | 3·7 | 24·2 | Dead | .... | 6·4 | 4·3 | 2·1 |

TABLE XXIII.—*Totals of Present Age of Mothers, of Respective Trades Classified, with Children Born, now Living, and Dead; and Total Ages of Married Women having no Children inserted under Respective Classified Ages and Trades.*

| | Under 20. | | | | | | 20 to 25. | | | | | | 25 to 30. | | | | | |
|---|---|---|---|---|---|---|---|---|---|---|---|---|---|---|---|---|---|---|
| | Age of Mother | | Difference in Years. | Children Born. | Children now Living. | Dead. | Age of Mother | | Difference in Years. | Children Born. | Children now Living. | Dead. | Age of Mother | | Difference in Years. | Children Born. | Children now Living. | Dead. |
| | When first child born. | Present Age. | | | | | When first child born. | Present Age. | | | | | When first child born. | Present Age. | | | | |
| Labourers | (1) 18 | 19 | 1 | 1 | 1 | ... | (16) 317 | 370 (282) | 53 | 39 | 24 | 15 | (44) 946 (5) | 1,197 (130) | 251 | 132 | 91 | 41 |
| Gunsmiths | (1) 17 (1) | 19 (19) | 2 | 2 | 2 | ... | (12)(13) 269 | 299 (62) | 30 | 22 | 15 | 7 | (28) 586 | 764 (77) | 178 | 101 | 68 | 33 |
| Gunmakers | ... | ... | ... | ... | ... | ... | (3)(5) 95 | 112 | 17 | 12 | 8 | 4 | (7) 143 (1) | 187 (25) | 44 | 25 | 20 | 5 |
| Shoemakers | (1) ... | (19) ... | ... | ... | ... | ... | (6) 112 (1) | 135 (22) | 23 | 18 | 9 | 9 | (21) 458 (1) | 558 (27) | 100 | 57 | 31 | 26 |
| Bricklayers | ... | ... | ... | ... | ... | ... | (2) 40 | 46 | 6 | 4 | 4 | ... | (3) 59 (1) | 78 (28) | 19 | 9 | 5 | 4 |
| Coopers | ... | ... | ... | ... | ... | ... | (5) 93 (2) | 115 (45) | 22 | 13 | 9 | 4 | (10) 213 (2) | 271 (54) | 58 | 34 | 22 | 12 |
| Engineers | (1) ... | (19) ... | ... | ... | ... | ... | (2) ... (1) | ... (48) | ... | ... | ... | ... | (5) 116 | 138 | 22 | 12 | 8 | 4 |
| Umbrella-makers | (1) ... | ... | ... | ... | ... | ... | (1) 18 (2) | 22 | 4 | 3 | ... | 3 | (2) 40 | 54 | 14 | 7 | 5 | 2 |
| Porters | (1) 16 | 17 | 1 | 1 | 1 | ... | (2) 38 (3) | 44 | 6 | 4 | 3 | 1 | (5) 106 | 133 | 27 | 17 | 14 | 3 |
| Carmen | ... | ... | ... | ... | ... | ... | (3) 57 (1) | 66 (25) | 9 | 6 | 6 | ... | (5) 114 (2) | 133 (110) | 19 | 10 | 9 | 1 |
| Butchers | (1) ... | (19) ... | ... | ... | ... | ... | (1) 21 | 22 | 1 | 1 | 1 | ... | (4) 43 | 56 | 13 | 7 | 4 | 3 |
| Sugar-bakers | ... | ... | ... | ... | ... | ... | (1) 18 (1) | 22 (22) | 4 | 2 | 1 | 1 | (5) 103 (1) | 133 (25) | 30 | 20 | 15 | 5 |
| Bakers | ... | ... | ... | ... | ... | ... | (1) 21 | 23 | 2 | 1 | 1 | ... | (5) 101 (1) | 130 (26) | 29 | 16 | 11 | 5 |
| Painters | ... | ... | ... | ... | ... | ... | ... | ... | ... | ... | ... | ... | (5) 101 (1) | 133 (22) | 32 | 18 | 12 | 6 |
| Watermen | ... | ... | ... | ... | ... | ... | (3) 52 | 68 | 16 | 6 | 5 | 1 | (4) 80 | 104 | 24 | 9 | 8 | 1 |
| Smiths | ... | ... | ... | ... | ... | ... | (5) 101 | 117 (89) | 16 | 9 | 8 | 1 | (5) 107 | 129 | 22 | 12 | 8 | 4 |
| Sailors | (1) 16 | 19 | 3 | 1 | 1 | ... | (2) 41 (5) | 45 (111) | 4 | 2 | 2 | ... | (14) 310 (4) | 387 (105) | 77 | 46 | 28 | 18 |
| Tailors | ... | ... | ... | ... | ... | ... | (3) 53 (1) | 64 (23) | 11 | 4 | 2 | 2 | (11) 240 (5) | 293 (130) | 53 | 36 | 27 | 9 |
| Cigar-makers | ... | ... | ... | ... | ... | ... | (8) 163 (1) | 183 (20) | 20 | 13 | 11 | 2 | (4) 93 | 106 | 13 | 8 | 8 | ... |
| Carpenters | ... | ... | ... | ... | ... | ... | (6) 107 (1) | 132 (23) | 25 | 17 | 13 | 4 | (6) 131 (1) | 159 (28) | 28 | 12 | 10 | |
| Gun-stock-makers | ... | ... | ... | ... | ... | ... | (1) 19 | 20 | 1 | 1 | 1 | ... | ... | ... | ... | ... | ... | ... |
| Tin-workers | ... | ... | ... | ... | ... | ... | (1) 22 | 23 | 1 | 1 | 1 | ... | (1) 19 | 26 | 7 | 3 | 3 | ... |
| Wheelwrights | ... | ... | ... | ... | ... | ... | ... | ... | ... | ... | ... | ... | (3) 64 | 78 | 14 | 6 | 5 | 1 |
| Shopmen | ... | ... | ... | ... | ... | ... | (2) 42 (1) | 47 (23) | 5 | 4 | 4 | ... | (2) 47 (1) | 52 (26) | 5 | 3 | 2 | 1 |
| Widows | ... | ... | ... | ... | ... | ... | (3) 59 | 70 | 11 | 6 | 3 | 3 | (8) 171 (2) | 240 | 69 | 23 | 14 | 9 |
| Policemen | ... | ... | ... | ... | ... | ... | (4) 85 | 91 | 6 | 4 | 3 | 1 | (2) 45 | 51 | 6 | 3 | 3 | ... |
| Printers | ... | ... | ... | ... | ... | ... | ... | ... | ... | ... | ... | ... | (3) 68 (2) | 84 | 16 | 11 | 8 | 3 |
| Clerks | ... | ... | ... | ... | ... | ... | ... | ... | ... | ... | ... | ... | (2) 47 | 55 | 8 | 6 | 5 | 1 |
| Miscellaneous | (1) 18 | 19 | 1 | 1 | 1 | ... | (25) 502 (10) | 567 (225) | 65 | 47 | 33 | 14 | (61) 1,289 (13) | 1,648 (343) | 359 | 200 | 142 | 58 |
| **Total** | (5) 85 (4) | 93 (75) | 8 | 6 | 6 | ... | (119) 2,345 (45) | 2,703 (1,016) | 358 | 239 | 167 | 72 | (271) 5,840 (44) | 7,377 (1,156) | 1,537 | 843 | 586 | 257 |

TABLE XXIV.—*Totals of Present Age of Mothers, of Respective Trades Classified, with Children Born, now Living, and Dead; and Total Ages of Married Women having no Children inserted under Respective Classified Ages and Trades.—Continued.*

| | 30 to 35. | | | | | | 35 to 40. | | | | | | 40 to 45. | | | | | |
|---|---|---|---|---|---|---|---|---|---|---|---|---|---|---|---|---|---|---|
| | Age of Mother | | Difference in Years. | Children Born. | Children now Living. | Dead. | Age of Mother | | Difference in Years. | Children Born. | Children now Living. | Dead. | Age of Mother | | Difference in Years. | Children Born. | Children now Living. | Dead. |
| | When first child born. | Present Age. | | | | | When first child born. | Present Age. | | | | | When first child born. | Present Age. | | | | |
| Labourers | (51)(34) 1104 | (188) 1634 | 530 | 259 | 142 | 117 | (50)(6) 1165 | (222) 1850 | 685 | 254 | 154 | 100 | (48)(2) 1123 | (86) 1993 | 870 | 305 | 173 | 132 |
| Gunsmiths | (9)(3) 193 | 288 | 95 | 48 | 35 | 13 | (8)(4) 184 | 257 | 102 | 41 | 28 | 13 | (4) 81 | 164 | 83 | 34 | 25 | 9 |
| Gunmakers | 63 | 96 | 33 | 15 | 9 | 6 | (4) 93 | 142 | 49 | 28 | 11 | 17 | ... | ... | ... | ... | ... | ... |
| Shoemakers | (13) 297 | (94) 413 | 116 | 62 | 47 | 15 | (11) 240 | 401 | 161 | 70 | 36 | 34 | (11) 254 | 466 | 212 | 90 | 46 | 44 |
| Bricklayers | (5) 101 | 155 | 54 | 31 | 18 | 13 | (5) 112 | 186 | 74 | 21 | 16 | 5 | (6) 128 | 243 | 115 | 48 | 29 | 19 |
| Coopers | (12)(11) 257 | 381 | 124 | 58 | 33 | 25 | (8) 176 | 300 | 124 | 28 | 17 | 11 | (8) 186 | 336 | 150 | 61 | 28 | 33 |
| Engineers | (5) 119 | (30) 160 | 41 | 20 | 16 | 4 | (4) 87 | 144 | 57 | 23 | 15 | 8 | ... | ... | ... | ... | ... | ... |
| Umbrella-makers | (1)(1) 52 | 32 | 10 | 6 | 5 | 1 | ... | ... | ... | ... | ... | ... | (1) 21 | 41 | 20 | 3 | 2 | 1 |
| Porters | (7) 148 | 221 | 73 | 46 | 26 | 20 | (4) 96 | 150 | 54 | 30 | 17 | 13 | (5) 118 | 209 | 91 | 28 | 19 | 9 |
| Carmen | (13) 298 | 410 | 112 | 60 | 33 | 27 | (5) 115 | (35) 185 | 70 | 27 | 16 | 11 | (7) 150 | 288 | 138 | 56 | 25 | 31 |
| Butchers | (1)(1) 21 | (30) 32 | 11 | 3 | 3 | ... | (2) 38 | 74 | 36 | 7 | 7 | ... | (2) 50 | 83 | 33 | 22 | 13 | 9 |
| Sugar-bakers | (1)(5) 119 | 154 | 35 | 18 | 11 | 7 | (6) 143 | 221 | 78 | 38 | 26 | 12 | (1) 18 | 40 | 22 | 10 | 5 | 5 |
| Bakers | (5) 111 | 157 | 46 | 24 | 18 | 6 | (1) 21 | 39 | 18 | 12 | 8 | 4 | (4) 104 | (40) 166 | 62 | 24 | 9 | 15 |
| Painters | (3)(7) 151 | (98) 219 | 68 | 31 | 18 | 13 | (2) 48 | 72 | 24 | 13 | 5 | 8 | (4) 104 | 161 | 57 | 24 | 17 | 7 |
| Watermen | (1)(31) ... | ... | ... | ... | ... | ... | (3) 53 | 114 | 61 | 25 | 10 | 15 | (2)(1) 40 | (41) 84 | 44 | 12 | 9 | 3 |
| Smiths | (6) 117 | (62) 189 | 72 | 29 | 21 | 8 | (2) 41 | 72 | 31 | 16 | 5 | 11 | (5)(1) 111 | (43) 209 | 98 | 40 | 17 | 23 |
| Sailors | (2)(9) 194 | 294 | 100 | 47 | 17 | 30 | (15) 361 | 548 | 187 | 73 | 41 | 32 | (5)(1) 116 | (40) 207 | 91 | 28 | 10 | 18 |
| Tailors | (11) 239 | 356 | 117 | 65 | 41 | 14 | (10) 215 | 364 | 149 | 71 | 50 | 21 | (8)(1) 192 | (40) 340 | 148 | 68 | 41 | 27 |
| Cigar-makers | (3) 57 | 96 | 39 | 17 | 10 | 7 | (3) 80 | 105 | 25 | 5 | 5 | ... | ... | ... | ... | ... | ... | ... |
| Carpenters | (9) 204 | 287 | 83 | 38 | 30 | 8 | (15) 357 | 555 | 198 | 89 | 53 | 36 | (8)(1) 182 | (40) 333 | 151 | 59 | 33 | 26 |
| Gun-stock-makers | (2) 42 | 63 | 21 | 14 | 6 | 8 | (1) 19 | 38 | 19 | 10 | 10 | ... | (1)(2) 25 | (43) 45 | 20 | 5 | 3 | 2 |
| Tin-workers | (1) 19 | 32 | 13 | 7 | 5 | 2 | (2) ... | ... | ... | ... | ... | ... | (2) 42 | 80 | 38 | 14 | 10 | 4 |
| Wheelwrights | ... | ... | ... | ... | ... | ... | (2)(1) 45 | (36) 74 | 29 | 18 | 9 | 9 | ... | ... | ... | ... | ... | ... |
| Shopmen | (2) 45 | 62 | 17 | 9 | 4 | 5 | ... | ... | ... | ... | ... | ... | ... | ... | ... | ... | ... | ... |
| Widows with incumbrance | (17) 378 | 548 | 170 | 63 | 43 | 20 | (19) 443 | 695 | 252 | 78 | 48 | 30 | (21) 497 | 872 | 375 | 118 | 79 | 39 |
| Policemen | (4) 88 | 122 | 34 | 14 | 12 | 2 | (3) 71 | 111 | 40 | 16 | 9 | 7 | (1) 24 | 40 | 16 | 4 | 4 | ... |
| Printers | (1) 22 | 30 | 8 | 2 | 2 | ... | (3) 71 | 114 | 43 | 19 | 10 | 9 | (2) 45 | 80 | 35 | 14 | 6 | 8 |
| Clerks | (2) 48 | 63 | 15 | 10 | 8 | 2 | (1) 31 | 38 | 7 | 4 | 3 | 1 | (1) 20 | 42 | 22 | 10 | 8 | 2 |
| Miscellaneous | (52)(3) 1157 | (91) 1652 | 495 | 220 | 141 | 79 | (32)(1) 771 | (37) 1182 | 411 | 171 | 118 | 53 | (40)(2) 933 | (81) 1676 | 743 | 279 | 174 | 105 |
| Total | (21) 5614 | (657) 8146 | 2532 | 1206 | 754 | 452 | (219)(9) 5076 | (330) 8061 | 2985 | 1187 | 727 | 460 | (197)(11) 4564 | (454) 8198 | 3634 | 1356 | 785 | 571 |

TABLE XXV.—*Totals of Present Age of Mothers, of Respective Trades Classified, with Children Born, now Living, and Dead; and Total Ages of Married Women having no Children inserted under Respective Classified Ages and Trades.—Continued.*

| | 45 to 50. | | | | | | 50 and upwards. | | | | | | Unknown. | | | | | |
|---|---|---|---|---|---|---|---|---|---|---|---|---|---|---|---|---|---|---|
| | Age of Mother | | Difference in Years. | Children Born. | Children now Living. | Dead. | Age of Mother | | Difference in Years. | Children Born. | Children now Living. | Dead. | Age of Mother | | Difference in Years | Children Born. | Children now Living. | Dead. |
| | When first child born. | Present Age. | | | | | When first child born. | Present Age. | | | | | When first child born. | Present Age. | | | | |
| Labourers | (30) 716 | 1404 (93) | 688 | 232 | 120 | 112 | (58) 1486 | 3263 (131) | 1777 | 408 | 192 | 216 | (2) 51 | Dead | ... | 12 | 7 | 5 |
| Gunsmiths | (3) 61 | 139 | 78 | 31 | 12 | 19 | (9) 222 | 492 | 270 | 87 | 44 | 43 | (1) 22 | Dead | ... | 13 | 7 | 6 |
| Gunmakers | (2) 33 | 93 | 60 | 13 | 7 | 6 | ... | ... | ... | ... | ... | ... | ... | ... | ... | ... | ... | ... |
| Shoemakers | (4) 81 | 185 (112) | 104 | 25 | 14 | 11 | (13) 359 | 740 | 401 | 75 | 46 | 29 | (½) 22 | Dead | ... | 11 | 9 | 2 |
| Bricklayers | (2) 43 | 95 | 52 | 25 | 7 | 18 | (3) 54 | 181 | 127 | 21 | 8 | 13 | (1) 27 | Dead | ... | 6 | 4 | 2 |
| Coopers | (5) 114 | 229 (88) | 115 | 33 | 19 | 14 | (8) 187 | 478 (50) | 291 | 68 | 25 | 43 | ... | ... | ... | ... | ... | ... |
| Engineers | (2) ... | (47) ... | ... | ... | ... | ... | (1) ... | ... | ... | ... | ... | ... | ... | ... | ... | ... | ... | ... |
| Umbrella-makers | (3) 83 | 142 | 59 | 32 | 15 | 17 | (2) 51 | 110 | 59 | 17 | 7 | 10 | ... | ... | ... | ... | ... | ... |
| Porters | (3) 65 | 136 | 71 | 21 | 7 | 14 | (4) 102 | 210 | 108 | 28 | 14 | 14 | (1) 20 | Dead | ... | 10 | 7 | 3 |
| Carmen | (2) 46 | 94 (48) | 48 | 11 | 11 | 3 | (5) 132 | 284 | 152 | 36 | 21 | 15 | ... | ... | ... | ... | ... | ... |
| Butchers | (1)(2) 45 | 92 | 47 | 12 | 7 | 5 | ... | ... | ... | ... | ... | ... | ... | ... | ... | ... | ... | ... |
| Sugar-bakers | (2) 40 | 93 | 53 | 7 | 4 | 3 | (2) 47 | 115 | 68 | 15 | 9 | 6 | ... | ... | ... | ... | ... | ... |
| Bakers | (1) 25 | 49 (47) | 24 | 5 | 2 | 3 | (2) 42 | 103 | 61 | 17 | 9 | 8 | ... | ... | ... | ... | ... | ... |
| Painters | (2) 50 | 90 (43) | 40 | 15 | 12 | 8 | (3) 65 | 168 | 103 | 34 | 11 | 23 | ... | ... | ... | ... | ... | ... |
| Watermen | (2)(1) 46 | 94 (43) | 48 | 16 | 11 | 5 | (2) 41 | 129 | 88 | 24 | 3 | 21 | ... | ... | ... | ... | ... | ... |
| Smiths | (2) 47 | 90 | 43 | 16 | 9 | 7 | (2) 44 | 124 | 80 | 19 | 9 | 10 | ... | ... | ... | ... | ... | ... |
| Sailors | (3) 70 | 145 | 75 | 18 | 10 | 8 | (7) 175 | 383 | 208 | 34 | 17 | 17 | ... | ... | ... | ... | ... | ... |
| Tailors | (9) 229 | 424 | 195 | 53 | 31 | 22 | (9) 223 | 555 | 332 | 73 | 31 | 42 | (1) 17 | Dead | ... | 8 | 7 | 1 |
| Cigar-makers | (1) 24 | 48 | 24 | 11 | 10 | 1 | (6) 138 | 336 | 198 | 55 | 21 | 34 | ... | ... | ... | ... | ... | ... |
| Carpenters | (8) 168 | 373 | 205 | 67 | 30 | 37 | (17) 426 | 947 | 521 | 143 | 74 | 69 | ... | ... | ... | ... | ... | ... |
| Gun-stock-makers | (1) 28 | 48 | 20 | 6 | 4 | 2 | ... | ... | ... | ... | ... | ... | ... | ... | ... | ... | ... | ... |
| Tin-workers | (4) 91 | 192 | 101 | 42 | 25 | 17 | (1) 34 | 57 | 23 | 8 | 3 | 5 | ... | ... | ... | ... | ... | ... |
| Wheelwrights | (1) 29 | 46 | 17 | 6 | 4 | 2 | (1) 35 | 56 | 21 | 3 | 2 | 1 | ... | ... | ... | ... | ... | ... |
| Shopmen | (3) 63 | 138 | 75 | 24 | 9 | 15 | ... | ... | ... | ... | ... | ... | ... | ... | ... | ... | ... | ... |
| Widows with incumbrance | (19) 441 | 883 (48) | 442 | 130 | 64 | 66 | (55) 1264 | 3339 | 2075 | 423 | 202 | 221 | ... | ... | ... | ... | ... | ... |
| Policemen | (3) 72 | 140 | 68 | 26 | 14 | 12 | (3) 70 | 152 | 82 | 24 | 5 | 19 | ... | ... | ... | ... | ... | ... |
| Printers | ... | ... | 71 | ... | ... | ... | (4) 99 | 213 | 114 | 24 | 13 | 11 | ... | ... | ... | ... | ... | ... |
| Clerks | (3) 66 | 137 | 762 | 18 | 11 | 7 | (58) ... | ... | ... | ... | ... | ... | ... | ... | ... | ... | ... | ... |
| Miscellaneous | (33) 787 | 1549 (48) | 1549 | 238 | 125 | 113 | (3) 1759 | 4136 (278) | 2397 | 476 | 251 | 225 | (11) 277 | Dead | ... | 61 | 41 | 20 |
| Total | (153) 3563 (14) | 7148 (651) | 3585 | 1136 | 594 | 542 | (285) 7015 (8) | 16571 (459) | 9556 | 3112 | 1017 | 1095 | (18) 436 | Dead | ... | 121 | 82 | 39 |

TABLE XXVI.—*Totals of present Age of Mothers of respective*

| Trades. | Under 20. | | | | | | 20 to 25. | | | | | |
|---|---|---|---|---|---|---|---|---|---|---|---|---|
| | Total Ages of Mothers | | Difference in Years. | Children born. | Children now living. | Dead. | Total Ages of Mothers | | Difference in Years. | Children born. | Children now living. | Dead. |
| | When First Child born. | Present Age. | | | | | When First Child born. | Present Age. | | | | |
| Labourers | 18 | 19 | 1 | 1 | 1 | .... | 317 | 370 | 53 | 39 | 24 | 15 |
| Gunsmiths | 17 | 19 | 2 | 2 | 2 | .... | 269 | 299 | 30 | 22 | 15 | 7 |
| Gunmakers | .... | .... | .... | .... | .... | .... | 95 | 112 | 17 | 12 | 8 | 4 |
| Shoemakers | .... | .... | .... | .... | .... | .... | 112 | 135 | 23 | 18 | 9 | 9 |
| Bricklayers | .... | .... | .... | .... | .... | .... | 40 | 46 | 6 | 4 | 4 | .... |
| Coopers | ... | .... | .... | .... | .... | .... | 93 | 115 | 22 | 13 | 9 | 4 |
| Engineers | .... | .... | .... | .... | ... | .... | .... | .... | .... | .... | .... | .... |
| Umbrella-makers | .... | .... | .... | .... | .... | .... | 18 | 22 | 4 | 3 | .... | 3 |
| Porters | 16 | 17 | 1 | 1 | 1 | .... | 38 | 44 | 6 | 4 | 3 | 1 |
| Carmen | .... | .... | .... | .... | .... | .... | 57 | 66 | 9 | 6 | 6 | .... |
| Butchers | .... | .... | .... | .... | .... | .... | 21 | 22 | 1 | 1 | 1 | .... |
| Sugar-bakers | .... | .... | .... | .... | .... | .... | 18 | 22 | 4 | 2 | 1 | 1 |
| Bakers | .... | .... | .... | .... | .... | .... | 21 | 23 | 2 | 1 | 1 | .... |
| Painters | .... | .... | .... | .... | .... | .... | .... | .... | .... | .... | .... | .... |
| Watermen | .... | .... | .... | .... | .... | .... | 52 | 68 | 16 | 6 | 5 | 1 |
| Smiths | .... | .... | .... | .... | .... | .... | 101 | 117 | 16 | 9 | 8 | 1 |
| Sailors | 16 | 19 | 3 | 1 | 1 | .... | 41 | 45 | 4 | 2 | 2 | .... |
| Tailors | .... | .... | .... | .... | .... | .... | 53 | 64 | 11 | 4 | 2 | 2 |
| Cigar-makers | .... | .... | .... | .... | .... | .... | 163 | 183 | 20 | 13 | 11 | 2 |
| Carpenters | .... | .... | .... | .... | .... | .... | 107 | 132 | 25 | 17 | 13 | 4 |
| Gun-stock-makers | .... | .... | .... | .... | .... | .... | 19 | 20 | 1 | 1 | 1 | .... |
| Tin-workers | .... | .... | .... | .... | ... | .... | 22 | 23 | 1 | 1 | 1 | .... |
| Wheelwrights | .... | .... | .... | .... | .... | .... | .... | .... | .... | .... | .... | .... |
| Shopmen | .... | .... | .... | .... | .... | ... | 42 | 47 | 5 | 4 | 4 | .... |
| Widows with incumbrance | .... | .... | .... | .... | .... | .... | 59 | 70 | 11 | 6 | 3 | 3 |
| Policemen | .... | .... | .... | .... | .... | .... | 85 | 91 | 6 | 4 | 3 | 1 |
| Printers | .... | .... | .... | .... | .... | .... | .... | .... | .... | .... | .... | .... |
| Clerks | .... | .... | .... | .... | .... | .... | .... | .... | .... | .... | .... | .... |
| Miscellaneous | 18 | 19 | 1 | 1 | 1 | .... | 502 | 567 | 65 | 47 | 33 | 14 |
| | 85 | 93 | 8 | 6 | 6 | ... | 2,345 | 2,703 | 358 | 239 | 167 | 72 |
| Married Women having no children | .... | 76 | .... | .... | .... | .... | .... | 1,016 | .... | .... | .... | .... |
| Total | 85 | 169 | .... | 6 | 6 | .... | 2,345 | 3,719 | .... | 239 | 167 | 72 |

*Trades, classified with Children Born, now Living and Dead.*

| 25 to 30 | | | | | | 30 to 35 | | | | | | 35 to 40 | | | | | |
|---|---|---|---|---|---|---|---|---|---|---|---|---|---|---|---|---|---|
| Total Ages of Mothers | | | | | | Total Ages of Mothers | | | | | | Total Ages of Mothers | | | | | |
| When First Child born. | Present Age. | Difference in Years. | Children born. | Children now living. | Dead. | When First Child born. | Present Age. | Difference in Years. | Children born. | Children now living. | Dead. | When First Child born. | Present Age. | Difference in Years. | Children born. | Children now living. | Dead. |
| 46 | 1197 | 251 | 132 | 91 | 41 | [1] 1104 | 1634 | 530 | 259 | 142 | 117 | 1165 | 1850 | 685 | 254 | 154 | 100 |
| 86 | 764 | 178 | 101 | 68 | 33 | 193 | 288 | 95 | 48 | 35 | 13 | 184 | 287 | 103 | 41 | 28 | 13 |
| 43 | 187 | 44 | 25 | 20 | 5 | 63 | 96 | 33 | 15 | 9 | 6 | 93 | 142 | 49 | 28 | 11 | 17 |
| 58 | 558 | 100 | 57 | 31 | 26 | 297 | 413 | 116 | 62 | 47 | 15 | 240 | 401 | 161 | 70 | 36 | 34 |
| 59 | 78 | 19 | 9 | 5 | 4 | 101 | 155 | 54 | 31 | 18 | 13 | 112 | 186 | 74 | 21 | 16 | 5 |
| 13 | 271 | 58 | 34 | 22 | 12 | [1] 257 | 381 | 124 | 58 | 33 | 25 | 176 | 300 | 124 | 28 | 17 | 11 |
| 16 | 138 | 22 | 12 | 8 | 4 | 119 | 160 | 41 | 20 | 16 | 4 | 87 | 144 | 57 | 23 | 15 | 8 |
| 10 | 54 | 14 | 7 | 5 | 2 | 22 | 32 | 10 | 6 | 5 | 1 | .... | .... | .... | .... | .... | .... |
| 06 | 133 | 27 | 17 | 14 | 3 | 148 | 221 | 73 | 46 | 26 | 20 | 96 | 150 | 54 | 30 | 17 | 13 |
| 14 | 133 | 19 | 10 | 9 | 1 | 298 | 410 | 112 | 60 | 33 | 27 | 115 | 185 | 70 | 27 | 16 | 11 |
| 43 | 56 | 13 | 7 | 4 | 3 | 21 | 32 | 11 | 3 | 3 | .... | 38 | 74 | 36 | 7 | 7 | .... |
| 93 | 133 | 30 | 20 | 15 | 5 | 119 | 154 | 35 | 18 | 11 | 7 | 143 | 221 | 78 | 38 | 26 | 12 |
| 01 | 130 | 29 | 16 | 11 | 5 | 111 | 157 | 46 | 24 | 18 | 6 | 21 | 39 | 18 | 12 | 8 | 4 |
| 01 | 133 | 32 | 18 | 12 | 6 | 151 | 219 | 68 | 31 | 18 | 13 | 48 | 72 | 24 | 13 | 5 | 8 |
| 80 | 104 | 24 | 9 | 8 | 1 | .... | .... | .... | .... | .... | .... | 53 | 114 | 61 | 25 | 10 | 15 |
| 07 | 129 | 22 | 12 | 8 | 4 | 117 | 189 | 72 | 29 | 21 | 8 | 41 | 72 | 31 | 16 | 5 | 11 |
| 10 | 387 | 77 | 46 | 28 | 18 | 194 | 294 | 100 | 47 | 17 | 30 | 361 | 548 | 187 | 73 | 41 | 32 |
| 10 | 293 | 53 | 36 | 27 | 9 | 239 | 356 | 117 | 55 | 41 | 14 | 215 | 364 | 149 | 71 | 50 | 21 |
| 93 | 106 | 13 | 8 | 8 | .... | 57 | 96 | 39 | 17 | 10 | 7 | 80 | 105 | 25 | 5 | 5 | .... |
| 81 | 159 | 28 | 12 | 10 | 2 | 204 | 287 | 83 | 38 | 30 | 8 | 357 | 555 | 198 | 89 | 53 | 36 |
| .. | .... | .... | .... | .... | .... | 42 | 63 | 21 | 14 | 6 | 8 | 19 | 38 | 19 | 10 | 10 | .... |
| 19 | 26 | 7 | 3 | 3 | .... | 19 | 32 | 13 | 7 | 5 | 2 | .... | .... | .... | .... | .... | .... |
| 54 | 78 | 14 | 6 | 5 | 1 | .... | .... | .... | .... | .... | .... | 45 | 74 | 29 | 18 | 9 | 9 |
| 47 | 52 | 5 | 3 | 2 | 1 | 45 | 62 | 17 | 9 | 4 | 5 | .... | .... | .... | .... | .... | .... |
| 1 | 240 | 69 | 23 | 14 | 9 | 378 | 548 | 170 | 63 | 43 | 20 | 443 | 695 | 252 | 78 | 48 | 30 |
| 15 | 51 | 6 | 3 | 3 | .... | 88 | 122 | 34 | 14 | 12 | 2 | 71 | 111 | 40 | 16 | 9 | 7 |
| 58 | 84 | 16 | 11 | 8 | 3 | 22 | 30 | 8 | 2 | 2 | .... | 71 | 114 | 43 | 19 | 10 | 9 |
| 47 | 55 | 8 | 6 | 5 | 1 | 48 | 63 | 15 | 10 | 8 | 2 | 31 | 38 | 7 | 4 | 3 | 1 |
| 89 | 1648 | 359 | 200 | 142 | 58 | 1157 | 1652 | 495 | 220 | 141 | 79 | 771 | 1182 | 411 | 171 | 118 | 53 |
| 40 | 7377 | 1537 | 843 | 586 | 257 | [2] 5614 | 8146 | 2532 | 1206 | 754 | 452 | 5076 | 8061 | 2985 | 1187 | 727 | 460 |
| .. | 1156 | .... | .... | .... | .... | .... | 657 | .... | .... | .... | .... | .... | 330 | .... | .... | .... | .... |
| 40 | 8533 | .... | 843 | 586 | 257 | 5614 | 8803 | .... | 1206 | 754 | 452 | 5076 | 8391 | .... | 1187 | 727 | 460 |

TABLE XXVI.—*Totals of present Age of Mothers of respective Trades,*

| Trades. | 40 to 45. Total Ages of Mothers | | 40 to 45. | | | | 45 to 50. Total Ages of Mothers | | 45 to 50. | | | |
|---|---|---|---|---|---|---|---|---|---|---|---|---|
| | When First Child born. | Present Age. | Difference in Years. | Children born. | Children now living. | Dead. | When First Child born. | Present Age. | Difference in Years. | Children born. | Children now living. | Dead. |
| Labourers | 1,123 | 1,993 | 870 | 305 | 173 | 132 | 716 | 1,404 | 688 | 232 | 120 | 112 |
| Gunsmiths | 81 | 164 | 83 | 34 | 25 | 9 | 61 | 139 | 78 | 31 | 12 | 1 |
| Gunmakers | .... | .... | .... | .... | .... | .... | 33 | 93 | 60 | 13 | 7 | |
| Shoemakers | 254 | 466 | 212 | 90 | 46 | 44 | 81 | 185 | 104 | 25 | 14 | 1 |
| Bricklayers | 128 | 243 | 115 | 48 | 29 | 19 | 43 | 95 | 52 | 25 | 7 | 1 |
| Coopers | 186 | 336 | 150 | 61 | 28 | 33 | 114 | 229 | 115 | 33 | 19 | 1 |
| Engineers | .... | .... | .... | .... | .... | .... | .. | .... | .. | .... | .... | |
| Umbrella-makers | 21 | 41 | 20 | 3 | 2 | 1 | 83 | 142 | 59 | 32 | 15 | 1 |
| Porters | 118 | 209 | 91 | 28 | 19 | 9 | 65 | 136 | 71 | 21 | 7 | 1 |
| Carmen | 150 | 288 | 138 | 56 | 25 | 31 | 46 | 94 | 48 | 14 | 11 | |
| Butchers | 50 | 83 | 33 | 22 | 13 | 9 | 45 | 92 | 47 | 12 | 7 | |
| Sugar-bakers | 18 | 40 | 22 | 10 | 5 | 5 | 40 | 93 | 53 | 7 | 4 | |
| Bakers | 104 | 166 | 62 | 24 | 9 | 15 | 25 | 49 | 24 | 5 | 2 | |
| Painters | 104 | 161 | 57 | 24 | 17 | 7 | 50 | 90 | 40 | 15 | 12 | |
| Watermen | 40 | 84 | 44 | 12 | 9 | 3 | 46 | 94 | 48 | 16 | 11 | |
| Smiths | 111 | 209 | 98 | 40 | 17 | 23 | 47 | 90 | 43 | 16 | 9 | |
| Sailors | 116 | 207 | 91 | 28 | 10 | 18 | 70 | 145 | 75 | 18 | 10 | |
| Tailors | 192 | 340 | 148 | 68 | 41 | 27 | 229 | 424 | 195 | 53 | 31 | 2 |
| Cigar-makers | .... | .... | .... | .... | .... | .... | 24 | 48 | 24 | 11 | 10 | |
| Carpenters | 182 | 333 | 151 | 59 | 33 | 26 | 168 | 373 | 205 | 67 | 30 | 3 |
| Gun-stock-makers | 25 | 45 | 20 | 5 | 3 | 2 | 28 | 48 | 20 | 6 | 4 | |
| Tin-workers | 42 | 80 | 38 | 14 | 10 | 4 | 91 | 192 | 101 | 42 | 25 | 1 |
| Wheelwrights | .... | .... | .... | .... | .... | .... | 29 | 46 | 17 | 6 | 4 | |
| Shopmen | .... | .... | .... | .... | .... | .... | 63 | 138 | 75 | 24 | 9 | 1 |
| Widows with incumbrance | 497 | 872 | 375 | 118 | 79 | 39 | 441 | 883 | 442 | 130 | 64 | 6 |
| Policemen | 24 | 40 | 16 | 4 | 4 | .... | 72 | 140 | 68 | 26 | 14 | |
| Printers | 45 | 80 | 35 | 14 | 6 | 8 | .... | .... | .... | .... | .... | |
| Clerks | 20 | 42 | 22 | 10 | 8 | 2 | 66 | 137 | 71 | 18 | 11 | |
| Miscellaneous | 933 | 1,676 | 743 | 279 | 174 | 105 | 787 | 1,549 | 762 | 238 | 125 | 11 |
| | 4,564 | 8,198 | 3,634 | 1,356 | 785 | 571 | 3,563 | 7,148 | 3,585 | 1,136 | 594 | 54 |
| Married Women having no children | .... | 454 | .... | .... | .... | .... | .... | 651 | .... | .... | ... | ... |
| Total | 4,564 | 8,652 | .... | 1,356 | 785 | 571 | 3,563 | 7,799 | .... | 1,136 | 594 | 54 |